Edward Conze

FURTHER BUDDHIST STUDIES

FURTHER BUDDHIST STUDIES

Selected Essays

by

EDWARD CONZE

BRUNO CASSIRER

ISBN 0 85181 009 8

Printed in Great Britain by
WILLIAM CLOWES & SONS LTD
London, Colchester and Beccles

Published 1975 *by*
BRUNO CASSIRER (PUBLISHERS) LTD
31 Portland Road, Oxford OX2 7EZ

Distributed by
LUZAC & CO LTD
46 Great Russell Street, London WC1

TABLE OF CONTENTS

Page

Foreword viii

I. Longer Articles

1. Dharma as a spiritual, social and cosmic Force 1
2. Buddhism and Gnosis 15
3. Love, Compassion and sympathetic Joy 33

II. The philosophical Background

1. The objective Validity of the Principle of Contradiction 56
2. Social Implications of logical Thinking 73
3. Social Origins of Nominalism 93

III. Shorter Articles

1. The Buddha's Bodies in the Prajñāpāramitā 113
2. Remarks on a Pala MS. in the Bodleian Library 116
3. The present State and future Prospects of Buddhism in Asia 125
4. Jung's Psychology and the Dharma 131
5. Professor Murti's Central Philosophy of Buddhism 137
6. Problems of Buddhist History 144

IV. Reviews

1. 1948: M-Th.de Mallmann, Avalokiteśvara 150
2. 1952–3: Upanishads 154
3. 1956: R. de Nevesky-Wojkowitz, Oracles and Demons of Tibet 156
4. 1956: K. W. Morgan, The Path of the Buddha 158
5. 1956: G. Tucci, Minor Buddhist Texts I 159
6. 1956: F. A. Bischoff, Mahābala Sūtra 161
7. 1956: T. Matsumoto, ed. The Questions of Suvikrāntavikrāmin 163
8. 1957: H. V. Günther, Abhidharma 166
9. 1958: R. Hikata, ed. The Questions of Suvikrāntavikrāmin 168
10. 1958: A. J. Bahm, Philosophy of the Buddha; M. Eliade, Yoga 171
11. 1958: B. Bhattacharya, Indian Buddhist Iconography 173
12. 1958: G. Tucci, Minor Buddhist Texts, II; A. Ferrari, Guide 176
13. 1959: A. F. Wright, Buddhism in Chinese History 178
14. 1959: D. L. Snellgrove, Hevajra Tantra 180
15. 1959: E. Zuercher, The Buddhist Conquest of China 182
16. 1960: D. Saunders, Mudrā 185
17. 1960: F. D. K. Bosch, The Golden Germ 188
18. 1960: Dr. Koestler and the Wisdom of the East 191
19. 1960: Ch. Luk, Ch'an and Zen Teaching I 194

20. 1961: Ch. Luk, Ch'an and Zen Teaching II 196
21. 1961: Asanga's Yogācārabhūmi 198
22. 1961: D. L. Snellgrove, Himalayan Pilgrimage 204
23. 1961: G. Tucci, Mandala 205
24. 1962: Ch. Luk, Ch'an and Zen Teaching III 208
25. 1962: A. Macdonald, Mañjuśrīmūlakalpa 209
26. 1962: J. Ph. Vogel, The Goose in Indian Literature and Art 211
27. 1963: R. B. Ekvall, Religious Observances in Tibet 212
28. 1963: A. Foucher, The Life of the Buddha, trsl. Boas 212
29. 1964: Thich Minh Chau, Madhyama Āgama and Majjhima Nikāya 214
30. 1965: F. Weller, Kāśyapaparivarta 216
31. 1967: Vimuktisena, ed. C. Pensa 220
Bibliography 222
Index 325

FOREWORD

When we brought out *Thirty Years of Buddhist Studies* in 1967, we announced that at some time in the future there would be a second volume, to be called *Further Buddhist Studies*. The idea was that it should garner and preserve for a while those of my shorter literary efforts which seemed to have a lasting value, and the fruition of this project had therefore to wait until the author's *oeuvre* appeared to be reasonably complete. This time has now come. A look at the Bibliography will show that production came to an end in 1968—some time before my 65th birthday. The five years since then have been devoted to teaching students at sundry universities, combating the infirmities of old age and preparing a definite edition, in three volumes, of my translations of *Prajñāpāramitā* texts. *Kataṃ karaṇīyam*. The task is both completed and accomplished. What I have had to say has been said. Nothing new occurs to me any longer, and there will be no more.

The *Bibliography* is more than a manifestation of personal pride—like a banner unfurled before battle. It acts as a sort of guide to the various publications which are quoted by the way they are arranged in the Bibliography: Capital letters for books, numbers for articles, small letters for reviews, numbers preceded by O for pre-Buddhist publications.

(I–III): The *articles*, both long and short, *on Buddhism* in the more narrow sense of the word, are self-explanatory and little need be said about them.

As for III.4, fifteen years after I wrote this article I was confronted with the problem of the relation between Jung and Buddhism in the Bay Area of San Francisco where the young seemed to regard the writings of Hermann Hesse as antidotes to the ills which beset American society. In lecture after lecture I had to explain that this kind of thing had nothing whatever to do with any recognizable form of Buddhism, that the formulations of the doctrine are quite at variance with those of the Buddhists,[1] and that the type of person whom Buddhists intend to produce is not at all the same which the Jungians have in mind, whether one takes the average product of a Jungian analysis, or such rather unpleasant fictional characters as Emil Sinclair, Demian, "Siddhartha" or the Steppenwolf; compared with the stifling atmosphere in which they live, Buddhism seems to take place in the clear air of the Himalayas.

III.1 is included not because of what is said about the somewhat unrewarding topic of the "bodies of the Buddha", but because there I enunciate what I regard as a very important methodological principle which should, I think, guide the evaluation of literary sources in any truly realistic history of Buddhist thought.

(II): Under the section heading "*The Philosophical Background*" we reprint three items which have no immediately obvious connection with Buddhism. A few words about my personal intellectual development may explain how they fit into the scheme of things.

In 1932 I had printed, though not published, a fairly large work on *Der Satz vom Widerspruch* which, modelling myself a bit on Arthur Schopenhauer, I was inclined to regard as my *Hauptwerk*. In fact it contains all my later ideas without exception. At that time, however, it was totally still-born, the Nazis ceremoniously burned it in Hamburg, no more than perhaps forty copies have survived and public indifference towards it has been total, unrelieved by any kind of interest anywhere at any time. When in 1933 I removed myself to England I regarded this book as my greatest, and in fact only, asset, and started to decant it into the English language—achieving, however, only the three articles which appear on pages 56–112.[2] What I had not reckoned with was that the traditional style of philosophizing, to which I had become accustomed in Germany, had gone out of fashion in England, and that my arrival there coincided with the victory of the

[1] This must become perfectly clear to anyone who reads the melodramatic accounts of "the Self" in volume XX of Jung's *Collected Works* (2nd ed., 1970).

[2] In addition there were, in 1935–6, two books, nos. 05 and 06. Orthodox marxists, like J. D. Bernal, a lapsed Catholic, criticized these as too mystical and anti-scientific—quite rightly as things have turned out.

comparatively rational logical positivism of my friend Alfred Jules Ayer, soon to be followed by the linguistic futilities which Ernest Gellner has so brilliantly described in his *Words and Things* (1959, Pelican 1968).

At the same time I endeavoured to neutralize the Marxist virus in my system—first by a number of political and semi-political books, culminating in *Spain To-day* in 1936, and then by composing a book on *The Psychology of Mass Propaganda* which argued for the futility of all political action on the ground that mass activities must necessarily be permeated and vitiated by self-deception, as well as by greed and hatred. This book was, on ideological grounds, never brought out by the publisher who had commissioned it, and it will probably be found among my posthumous papers.

The upshot of all these convulsions and heartaches was a revival of an earlier interest in Buddhism, which goes back to my adolescence and had come to some prominence in my Heidelberg days in 1923 and 1924. Still continuing to think with pen in hand I composed a vast treatise on *Contradiction and Reality*, of which a *Summary* was printed at the outbreak of the war at the expense of a friend. The war itself drove me into Dr. Aubrey Westlake's wood in Godshill in Hampshire where, as later in a caravan in Ewelme, Oxon., I attempted to realize in meditation the teachings which I had speculatively developed in that *Summary*. Thereafter I decided to adopt an indirect approach and thus between 1946 and 1968 remained content to edit and expound the ancient Sanskrit texts of the *philosophia perennis*.[1]

The component of my views which sticks most of all in the gullets of my academic contemporaries is the acceptance of *magic*. This was stated as clearly in 1934 (s. pp. 81–2) as in 1964 (s. pp. 9–14), and it induced the then president of the Aristotelean Society, who was also the first female professor of logic[2] in modern history, to absentee herself from the meeting of November 19th where she should have chaired my paper. And yet all who have studied the history of ideas must

[1] About this term see *S* 212–215.

[2] Bertrand Russell pointed out to me at the time that this compound shows the importance of word order in English. What would happen if "female" became the penultimate word?—And she loved him so much!

be aware that a fusion between philosophy and magic is a normal stage in the history of many philosophical systems. In Indian Buddhism it took place from at least the third century A.D. onwards,[1] and in the Greco-Roman world it was carried out by Stoics, Gnostics (s. pp. 15–32) and Neoplatonists, to mention only a few. The later stages of Neoplatonism, as represented by Jamblichus, Proclus and Damascius, correspond closely to my own point of view. Modern philosophers usually deal with these people by summarily ejecting them from the premises, on the ground that they fall outside some narrow definition of 'philosophy', or they somewhat quaintly complain about aspects of Neoplatonism" which makes it totally unacceptable to an empiricist".[2] Classicists are taught to disparage them; e.g. Jamblichus "corrupted Plotinus' teaching by introducing theosophical phantasies from alien sources; and his tendency is to substitute magic for mysticism".[3] Historians of philosophy have treated them very shabbily, by providing no editions or translations, or anything that might be considered to be an even tolerably adequate treatment, until 1972 when R. T. Wallis, a British exile in Oklahoma, published his *Neo-Platonism*.

It may be more than a mere coincidence that both Jamblichus and I are fated to live in an effete and excessively urbanized civilization, at a time when the joint activities of the internal and external proletariat combine to put a stop to the few remaining educated people, and when the massive overweight of the political superstructure crushes the bones of everyone and everybody. On the other hand, some of the responsibility for my views may lie with some congenital disposition. When we both lived in London, Prof. Eichhorn, a Sinologue now in Tuebingen, assured me that, to his great surprise, my views were exactly those of a Chinese of the Han period (200 B.C.–A.D. 200). No compliment could have been more welcome! For, as Roy Fuller so aptly put it, "Anyone

[1] See *S* 82–84.

[2] *The Concise Encyclopedia of Western Philosophy and Philosophers*, ed. J. O. Urmson, 1960, p. 277.

[3] *The Oxford Classical Dictionary*, 2nd ed., 1970, p. 538b. Oh these aliens! Who has not heard of Heinrich Heine's, "Ausländer, Juden sinds zumeist", and so on.

happy in this age and place Is daft or corrupt. Better to abdicate," etc. etc.

Even in modern times a resurgence of magic is attested by the portent of Carl Gustav Jung, and other rather more powerful[1] tokens. It is quite an important component in the "counter-culture" which I encountered during my last stay in Berkeley. After being accused of "obscurantism" for so many years I was really gratified to be treated for once as a kind of culture hero. Students habitually handed me their horoscopes for my appraisal, and little girls, locally known as "co-eds", reverently held the hand of the master so as to ascertain more clearly the configuration of his heart line.[2] *Tempora mutantur sed non mutamur in illis.*

Leaving aside these unseemly jokes, I wish to point out that it was not an Indian, but Glycon, a Greek, who said:[3]

> *πάντα γέλως καὶ παντα κόνις καὶ πάντα τὸ μηδέν.*
> *πάντα γὰρ ἐξ ἀλόγων ἐστὶ τὰ γινόμενα*

Oriental philosophy cannot possibly be understood if one assumes that the minds of Orientals are qualitatively different from those of Westerners, and that it contains some "mysterious" elements which can never have a living meaning to men brought up in the West. I regard Buddhist philosophy, as preached in the *Prajñāpāramitā* and argued by Nāgārjuna and Candrakīrti as the most likely, or at least as the least unlikely, of all philosophical attitudes. I arrived at it by the logical development of elements which form part of "Western" tradition for thousands of years, and I had reached the basic tenets (as shown in *o2*) long before I had made a study of the Sanskrit sources. When I was a student, it was well nigh

[1] In my 1939 typescript of *The Psychology of Mass Propaganda* a special chapter on Magical Beliefs gives examples drawn from the "blood and soil" of a Germany tortured by Hitler and his Nazis, from the mummy-worshipping atheists of Stalin's Russia, etc. A fine survey of recent trends in L. Pauwels and J. Bergier, *Le matin des magiciens,* 1960 ("The Dawn of Magic", 1964, 1967).

[2] The usual reaction, incidentally, was, "I am glad that I am not married to *you*!" This shows that the little girls knew what they were about.

[3] *Anth. Pal.* 10, 124.

impossible to get any real information about the Mahayana, the Gnostics and the later Neoplatonists. There must have been hundreds and hundreds of us who wanted to know more—how otherwise could one account for the immense upsurge in the scholarly study of these three systems of thought over the last fifty years? It is in order to illustrate points such as these that I offer up to kindred spirits the sixty pages devoted here to the "Philosophical Background".

(IV): Out of 143 *reviews* we have chosen to reprint 31. These either contain useful scholarly information, chiefly about my own chosen field of Mahayana literature, or they treat of problems, tendencies, misconceptions and significant personalities who are still with us in the seventies. Some of the reviews may seem unduly polemical. But, if we may pursue the topic of magic a bit further, those who know about these things are aware that a conjunction of Mars and Moon in Aries in the ninth house inclines the native to religious invective and controversy. May this reference to my natal chart (March 18, 1904, 3 p.m. London, Lewisham) act as a balm to the victims' bruised feelings!

The articles have generally been printed as they stood. Occasionally I have used the opportunity to introduce some *Retractationes* or to add references to later publications in which the topic on hand has been treated more fully. For one of my reviews (i.e. zcv) I must apologize outright, because I wrote about something I knew nothing about. In the article II.1, on "Objective Validity", I had to improve the English style in this, my very first effort in English. Some of it (esp. pp. 61–2) is rather heavy going, has an indefinable Teutonic flavour and seems to resist further anglicizing. As in the case of *Thirty Years* the usage of diacritical marks, italics, capitals, etc., is that of the articles as they appeared at the time, and therefore varies from place to place.

We thank the following for allowing us to reprint material which appears here: *Akten* des 24.Or.Kongress München 63; *The Aristotelean Society* o3; *The Aryan Path*, zad; *Asia Major*, zaf, zbm; Anthony Blond Ltd., 84; *Bulletin of the London School of Oriental and African Studies*, zbx, zcz; *The Hibbert Journal*, zo, zba, zbp, zbz; *Indo-Iranian Journal*, zau, zbf, zdc, zdd, zdo, zdr, zdx; *Journal of the American Oriental Society*, zdi; *The Journal of the Royal Asiatic Society*, zdm; *Marxist Quarterly* 08; *The Middle Way* 23, 24, 25, 29, 42, i, zm, zn, zr, zaw, zbu, zbq, zcq, zdu; *Oriental Art* 7, e, zaa, zaz, zbv, zbw, zci, zck, zcx, zdk; *Philosophy* 04; *Philosophy East and West* 22; *Self-Knowledge* 20; Supplements to Numen 89; University of Washington Press 91.

In this Foreword I have, at the prompting of some friends, let my hair down quite a bit, and much, probably too much, of it is about my own dear self. This should not allow me to forget that during the last twenty-five years I have been helped by many people. Two of these should perhaps be singled out. The one is my wife Muriel who has stood by me during all this time. The other is George Hill, my Oxford publisher, who was the first to make my reputation and who has shown that a publisher can also be a friend.

Foxwell, Marston Road
Sherborne, Dorset

I. LONGER ARTICLES

1

DHARMA AS A SPIRITUAL, SOCIAL, AND COSMIC FORCE

Buddhists do not normally speak of their own relgion as "Buddhism," but usually refer to it as "the Dharma". The word "Dharma" is a Sanskrit term that comes from the root *dhṛ*, which means "to uphold", and to it also such words as *thronos*, *firmus*, and *fretus* are related. We read, for instance in the *Mahābhārata* (*Śāntiparvan* 109.11): "They call it 'Dharma' because of its 'holding' (*dhāraṇād;* keeping things as they are); it is through Dharma that the people are severally held in their places (*vi-dhṛ-tāḥ*). That which is conjoined with holding (*dhāraṇa*, i.e., either 'upholding' or holding down'), that is determined as 'Dharma'." In this basic meaning the term is still alive in India. Recently I looked into a copy of a pamphlet entitled *Sikh Mysticism*, by Dr. Mohan Singh Uberoi and the first sentence my eyes lighted upon was 'Dharma (Norm, Law), in its field, deals with the laws that sustain the universe", with a footnote to the effect that "Dharma operates as the support, duty-binding",[1] This is exactly how the Buddhists have always fundamentally understood the term. In Buddhist writings it has acquired a great, and to some extent even bewildering, variety of meanings. These I have sorted out from a philosophical point of view,[2] and long before me, in 1920, M. and W. Geiger collected all the relevant passages concerning Dhamma (Pali equivalent of the Sanskrit "Dharma") from the Pali Canon, distinguishing dozens of meanings and submeanings.[3]

[1] Mohan Singh Uberoi, *Sikh Mysticism* (Amritsar, 1964), p. 12.

[2] Edward Conze, *Buddhist Thought in India* (London: George Allen and Unwin, 1962), pp. 92–106.

[3] M. and W. Geiger, *Pāli Dhamma vornehmlich in der kanonischen Literatur* (*Abhandlungen der bayrischen Academie der Wissenschaften Philosophisch-Historische Klasse*, vol. XXXI, No. 1, 1920).

I

In the present context we will ignore all these finer shades, and concentrate on that side of "Dharma" which makes it to some extent analogous to what we nowadays call "order." The *Pali-English Dictionary* speaks of "dhamma as the interpreted Order of the World," and says:

> That which the Buddha preached . . . was the order of law of the universe, immanent, eternal, uncreated, not as interpreted by him only, much less invented or decreed by him, but intelligible to a mind of his range and by him made so to mankind as bodhi: revelation, awakening. The Buddha is a discoverer of this order of the Dhamma, this universal logic, philosophy or righteousness ("Norm"), in which the rational and ethical elements are fused into one.[1]

Taken in and by itself, the Dharma is what we would call the "Absolute", one and single, without any duality or multiplicity in it; its inward unity and, if I may coin the term, its "unicity" preclude it from the very possibility of disorder. In its manifestations the Dharma pervades the universe and furnishes it with a certain number of fixed regularities, or fixed causal sequences—the final and indubitable facts of life which must be taken into account if we want to live fruitfully and serenely. Although it is the unconditioned One, it is not some barren remoteness, but infuses order into the multiple appearances of the conditioned world, and conformity to it is the basis of the spiritual life. In Buddhism impermanence is a sign that there is something wrong with a thing, whereas the perfect Dharma and its irradiations abide for ever. To describe these dharmic laws would be to enumerate all the essential items of Buddhist doctrine, and I must be content with one single example, a verse from the *Dhammapada* (I 5) which says: "Never can hatred be appeased by hatred; it will be appeased only by non-hatred. This is an everlasting (*sanantano*) dharma."

Special terms, like *dhamma-niyāmatā*, and so forth, denote the orderliness of dharmic processes, and we often hear that "whether Tathagatas do or do not appear, that state of Dharma, that established order of Dharma, that fixed sequence of Dharma is firmly established, i.e., that all compounded

[1] *Pali-English Dictionary*, ed. T. W. Rhys Davids and W. Stede (London: Pali Text Society, 1921), p. 171.

dharmas are impermanent, ill, not-self".[1] There is, however, nowhere an attempt to *prove* that either the Absolute or its workings in the world are orderly rather than chaotic or disorderly. One of the reasons may have been that the *a-dharma*, "that which is not Dharma", is manifestly so disorderly that one may infer that Dharma, its opposite, will represent Order. Those parts of the world which have escaped the control of Dharma are marked by strife (*raṇa*) and turmoil (*ḍamara*). On a more or less poetical and allegorical level this is often shown in the scriptures by contrasting the serenity, peace, and harmony of the world which is dominated by the Buddhas and Bodhisattvas (who are channels through which the transcendental Dharma reaches the world) with what is going on in the hells or among Mara's hosts. It is quite in keeping with Buddhist stylistic conventions that there are few, if any, attempts to give a positive definition of the glory of the order of Dharma. Instead one is content to infer it by copious descriptions of the disorders that result when one departs from the dharmic order. The spiritual realization (*sākṣātkriyā*) of this Dharma can be effected only by those who have left home and have become either monks or wandering ascetics. By a combination of "transic" meditation and gnosis they gain a direct intuition of the Dharma which "must be known by the wise, each one by and for himself (*paccatam veditabbo viññūhi*)". When they have done so, the fetters of this world drop off, and Nirvana, the ultimate goal of Buddhist endeavour, is achieved.

II

From the Dharma of the monks we now move on to the Dharma of the kings. From at least the time of Asoka onward two kinds of Buddhism must be distinguished: that of the kings, at grips with the realities of the social world; and that of the monks, tranquilly renouncing the world and its agitations, provided the kings furnished them with the means to do so. It is well known that the inscriptions of Asoka make no reference to Nirvana, to the four holy truths, or to the other stock items of monastic Buddhism. But, when speaking of the distinguishing marks (*guṇa*) of Dharma, the great king tells his subjects that

[1] See Conze, *Buddhist Thought in India*, p. 93.

"it is commendable to abstain from slaughtering living beings", and that "it is also commendable not to spend or hoard too much".[1] It is impossible here to describe in detail the code of social conduct as laid down by Asoka. In any case, to observe Dharma brings happiness in this world and the next, whereas its disregard is bound to be punished at some time or other. In view of the predilection of Puritans for condemning the sins of the flesh, it is noteworthy that when Asoka describes non-dharmic conduct, which he calls "evil" (*pāpam*), he concentrates on sins of hate, i.e., fury, cruelty, anger, pride, and envy.[2]

The bilingual edict of Kandahār renders "Dharma" by *eusebeia* (piety), and this makes Asoka a kinsman of those ancient Romans who attributed their imperial successes to their *pietas*, to their scrupulous religious observances. "'Tis by holding thyself the servant of the gods that thou dost rule; with them all things begin, to them ascribe the outcome,"[3] wrote Horace, speaking poetically. At the same time the Stoic philosophers provided the Roman Empire with a philosophical ideology, which formulated certain precepts of "natural" as distinct from conventional law. This "natural law" is the closest parallel we have in Europe to the Dharma of Asoka and his successors.

What is the relation between the spiritual and the social side of Dharma? It seems to me obvious that the Buddhists could not have maintained themselves for so long in society if they had not contributed anything to its functioning. And they may also very well have had a doctrine about society, in spite of the fact that the canonical writings say so little about it. But that may be because the canonical writings concentrate on the problems concerning salvation from the world, and, just as the Gospels do, say almost nothing precise about the regulation of the world itself.

Where, then, have the Buddhists been able to practice their doctrine? That depended, of course, on their relative strength in

[1] R. K. Mookerji, *Asoka* (3rd ed.; Delhi: Motilal Banarsidass, 1962), p. 135.

[2] Mookerij, *Asoka*, pp. 71, 176.

[3] Horace, *Odes*, iii.6: "dis te minorem quod geris imperas: hinc omne principium; huc refer exitum".

relation to that of the secular ruler. One extreme would be Tibet, where during the last four hundred years there was in theory a pure theocracy, in which the spiritual head of the Samgha was also the ruler of the country, although in practice, of course, Chinese interference counted for a great deal. The other extreme would be the Japan of the Tokugawa period, where the monks were reduced to the position of tame pensioners of the state and deprived of nearly all social influence and initiative.

The normal pattern was a collaboration between the monks (Samgha) and an absolute and divine king. The monasteries were subject to the general control of government officials, and the kings themselves often had the last word in doctrinal disputes, deciding which was the orthodox sect and which was not. This kind of subordination of the church is known in Europe as Erastianism and has generally appeared quite normal and unobjectionable to Buddhists, who indeed find it hard to maintain monastic discipline on their own, as was shown in Ceylon and Burma. At the same time the government provides the Samgha with material necessities, and a varying proportion of the national income is drained away into the support of the monks, into the casting of images, into religious buildings, and so on. The Buddhists in their turn greatly influenced the general tone of government policy, although not so much its details. In Burma, for instance, "the monks, to whom even the king had to bow, are known, in history, to have intervened on the side of the oppressed and to have diverted royalty from feats of arms to feats of architecture, scholarship and husbandry."[1] The Buddhists also reinforced the belief that the king had divine sanction by associating him or his family with some member of the Buddhist pantheon. In this way the Manchu dynasty was somehow identified with the Bodhisattva Monju (Mañjuśrī), and so on.

At the same time, in Burma and elsewhere the kings showed their fitness to rule by protecting and purifying the religion. This pattern began with the emperor Asoka, the "Beloved of the Gods", about 250 B.C. and for seventeen hundred years most of the great rulers of Asia have sought and won the

[1] M. Mendelson, "Religion and Authority in Modern Burma", in *The World To-day* (London: Oxford University Press, 1960), p. 111.

collaboration of the Buddhist community. During the twentieth century this system has by now reached a condition of virtual extinction. Asoka embodied the ideal of a "universal ruler", or *cakravartin*, "who has conquered the earth from ocean to ocean, and rules it not by the rod or by the sword, but by Dharma". The *cakravartin* is a figure of cosmic significance, he has seven "treasures" which are his magical insignia, and he is to society what the Buddha is to the world of the spirit, his exact counterpart. This idea of a *cakravartin* has dominated Buddhist social thinking for seventeen hundred years, and each ruler who supported the Samgha was viewed as one. The pre-Asokan contractual theory of the origin of kingship is now replaced by the theory that the king holds his office by the authority of the gods, who have first ordained him, and is therefore entitled to be addressed as *deva* or *devaputra*. As Basham says, "this doctrine of divine appointment may be compared with that widely proclaimed in England during the Stuart period, and it is also closely akin to the Chinese doctrine of the 'Mandate of Heaven'."[1] So what Buddhism seeks in the social sphere is a *dharma-rājā*, a king of Dharma. The same Dharma which rules the spiritual should, in other words, also dominate the social sphere.

The kind of society which Buddhists would regard as being in harmony with Dharma has at least four essential features.

1. First of all, Buddhism is obviously in favor of peace and against violence. Nonviolence (*ahimsā*) was what attracted Asoka to Buddhism, and it became the great inspiration of his reign. The scriptures naturally contain many admonitions in this direction. In the *Suvarṇaprabhāsa*, for instance, we hear:

> Turn back the troops of their enemies and create in all the earthly kings of India a desire to avoid fighting, attacking, quarrelling, or disputing with their neighbours. These kings will gain their thrones by the due accumulation of the merit of former deeds; they will be satisfied with their own kingly state, and will not destroy one another, nor show their mettle by laying waste whole provinces.[2]

[1] A. L. Basham, "Jainism and Buddhism", in *Sources of Indian Tradition*, ed. William T. De Barry *et al.* (New York: Columbia University Press, 1958), pp. 132–6, 185.

[2] *Ibid.*, p. 184. trsl. R. E. Emmerick, 1970, pp. 27–8.

This is the precept, and some remarkable achievements may be recorded. In India, between 300 B.C. (the account of Megasthenes) and A.D. 400 (the report of Fa-hsien), there had been considerable progress in the direction of mildness and nonviolence. The death penalty, very frequently and cruelly inflicted in 300 B.C., had gone quite out of use. In Megasthenes' days all classes ate meat, while in the time of Fa-hsien only the outcasts did so. Buddhists abhor bloodshed of any kind. Among the Tibetans and Mongols they abolished animal sacrifices and made these fierce warriors quite pacific. A Buddhist society will therefore know no militarism, and the armed forces will be small and inefficient. Such things as vivisection are quite unthinkable, and also hunting and fishing will be left to the lowest of the low. In suppressing these misdemeanors, Buddhism relies not so much on repression as on convincing people that these are low-class ways of behaving and on confining them to the low-class people of whom there is a certain number in every society. Let there be butchers, but let them be ashamed of being butchers! Let there be hunters, fishers, and soldiers, but let them realize what a beastly crowd they are! In this way the whole tone of society will be raised. And, as a corollary, the rights of others should be respected, and Man should humbly coexist with others. We shall say more about that later.

2. Material prosperity is not altogether a bad thing, but frugality is desirable because greed is evil. One should not hoard because generosity is a great virtue, and material happiness is quite unimportant, "not worth one sixteenth part" of the spiritual happiness arising from a faultless and good life.

3. Buddhism clearly favors stable rather than "progressive" societies, and in the latter kind it is likely to die. From Asoka's edicts we see that everything which strengthens respect for tradition (*purāṇa*) seemed desirable to him, and among his "regulations of Dharma" (*dharma-niyama*) obedience to parents, elders, and teachers (*guru*) figures quite prominently.[1]

4. Buddhism also prefers a religious to a secular society. The latter would appear to be both undesirable and impossible. It is undesirable because it does not allow the centers of spiritual life to function, and because the surplus wealth is spent on armaments, dope, and feminine vanity rather than for religious

[1] Mookerji, *Asoka*, pp. 116, 169.

purposes. It is also impossible because, among other things, it must become so drab that it cannot last.

That is all, and someone who expects from the Buddhists a nice blueprint of a dharmic, or ideal, society must be disappointed. The reason is that all technical details depend on the concrete circumstances, whereas ultimately social prosperity is derived not from these but from spiritual and magical conditions.

In a time like ours, when society has become so thoroughly disordered that constant manipulation is needed to keep it going, it must seem most naïve and unsatisfactory to be told that one has only to honor the Dharma, and everything in the social world will be all right. Yet this is what we read in "The Sutra on Perfect Wisdom, explaining how Benevolent Kings may protect their countries", where the Buddha says (*T* p. 174):

> Now I shall proclaim the Dharma which allows you to protect your countries. In all countries, when riots are imminent, calamities are descending, or robbers are coming to destroy (the houses and possessions of the inhabitants,) you, the kings, ought to receive, keep and read this Prajñāpāramitā, solemnly adorn the place of worship, to place (there) a hundred Buddha-images, a hundred images of Bodhisattvas, a hundred lion-seats, and to invite a hundred Dharma-master that they may explain this Sutra. And before the seats you must light all kinds of lamps, burn all kinds of incense, spread all kinds of flowers. You must liberally offer clothes and bedding, food and medicine, houses, beds and seats, all offerings, and every day you must read this Sutra for two hours. If kings, great ministers, monks and nuns, male and female lay members of the community listen to it, receive and read it, and act according to the Dharma, the calamities shall be extinguished. Great kings, in the countries there are innumerable demons and spirits, each of them with innumerable followers; if they hear this Sutra, they shall protect your countries. If riots are imminent, the demons and spirits are uproarious beforehand; and it is for this reason that the people revolt; then robbery arises, and the people perish; the kings and the crown princes, the princes and the hundred magistrates mutually do right and wrong. If unnatural things happen in heaven and on the earth: the sun, the moon and the stars lose their times and their courses, and great fires, inundations and storms are prevalent, if all these calamities arise, all people must receive, keep and read this Prajñāpāramitā.

The ideas of causality implied here are certainly strange to our way of thinking. It was the belief of the Buddhists, shared by the Hindus and Chinese, that the welfare of the whole land, and even the regularity of the calendar and of heavenly phenomena generally, are dependent on the king, who is at the centre of society, being attuned to the Dharma. When the king gets out of tune with the Dharma, then, to quote the *Suvarṇaprabhāsa:*

> Then the land is afflicted with fierce and terrible crime,
> And it perishes and falls into the power of the enemy.
> Then property, families, and hoarded wealth all vanish,
> And with varied deeds of deceit men ruin one another.
> Whatever his reasons, if a king does not do his duty
> He ruins his kingdom, as a great elephant a bed of lotuses.
> Harsh winds blow, and rain falls out of season,
> Planets and stars are unpropitious, as are the moon and sun,
> Corn, flowers and fruit and seed do not ripen properly,
> And there is famine, when the king is negligent.
> From the wrath of the gods his kingdom will perish.
> All living beings will be ugly, having little vigour, very weak;
> They will eat much, but they will not be filled.
> They will have no strength, and no virility—
> All the beings in the land will be lacking in vigour.[1]

III

The third part of this paper concerns a topic so inherently incomprehensible to modern Americans that I fear very much that I will fail to make my meaning perfectly clear. I speak of the topic of magic. The whole functioning of Buddhism cannot be understood unless we realize that not only the monks and kings must be considered, but also a third class of people, who have been present in large numbers wherever Buddhism

[1] Basham, "Jainism and Buddhism", pp. 186–7. trsl. R. E. Emmerick, 1970, pp. 59–61.

has struck root. These are the magicians. In present-day Burma, for instance, there are hundreds of groups of *gaings* who manipulate "various magical techniques associated with alchemy, *mantras*, medicine and cabbalistic signs".[1] By undergoing various rules of abstinence, they hope to gain a very long or even eternal life, and their highest aim is to see and hear the future Buddha Maitreya and to reach Nirvana by means of his sermons. The *gaings* are the successors of the Mahayana Tantrists, and they keep alive the longing for kingship. "The remarkable fact is that there are still, all over Burma, future kings and messiahs (these notions are very mixed up at the popular level) with courts of attendants waiting upon them daily until such time as they will mount the throne of the Land of Gold on earth or in heaven (this again is never too clear) and shower blessings and gifts on their devotees."[2] Mendelson calls this "messianic Buddhism", and it has a great importance in politics, since "the ideology of the *gaings* . . . permeates the life of all Burmese to some degree or other and countless soldiers, lawyers, civil servants, government officials and business men model their lives and decisions on the teachings of their *gaing* masters". With these magicians "involvement in the world and rejection of the world are two sides of one medal".[3] It is they who bridge the gulf between the wordliness of the layman and the unworldliness of the monk. And so it has always been.

To take another nearly contemporary example, the magical connotations of sovereignty have been particularly clear in Tibet. In a very fine essay Marco Pallis has recently defined the exact function of the Dalai Lama as an "activity of presence".[4] It is more a magical than a rational notion to believe that the Panchen and Dalai lamas are the great and precious "protectors" of Tibet not because of anything they actually do, but because their very presence assures the prosperity and happiness of all.

"Magical" in this sense is a term that covers those methods by

[1] Mendelson, "Religion and Authority in Modern Burma", p. 115.

[2] *Ibid.*, p. 117.

[3] *Ibid.*, pp. 117, 118.

[4] Marco Pallis, *The Way and the Mountain* (London: Peter Owen, 1960), pp. 160–76.

which nomadic and agricultural populations all over the world have always regulated their lives, as contrasted with "scientific" methods, on which industrialized societies are based. The basic difference in their approach is that magic aims at producing harmony with the cosmos, whereas science increases our control over nature. For example, let us represent science by modern astronomy and magic by astrology. Astronomy became scientific only after it had discarded the ancient fables about "the harmony of the spheres" and the divinity of the stars; it then "discovered" that the celestial realm consists of nothing but a large number of pieces of matter, with a lot of space and all kinds of rays in between. Once it had accumulated sufficient knowledge it then proceeded to throw pieces of metal into that space, some of them even hitting the serene face of the moon. The Greeks would have been a bit doubtful about the wisdom of these activities, regarding them as a gross act of impiety which one day would surely provoke the thunderbolt of Zeus. A scientist can only shrug his shoulders at such childishness and will point out to you how much we have progressed since those days.

Quite different is the attitude of astrology—and may I add at once that I wish only to illustrate its methods without necessarily attributing validity to it. In astrology you rejoice to find that a gloomy person with a strong sense of duty is a Capricorn, that a "family man" is a Cancer, or that an overprecise, oversensitive, and overscrupulous person is a Virgo. You rejoice because this identification explains to you the behavior of these people and shows you to what you must adjust yourself. But it would not occur to you for a moment to try to make a Capricorn permanently cheerful, or in any other way to alter the characteristics of a person as indicated by his horoscope. The only result would be to make him into a bad and neurotic Capricorn, and so on. The central point is that astrology deals with an "ordered pattern", a "cosmos" that must be respected and that would merely be brought into disorder if it were interfered with. These categories do not apply to "nature" as understood by the natural sciences, which assume that nature has no such pattern, that it has no will of its own, and that it therefore behoves Man to control it for his own convenience. In terms of housebuilding, the symbol of magic would be the *Feng-shui*, that of science the bulldozer. We all know what a bulldozer is. The *Feng-shui*, Chinese for "Wind and Water", are the occult influences that determine the character of a locality and that must be preserved at all costs because, if they are obliterated, beauty and harmony will surely be crushed. In the *Feng-shui* system you make yourself quite small; in the bulldozer system you get bigger and more powerful all the time.

A little reflection will show that when you speak of achieving, or rather maintaining, harmony with the cosmos, you thereby imply two kinds of cosmos: yourself, who are the microcosm; and the universe around you, which is the macrocosm. Again in terms of astrology, the human body is a microcosm that corresponds to the zodiac, which is the macrocosm. In this way the head corresponds to Aries, the neck to Taurus, and so on until we come to Pisces, who must be content with the feet. If this correspondence were widely held to be true, it would have far-reaching consequences for medicine. But because magic and science are mutually incompatible there is no great likelihood that this lore will be admitted into the curriculum of our universities. It is interesting to note that in tantric Buddhism also an elaborate system was worked out which, based on the equivalence of events in macrocosm and microcosm, viewed the human body as a replica of the cosmos and treated it as an instrument of salvation and as the scene of the quest for enlightenment.

It was because Buddhism assured this harmony with the cosmos on which all social welfare depends that the laity was so eager to support the Order, house its members, and erect fine monuments in honour of their teachings. The world would not have put up for long with a community of monks who would turn their backs on those who fed them if they had not given something priceless to the world which it could not get in any other way. The visible manifestations of this concern for cosmic harmony are the magnificent stupas that adorn all parts of the Buddhist world and are the tangible focus of the religion. It was the business of the laity to build those stupas, though only the relics of the Lord Buddha could give them life. The stupas are as fundamental to Buddhism as the four holy truths, and it has been shown beyond doubt that they have a cosmic significance, that they are representative of the universe—not only the stupa at Borobudur, but also those at Sanchi, Bharhut, and Shwe Dagon. This "cosmic architecture represents the world as a theatre for the working-out of the Dharma and for the awakening of all beings by its piercing rays."[1] Each stupa is an "imitation" of the life, or rather lives, of the Tathagata (an epithet of the Buddha), they allowed a whole society to unite in one common celebration, and thus had not only great moral, but also political consequences.

It was the French scholar Paul Mus who in his monumental work on Borobudur proved that the works of architecture, properly interpreted, show that the Buddhists felt responsible for the welfare of society as a whole, and that the Samgha, the community of monks, aimed at fostering and maintaining that cosmic harmony which is the source and basis of all social prosperity.[2] The great stupas of the Buddhists are the descendants of the Assyro-Babylonian ziggurats and the imperial cities of the Iranian kings, and they fulfill the same purpose. They were in fact mandalas, or magic circles, and it was Professor G. Tucci who first gave us a comprehensive survey of the often obscure metaphysical and psychological assumptions that activated the minds of those Buddhist thinkers who regarded mandalas as a means of salvation.[3] Some of these are archaic concepts that are found nearly everywhere in preindustrial cultures. There is, first, the universal magical practice of marking off a sacred, ritually pure spot by means of a circle. Then there is the idea of a diagram of the cosmos which, in its Buddhist form, is considered "as a vital process which develops from one essential Principle and rotates round one central axis, Mount Sumeru, the axis of the world."[4] This diagram was reproduced in ritual vases, royal palaces, stupas, temples, and mandalas. A vast complex of magical identifications, correspondences, transformations, and transfigurations was woven around these basic ideas. The Indians may have added the symbolism of the lotus and the evocation of

[1] Paul Mus, "Introduction", *Présence du Bouddhisme* (*France-Asie* [Saigon], Vol. XVI, 1959), pp. 187–200.

[2] Paul Mus, *Borobudur* (2 vols.; Hanoi, 1935).

[3] G. Tucci, *The Theory and Practice of the Mandala* (London: Rider and Company, 1961). See below IV 23.

[4] *Ibid.*, p. 23.

deities by means of syllables which "constitute their occult principle."[1] The whole, taken together, makes it possible to express the basic cosmic and spiritual forces that govern our destiny "by means of symbols which, if they be wisely read by the initiate, will induce the liberating psychological experience".[2] What is assumed is that through symbols "one can give form to the infinite possibilities which lie in the depth of the unconscious, to unexpressed fears, to primordial impulses, and to age-old passions."[3]

It has been necessary to speak at such length about the magical side of Buddhism in order to present a balanced exposition of the Dharmah; for Dharma is a sort of tripod that needs all its three feet equally: the spiritual, the social, and the cosmic. I do not wish to conceal, however, a subsidiary reason, and that is to present the idea that these notions about "harmony with the cosmos" might be well worth re-examining at the present time. Recently I found myself in an airplane with a natural scientist, a colleague from the University of Wisconsin. When he learned that I am a professor of Buddhist studies, he wondered why anybody should wish to study a subject as useless as Buddhism. I gave him various reasons, one of them being that Buddhism might conceivably contain some kind of wisdom that would enable us to make a more intelligent use of the vast knowledge we have recently acquired. He really did not think much of that one. For three quarters of an hour we circled over the thick fog that covered Chicago, and after a time we became slightly apprehensive. Suddenly my colleague turned to me and said, "Just think what we would feel if, while circling up here six thousand feet above Chicago, we were now told that there is no pilot on board. That exactly is the present situation of mankind"—and I had the chilling realization that this is precisely what has happened. The only thing a society based on Dharma can with absolute certainty claim in its favour is that it is bound to prevent such a situation as described by my friend from the department of oncology.

[1] *Ibid.*, pp. 30–7.
[2] *Ibid.*, p. 22.
[3] *Ibid.*

2

BUDDHISM AND GNOSIS

The topic of my paper has a fairly long ancestry. Already in 1828 Isaac Jacob Schmidt, a German living in Russia, published a pamphlet entitled "Über die Verwandtschaft der gnostisch-theosophischen Lehren mit den Religionssystemen des Orients, vorzüglich dem Buddhaismus",[1] which Arthur Schopenhauer in his collected works recommended no fewer than three times. Much has been learned in the intervening 138 years, and to-day a German living in England will try to outline briefly the present state of the question as he sees it.

By "Buddhism" I mean in this context the Mahāyāna form of that religion which developed as a distinctive trend from about 100 B.C. onwards, and had its greatest creative period in the first centuries of the Christian era. Not all the doctrines I shall adduce in this paper are, however, *exclusively* mahāyā-nistic. Some of them can also be found in the "Hīnayāna",

[1] Leipzig, IV + 25 pages, 4to. I. J. Schmidt said "daß die Gnostiker ihre Ideen aus den Religionssystemen des Orients geschöpft haben" (p. iii; also p. 16) and on p. 20 he says that "diese Lehrsätze (of the Gnostics) fast genau so klingen als wären sie wörtlich aus den buddhaistischen Schriften vorgetragen oder abgeschrieben". These were the views of a period which had "die Überzeugung, daß alle Cultur, die sich in Europa zu eigenem Leben zu entfalten Raum fand und deren Früchte wir jetzt geniessen, ihren Ursprung aus Asien hat" (*Über einige Grundlehren des Buddhaismus*, 1829, p. 2). (In 1952 Widengren described Gnosis as "a principally Indo-Iranian movement"). I. J. Schmidt's description of Buddhism, which he had derived from its "geachtetsten Religionsschriften" (p. 13, n. 4) concerns naturally the Mahāyāna in its Lamaist form with which alone, as a resident of Russia, he could at that time be familiar. Another person who has worked on this subject is A. Lloyd, a missionary in Japan. His book *The Creed of Half Japan* (1911) and his article *Kirchenväter und Mahayanismus* in *Mitteilungen der deutschen Gesellschaft für Natur- und Völkerkunde Ostasiens*, vol. XI, Tokyo 1909, contain many hopeful suggestions, but it is not always easy to separate the wheat from the tares.

either because they represent an earlier tradition accepted by all Buddhists, or because the "Hīnayānists" had at some time or other absorbed the new doctrines. For the Mahāyāna has in the main four components, (1) ancient Buddhist teachings which had been neglected and now receive greater emphasis; (2) logical deductions which had not previously been made; (3) reactions to non-Indian thinking, and (4) absorption of the customs and thought-forms of popular piety.

This Buddhism I propose to compare with "Gnosis" rather than "the Gnostics," because the connotation of the latter term is still so uncertain that this Congress has been specially convened for the purpose of defining it. The adherents of Gnosis in my view are those who share the eight assumptions which I will outline in my paper and which can be found in varying degrees in most forms of Hellenistic mysticism and its offshoots.[1] All these traditions are one in spirit, and while the differences between them must seem important to the Near Eastern specialist, for comparative purposes they are of a fairly minor order. Some doctrines are, of course, nearer to Buddhism than others. For instance, a Buddhist who had to take sides on the question whether the world (*kosmos*) is irremediably evil (*kakon*), would on principle have to decide against Plotinos[2] (because to him all conditioned things would be *duḥkha*, ill). The brevity of this paper forces me to concentrate on essentials.

Now I will describe the eight basic similarities between Gnosis and Mahāyāna Buddhism:

(1) (a) *Salvation* takes place through *gnōsis* or *jñāna*, and nothing else can finally achieve it. Both words are etymologically derived from the same Indo-European root. Their meaning also is quite similar. "Not Baptism alone sets us free, but gnosis,—who we were, what we have become; where we

[1] i.e. the Hermetic tradition, the Christian Gnostics, the more spiritual mystery religions (J 38), the neo-Pythagoreans, neo-Platonists, Mandeans, and Manicheans (P 69–72). For the convenience of my fellow Buddhologues I have documented the principal Gnostic tenets from two easily accessible books, i.e. H. Jonas, *The Gnostic Religion*, 1963 (abbreviated as J) and H.-C. Puech, *Le Manichéisme*, 1949 (abbreviated as P).

[2] *Enn.* II.9. Though, of course, some of the views of the Gnōstikoi would be none too palatable either.

were, whereinto we have been thrown; whither we hasten, whence we are redeemed; what is birth and what rebirth"—so the *Excerpta ex Theodoto*.[1] Buddhism in its turn claims that the cognition of conditioned co-production, which the Buddha attained shortly before his enlightenment, dispels all misconceptions on precisely the points enumerated in the Valentinian statement.[2] In both cases the mere insight into the origination and nature of the world liberates us from it, and effects some kind of re-union with the transcendental One, which is identical with our true Self.

(b) As a negative corollary to this, Buddhism teaches that *ignorance* (*avidyā*) is the root evil and the starting point of the chain of causation. This ignorance is in part blindness to the true facts of existence, and in part a self-deception which, misdirecting our attention towards a manufactured world of our own making, conceals the true reality to which wisdom, the highest form of gnosis, alone can penetrate.[3] In the Mahāyāna it means that fictitious beings indulge in a multiplicity of vain and baseless imaginings which cover up the ultimate One. Likewise some, though not perhaps all, Gnostic systems explicitly declare ignorance to be the basic fault[4] which has alienated us from true reality.

(c) This gnostic knowledge is derived solely from revelation,[5] although each one has to experience it within himself.

[1] 78;2. For parallels see P n. 279.

[2] e.g. Buddhaghosa, *Visuddhimagga*, ed. H. C. Warren, 1950, xvii 112-9.—A good collection of Buddhist descriptions of *jñāna* in *Hōbōgirin*, s.v. Chi.—J 34–7, 284–5. Also R. Bultmann's (*Theologie des Neuen Testaments*, 1958, p. 168) definition of *gnōsis* as "das Wissen um die himmlische Herkunft des Selbst" would fit the Mahāyāna quite well.

[3] For more details see my *Buddhist Meditation*, 1956, p. 153, which is based on the *Visuddhimagga*.

[4] e.g. Hermetics x:8. The Valentinian *Gospels of Truth* ascribes creation to Error personified (J 76).—The world is bad, under the control of evil, ignorance or nothingness. The Manicheans: "L'âme s'oublia elle-même; elle oublia sa demeure primitive, son centre véritable, son existence éternelle", quot. P 156. J 63, 71, 127, 131, 174–5, 183, 194, 197, 254. See Bultmann (pp. 169–70) about the "Anfang des des Dramas, das tragische Ereignis der Urzeit". For the Christian Gnostics see also *ibid*. p. 180.

[5] *Buddhism and Culture*. Suzuki Commemorative Volume, ed. S. Yamagucchi, 1960, p. 30. *Buddhist Thought in India*, 1972, pp. 28–30.

(2) We secondly consider the teaching concerning the *levels of spiritual attainment*, and that under three headings:

(a) There is a very sharp division between the aristocracy of the *perfecti* or Elect, and the ordinary run of the *auditores*.[1] To it corresponds in Buddhism that between the *āryas* ("holy" or "noble" men) and the "foolish common people" (*bāla-pṛthagjanā*), who occupy two distinct planes of existence, respectively known as the "wordly" and the "supramundane". Ordinary people are entirely absorbed in the pursuit of sensory objects, or the flight from them, while the saints have undergone a spiritual rebirth, have turned away from this world to the world of the spirit, and have won sufficient detachment from conditioned things to effectively turn to the Path which leads to Nirvāṇa.[2]

(b) There is a *qualitative* difference between the highest ranks of the spiritually awakened and the ordinary run of mankind. They have attained a positively superhuman stature and no common bond of humanity unites them with the rest of us. They have conquered death and become immortal;[3] they have become divine, equal to God,[4] and deserve to be worshipped; the Tathāgatas are absolutely pure, completely omniscient,[5] and omnipresent. The process of salvation is based on the kinship (*syngéneia*) of saviour and saved, because

J 45. For a masterly survey of the modes of revelation see Le R. P. Festuguière, *La révélation d' Hermès Trismégiste*, I, 1950, pp. 59–60, 309–354.

[1] The two classes are "wesenhaft verschieden", Reitzenstein quot. in H. Jonas, *Gnosis und spätankiker Geist*, I, 1934, p. 212; cf. *ibid.* 212–4 for the two, respectively three, classes of men. P 88–9, n. 374; 91, n. 393; J 232–3, P 86–7 and n. 362 about the Manichean hierarchy.

[2] For further information see my *Buddhist Wisdom Books*, 1958, pp. 38–9.

[3] e.g. Apuleius in book XI describes a rite of deification which purges man of his mortality, reconstructs him as an immortal being, and fills him with divine power.

[4] Hermetists: In his essential being man is *nous*, which is divine, "wherefore some men (who know their true nature) are divine, and their humanity is nigh unto divinity" (xii:1). "If thou canst not make thyself equal to God, thou canst not know God" (xi-20). *Manichaeus qui se mira superbia adsumptum a gemino suo, hoc est spiritu sancto, esse gloriatur*. P 44. U. Bianchi 165. J 45, 107, 153, 166, 296–7.

[5] e.g. *Saddharmapuṇḍarīka*, ed. U. Wogihara, 1958, II p. 29.

both have a divine origin. The doctrine of the divine spark, which is our true Self,[1] is indeed fundamental in both systems. For the Mahāyāna the intimate essence of man's being is "the celestial nature itself, purest light, *bodhicittaṃ prakṛtiprabhāsvaram*".[2] In salvation the god within has united with the god outside.[3]

(c) The division between the "saints" and the "foolish worldlings" is found in all Buddhist sects and must go back for a long time. It is only after about A.D. 200 that some Mahāyānists superimposed upon it another division which distinguishes three classes (*gotra* or *rāśi*) of people, i.e. those destined for salvation (*samyaktva-niyata*), those destined for perdition (*mithyātva-miyata*) and those whose destiny is not fixed either way (*aniyata*).[4] This classification, as Tucci has pointed out,[5] corresponds to the well-known gnostic division into those who possess the divine essence (*spermatikoi*), those who, devoid of the divine Self, can by their very material nature not be saved (*hylikoi*), and those who may or may not be saved according to the circumstances (*psychikoi*). Tucci assumes a Gnostic influence, and I am prepared to agree with him. First of all, those who were excluded from salvation, as being destitute of the Buddha-nature, became sometimes known as *icchantika*. So far no one has found a convincing derivation for this term, and everything said about it is guesswork or belongs

[1] J 44, 122–3, 263–4, 271; P 71, 85, n. 275.

[2] G. Tucci, *Tibetan Painted Scrolls*, I, 1949, p. 211. The "self-luminous thought" which is at the centre of our being and has been overlaid by "adventitious defilements" (*āgantukehi upakkilesehi*) becomes in the Mahāyāna "the embryo of the Tathāgata" (see now: D. S. Ruegg, *La théorie du tathāgatagarbha et du gotra*, 1969). To see through to one's own "Buddha-self" became the chief preoccupation of the Zen sect. The Manicheans likewise speak of "our original luminous nature" (J 123), "those around Basilides are in the habit of calling the passions 'appendages'" (J 159) and "in the *Poimandres* the ascent is described as a series of progressive subtractions which leaves the 'naked' true self" (J 166).

[3] e.g. *Buddhist Texts*, 1954, n. 185. A good explanation in E. Obermiller, *Analysis of the Abbisamayālankāra*, 1933, 86–94.

[4] e.g. *Aṣṭādaśasāhasrikā prajñāpāramitā*, ed. E. Conze, 1962, pp. 141–2.

[5] *Jñānamuktāvalī. Commemorative volume in honour of J. Nobel*, New Delhi, 1959, p. 226.

to the realm of Volksetymologie.[1] Secondly, it is hard to see how the determinist and almost Calvinistic postulate that these people are permanently damned, because totally without merit,[2] could possibly be derived by logical steps within Buddhism itself from its own presuppositions. And, thirdly, within the Mahāyāna it is clearly a foreign body and in direct conflict with its basic teaching that the Absolute, or the "Buddha-nature", is the same in all conditioned dharmas and therefore also in all beings. In consequence, this concept became the subject of prolonged discussions,[3] also in China, and numerous attempts were made to abolish it and to find some loophole by which the force of supernatural compassion could somehow redeem these people.

(3) Our third point concerns the crucial role which *Wisdom* plays in both systems. We will consider wisdom under three headings, (a) as a kind of archetype, (b) in her cosmogenic function, and (c) as a feminine deity.

(a) As to the first, I may well be said to be stretching a point by introducing some of the "Wisdom Books" of the Old Testament. But they obviously belong to the same religious complex, and were the work of the immediate predecessors of the Gnostics as well as a source of inspiration to many of them. It seems to me remarkable that during the same period of time—i.e. from *ca.* 200 B.C. onwards—two distinct civilizations, one in the Mediterranean, the other in India, should have constructed a closely analogous set of ideas concerning "Wisdom", each one apparently independently, from its own cultural antecedents. Here are some of the similarities between Chochma[4] and Sophia on the one side and the Prajñāpāramitā on the other:[5] Both are feminine, and called 'mothers' and "nurses". They are equated with the Law (tōrā and

[1] See F. Edgerton, *Buddhist Hybrid Sanskrit Dictionary*, 1953, s.v. D. T. Suzuki, *Studies in the Lankavatara Sutra*, 1957, p. 219 n.

[2] Lit. "they have lost all merit", *sarvakuśalamūlotsarga. Lankāvatāra Sūtra*, ed. B. Nanjio, 1923, p. 66, l.

[3] The Manicheans also were divided on this issue. P 85.

[4] For my information about the Hebrew side I rely on H. Ringgren, *Word and Wisdom*, 1947.

[5] The references can be found in *Oriental Art*, I, 4, 1948, pp. 196–7 (= *S* 207–209).

Dharma), have existed from all times, are the equivalent of God or the Buddha, the consort of Jahve or Vajradhara,[1] extremely elusive, respectively a gift of God or due to the Buddha's might, dispense the waters of knowledge and the food of life, are extremely pure, related to the sky or ether, connected with trees and compared to light. We are urged to "lean on" them and to accept their chastisement. They are vitally important to kings and will disappear in the chaos of the last days.

(b) The *cosmogenetic function* of Sophia is quite pronounced in many Gnostic systems. Until a few years ago every Buddhist scholar would have asserted categorically that *Prajñā* (even in a debased or fallen form, if such a thing were conceivable) could not possibly have anything to do with the creation of the world, being entirely occupied with its removal. Then in 1959 we had the first critical edition of a Buddhist Tantra, and there, in the *Hevajra Tantra*,[2] we unmistakably read that "*Prajñā* is called Mother, because she gives birth to the world." Dr. Snellgrove, the editor, stresses the presence in this text of "notions that are not Buddhist, in the sense that they are not properly assimilated, and seem to exist in contradiction with the wider context".[3] This particular idea about *Prajñā* is so much at variance with what is possible within the orbit of Buddhist thinking that it must have come from the outside, and the Gnostics seem the most likely source. If we bear in mind that there are literally thousands of Tantras which have never yet been critically investigated by Europeans, many more surprises are likely to be in store for us.

(c) Perhaps the most radical innovation of the Mahāyāna was the introduction of *feminine* deities. As usually the dates are none too certain, but by A.D. 400 female deities, among them the *Prajñāpāramitā*, were definite cult objects. Much earlier the *Prajñāpāramitā* had been proclaimed as the Mother

[1] Likewise the Valentinians spoke of the marriage of Sophia and Jesus.

[2] ed. D. L. Snellgrove, 1959, I, v, 16: *Jananī bhaṇyate prajñā janayati yasmāj jagat*. For my further comments on this passage see BLSOAS, xxiii, 3, 1969, p. 604 = p. 215 below. In Irenaeus, *adv. haer.* I, 23, 2 the Helene of Simon is called *mater omnium*.

[3] p. 7: cf. 11, 18. J. 306: The different versions of the *Apocryphon of John* "show the ease with which heterogeneous material was accepted into gnostic compositions of well established literary identity".

of the Buddhas.[1] To cut it short, if it gives sense to distinguish between "matriarchal" and "patriarchal" religions, then surely the Mahāyāna and Gnosticism are more "matriarchal"[2] than, say, the "Hīnayāna" and Protestant Christianity. Later on, in the Tantras, the consorts of the Buddhas and Bodhisattvas, and by implication the girls involved in ritual intercourse with the Tantric *siddhas*, were known as *prajñās* and *vidyās*.[3] It is a noteworthy coincidence that a few centuries before their time Sophia should have been described as suitable for sexual intercourse[4] and that a bit later the Gnostic Simon should have called his consort Helene, a harlot[5] he had found in a brothel in Tyre, by the names of "Sophia" (= *prajñā*) or "Ennoia" (= *vidyā*).[6]

(4) Both Mahāyāna and Gnostics are indifferent to *historical facts* and tend to replace them by *myths*. This shows itself in at least two ways:

(a) A *docetistic* interpretation of the Founder's life. It would be unsuitable for me to tell this audience about the Docetism of the Gnostics.[7] In the Mahāyāna it takes the form of asserting that the Buddha's physical body, his human and earthly life, his birth, enlightenment and death, were not really real, but a mere show conjured up to teach and awaken people. To quote *The Lotus of the Good Law*: "Although the Tathāgata has not actually entered Nirvāṇa, he makes a show of doing so,

[1] For the *Ratnaguṇasaṃcayagāthā* see *Suzuki Commemorative Volume* 1960, pp. 25–6. (= *S* 125).

[2] For the Gnostics see e.g. E. O. James, *The cult of the mother goddess* 1959, pp. 192–4. In greater detail see *Gnosis und spätantiker Geist*, I, 1934, where H. Jonas distinguishes a "männliche Gruppe" (335–51) and a "weibliche Gruppe" (371–75); p. 352: "daß z.B. die spekulativ zentrale weibliche Gottheit von der Gestalt einer syrisch-phönizisch-ägyptischen Mond-, Mutter- und Geschlechtsgöttin hergeleitet ist, hat Bousset nachgewiesen".

[3] The term *śakti* is exclusively Hindu and never used by Buddhists.

[4] Ringgren, p. 119; cf. p. 106.

[5] In the Mahāyāna, by contrast, the Bodhisattvas Samantabhadra (D. T. Suzuki, *Essays in Zen Buddhism*, III, 1934, p. 372) and Avalokiteśvara (F. Sierksma, *The gods as we shape them*, 1960, pl. 28) manifest themselves as harlots.

[6] J. 104, 107.

[7] J 78, 128, 133, 195.

for the sake of those who have to be educated".[1] The real Buddha should not be mistaken for the historical Buddha, who is no more than a phantom body displayed by Him.

(b) The scriptural tradition is authenticated by reference to persons and events which have often no clearly defined place within the framework of observable and verifiable human history, and their initial revelation normally takes place neither on earth nor among men,[2] and often at the beginning of time. The *Pistis Sophia* is the teaching of the Risen Christ, another text is ascribed to "Poimandres, the Nous of the Absolute Power",[3] the Manichean *Kephalaia* have been revealed by "the Living Paraclete"[4] and the Hermetic tradition dates back to Hermes Trismegistos who is identified with Thoth. Just so all Mahāyāna scriptures were inspired and compiled by mythological personages, such as Maitreya, Amitābha, Avalokiteśvara, or Mañjuśrī.[5] The lineage of the *Guhyasamāja*, for instance, gives first the Buddha Vajradhara and the Bodhisattva Vajrapāṇi, and only then a number of historical names.[6] The Hermetists were in the habit of unearthing books hidden away by godlike sages in the remote past (*exemāsteuse* is the technical term), and likewise the Tibetan Nyingmapas and Kahgyutpas put their faith in the *gter-ma*, or buried

[1] *Buddhist Texts through the Ages*, ed. E. Conze, 1954, no. 135.

[2] E. Lamotte, *Sur la formation du Mahāyāna*, in *Asiatica*, Festschrift Friedrich Weller, 1954, pp. 381–6. The Mahāyāna scriptures are said to have been compiled on Vimalasvabhāva, a mythical mountain, by a council composed of Bodhisattvas, presided by Samantabhadra—Mañjuśrī reciting the Abhidharma, Maitreya the Vinaya and Vajrapāṇi the Sūtras. They were miraculously preserved for five centuries in hidden places, such as the palace of the king of the Gandharvas, or of the king of Nāgas, etc. Some of the scriptures were also due to Mahāyāna saints going up into the Tushita heaven and being there instructed by the Bodhisattva Maitreya. Tucci, p. 210: "Some Tantras were spoken on Sumeru, to an assembly of bodhisattvas, or of divine beings. Others in the Akaniṣṭha paradise, others among the Śuddhāvāsa gods and so on".

[3] J 148.

[4] J 208.

[5] E. Lamotte, *Manjuśrī*, in *T'oung Pao*, XLVIII, 1960, pp. 5–8, 40–8. Alternatively Maitreya descends on earth to recite Sūtras, or "one sees the face of Manjuśrī" and learns from him. See n. 5 on p. 17.

[6] A. Wayman in JAOS 75, 1955, p. 258.

texts, which were hidden by Buddhas or Saints (esp. Padmasambhava) and later on recovered by predestined persons, often with the help of the *ḍākinīs*, or "sky-walkers".[1]

(5) A tendency towards *antinomianism* is inherent in both systems. This ticklish theme can be discussed on the plane of either theory or practice. As far as *theory* is concerned, there is no difficulty. The exalted spiritual condition generated in the perfect by the power of full understanding must of necessity cause a certain disdain for the puny demands of conventional morality. In consequence some Gnostic sects taught that once a man has gained salvation, he is free to disregard moral obligations.[2] Likewise some Mahāyānists were so intoxicated by the heights to which the perfection of wisdom had carried them that they regarded the practice of morality as unworthy of their attention, while others went out of their way to demonstrate their spiritual freedom by deliberately breaking all the moral precepts intended only for the lesser breed.[3] As for the actual *practice*, the case is different. How far did sexual symbolism imply sexual activity? Did these saintly men ever commit any of the abominations which they so freely commended in words? The answer is, I suppose, that while some did and some did not, their opponents would make the most of those who did. The Fathers of the Church were most eloquent about the misdeeds of the Gnostics, but the books recently found in Chenoboskion hardly bear them out. This is all that need be said, and a closer scrutiny of the actual behaviour of these people would only serve to gratify a vulgar and prurient curiosity.

(6) As distinct from the theistic religions, both Mahāyāna

[1] Le R. P. Festugière, *La révélation d' Hermès Trismégiste*, I, 1950 pp. 76, 78, 319–24; H. Hoffmann, *Die Religionen Tibets*, 1956, pp. 45, 49, 54, 175; W. Y. Evans-Wentz, *The Tibetan Book of the Dead*, 1957, LIV-LV, 73–7.

[2] For a very fine account of Gnostic antinomianism see J 266–77; also J 46, 110, 136.

[3] Śāntideva, *Sikṣāsamuccaya*, ed. C. Bendall, 1902, p. 97 and *Suzuki Commemorative Volume* pp. 38–9; D. L. Snellgrove, *The Hevajra Tantra*, I, 1959, pp. 8–9, 18, 42–4, 81; E. Conze, *Buddhism*, 1951, pp. 177–8, 195–7; S. B. Dasgupta, *Introduction to Tāntric Buddhism*, 1950, pp. 113–8, 198–211. For a fairly early statement see *Kāśyapaparivarta*, par. 103. trsl. F. Weller, 1965, pp. 122–3.

and Gnosis differentiate between the still and quiescent *Godhead*, and the active *creator god*, who is placed at a lower level. Of the first, the Hermetists said that "of Him no words can tell, no tongue can speak, silence only can declare Him".[1] And so the Buddhists on countless occasions about the Absolute which they identified with Nirvāṇa, the Buddha, the Realm of Dharma, Suchness, etc. The demiurge, in his turn, is a secondary divine being who, himself a proud, ambitious and impure spirit, has created this most unsatisfactory world.[2] His Buddhist counterpart is to some extent the Hindu god Brahmā who in his stupidity boasts about having created this cosmos,[3] when in fact it is the automatic product of cycles of evolution and involution going on over the ages. But, how ever the world may have come about, at present it is, in any case, the domain of an evil force, of Satan or of Māra the Evil One.[4]

(7) Both systems despise easy popularity, and their writings aim at initiates and exclude the multitude. In consequence there is everywhere a predilection for the mysterious, the secret, the enigmatic, the hidden, the esoteric. In Buddhism it increased as time went on. The first step was, about A.D. 300, the largely Yogācārin concept of *saṃdhābhāṣya*, according to which words had both an obvious and a hidden meaning, and works composed under Yogācārin influence made much of this "hidden meaning".[5] The second step was the wholesale

[1] I:31—In both systems immense efforts were made to guard the transcendental character of the ultimate reality. J 251: "The true God . . . is the Unknown, the totally Other, unknowable in terms of any worldly analogies". This might have been said of Nirvāṇa. So also J 42, 288–9. Or J 142: "There is no trace in all nature from which even his (the true God's) existence could be suspected". He is altogether "Beyond" (J 51), and *pāram* is one of the keywords of Buddhism.

[2] J xiii, 109–10, 134–6, 191 n., 295–8; P 71 and n. 274.

[3] *Dīgha Nikāya* I 18. In popular belief he is "Victor, Unvanquished, All-seeing, Controller, Lord, Maker, Creator, Chief, Disposer, Master, Father of all that have become and will be".

[4] T. O. Ling, *Buddhism and the Mythology of Evil*, 1962, pp. 58–9, 86. J 211, 224. Bultmann, p. 173. For the Mandean Ruha see J 72.

[5] For a definition see Asanga, *Mahāyānasaṃgraha*, in E. Lamotte, *La Somme du grand Véhicule*, II, 1, 1938, pp. 129–132, with further literature at 23*, and for examples see *Suzuki Commemorative Volume*, 1960, pp. 40–1 (= *S* 142). An early example is *Dhammapada* 294–5,

adoption of an esoteric terminology which was unintelligible without the oral explanations of a *guru*, and thus tended to conceal rather than reveal the message conveyed. Many Tantras, and also some Ch'an works,[1] were composed in this fashion.

(8) Last, but not least, both systems adopted a metaphysics which is *monistic* in the sense that it enjoins an intellectual, emotional and volitional revulsion from multiple things, and advocates, more or less explicitly, a re-union with a One which transcends the multiple world.[2] Occasionally both systems also adopt a dialectical critique of all thought-constructions which shows them to be untenable and self-contradictory figments of the imagination which have to be paradoxically both discarded and somehow preserved for the vision of the ineffable One to become possible.[3]

These are my eight chief points. There is no room for the discussion of numerous minor analogies. In any case, if these are the similarities, what then are the *differences*? They are, I think, basically threefold: (1) The intellectual categories in which these theories are clothed are indigenous and therefore in one case taken from the Abhidharma, in the other from Greek philosophy; and also the mythological figures vary accordingly. (2) Compared with the Mahāyāna, some Gnostics seem guilty of excessive myth-mongering, though I feel that some Christian authors, both ancient and modern, have somewhat exaggerated its importance. From this point of view Prof. F. R. Hamm was right when he argued against me that "der Tenor" of gnostic literature is essentially different from

unless these two verses foreshadow the later antinomianism.—Likewise the Valentinians in "their pneumatic exegesis of Scripture stressed the difference between the manifest meaning open to the 'psychics' and the hidden one accessible to themselves" (J 206).

[1] e.g. "The Stories of the founders of the five Ch'an sects". See my review in *The Middle Way*, xxxvi, 1961, pp. 136–7 (= p. 197 below).

[2] For both Buddhists and Gnostics the world of divine freedom is strictly *transcosmical*. Nirvāṇa is defined as the place "where do water, earth and fire,—where does air no footing find", or "where these four great elements cease to exist without leaving any trace of them". *Dīgha Nikāya*, I, 222, in F. L. Woodward, *Some Sayings of the Buddha*, 1925, p. 321. About Gnostic Monism see J 60–1.

[3] R. Gnoli, in *La Parola del Passato*, LXXVII, 1961, pp. 155–8, about Damaskios and Nāgārjuna.

that of the Buddhist wisdom books.[1] (3) Assuming that man has fallen into this world from a more perfect condition, the Gnostics expended much ingenuity on trying to describe the process which brought about this fall. Classical Buddhism shows no interest in what may have preceded ignorance. All one wanted to know was how salvation can be achieved, and not how it became necessary. But there is the proviso that the later Yogācārins, particularly in China, devoted much attention to the stages by which the world is derived from an originally pure "store-consciousness" (*ālayavijñāna*).

Making allowance for the differences, I still think that the similarities between Gnosticism and Mahāyāna Buddhism are remarkably close, and do not concern only fortuitous details, but the essential structure itself.[2]

Here are a few more apparent, and at least possible similarities:

(1) Both systems are fond of Serpents (*nāgas*) as beings connected with wisdom (J 93–5, 228).

(2) Both hold astrology in high esteem (J 157, 254–65); the principal Buddhist literary source is the late *Kālacakra-tantra*, but the actual practices are almost universal in Buddhist countries.

(3) Both rely on the power of secret formulas, *mantras* or spells.

(4) Both place a great emphasis on Light (*phōs* and *āloka*).

(5) Both show a tendency towards syncretism, borrow from ancient mythologies and revive the most archaic ideas. In this connection I must refer to U. Bianchi's "Le problème des origines du gnosticisme et l'histoire des religions", *Numen* xii, 1965, 161–178, who has well shown not only that Gnosticism as a "complexe idéologique" is foreshadowed already in Orphism, but also that many of its basic ideas are of great antiquity[3] and that some can be traced back to prehistoric times. Bianchi has also seen the affinity with Buddhism in

[1] OLZ 58, 1963, p. 188.

[2] See also G. Tucci, p. 210, "The Tantras may in fact be best defined as the expression of Indian gnosis"; p. 211, "Gnosis was born in India a little later than in the West and Iran", but in spite of all contacts Tucci regards it as "a spontaneous germination of India" (p. 212).

[3] See also R. Crahay, on pp. 323–39.

"Initiation, Mystères, Gnose," *Initiation*, ed. C. Bleeker, 1965, pp. 167–9.

(6) In both the perfect can demonstrate their high degree of spirituality by the display of wonderworking powers; there is indeed a close affinity between some of the later Neoplatonists, such as Proclus (see A. J. Festugière's paper in the Colloquio[1]) and the later Tantric professors at Nālandā University in the eighth century, in that both combine (1) a sober and perfectly rational philosophical dialectic with (2) a yearning for union with the One and (3) a cultivation of magical prowesses of various kinds (for parallels to Festugière from the Mahāyāna see my *A Short History of Buddhism*, 1960, p. 63).

(7) The more philosophical authors and the *Prajñāpāramitā* texts show many verbal coincidences; here Sophia as the *oikía* of the wise, there the P.P. as their *vihāra* (dwelling); the epithet *phōsphóros* corresponds to *ālokakarī* (Light-bringer), *achrāntos* to *anupalipta* (immaculate), etc. etc. The *Heart Sūtra*, both in structure and content, shows much similarity to Dionysius Areopagita's *Divine Theology* (I 2, II 1, III 1, IV–V), and in general the "negative theology" (J 268) uses the same approach as the *Prajñāpāramitā* Sūtras which employ negations to such an extent that their philosophical exegesis by the Mādhyamikas consists largely in clarifying the logic of negative propositions. Some attempts are made in both systems to somehow mediate between the absolutely transcendental One and the completely incommensurable conditioned world. So in the "Questions of Maitreya" in the *Pañcaviṃśatisāhāsrikā prajñāpāramitā* (fol. 580 no. 31) we read: "But if the inexpressible realm were quite other than the entity which is the sign of something conditioned, then even just now that sign could not be apprehended through which there would be a penetration into this inexpressible realm". This statement may, or may not, be connected with what Proclus (*The Elements of Theology*, ed. E. R. Dodds, 1933) says (pp. 109–11, prop. 123), i.e. "All that is divine is itself ineffable and unknowable by any secondary being because of its supra-existential unity, but it may be apprehended and known from the existents which participate in it".

(8) There may be some relation between the "Counterfeit

[1] Not published in the *Numen* Supplement.

Spirit" (J 92, 205, 226) and the *prativarṇikā prajñāpāramitā* (e.g. *Aṣṭasāhasrikā prajñāpāramitā*, ed. R. Mitra, 1888, v, 112–3) or the "Counterfeit Dharma" of Chinese Buddhist tradition.

(9) The figure of Yama, god of death, seems to be inspired by Gnosticism (J 87).

(10) The Gnostics attach importance to "Seals' (J 119–20) and in later Buddhism the term *mudrā* is increasingly used.

(11) Some sub-sects give allegiance to persons violently repudiated by the main tradition, e.g. to Cain (J 95) and Devadatta.

(12) The formula "because this is so, therefore this is so" (J 310) looks very much like the famous *evaṃ sati idaṃ hoti*.

(13) Both show fondness for sexual imagery.

(14) Salvation is likened to an "awakening" (J 80 sq.), and in consequence there is a tendency to regard this world, as it appears, as a dream (J 70), wholly unsubstantial (J 84) and "a Nothing" (J 184n.); see also R. Crahay's paper on p. 328.

(15) In both systems sexual intercourse (J 72) and coarse food (J 114) played a decisive part in the gradual deterioration of mankind (for the Buddhists see e.g. *Buddhist Texts*, ed. E. Conze, 1954, no. 206); and likewise in both cases the size of people corresponds to their spiritual stature (see Böhlig's paper p. 126).

(16) There is also a striking similarity between some of the similes used as well as the conclusions drawn from them. One may compare: "As gold sunk in filth will not lose its beauty but preserve its own nature, and the filth will be unable to impair the gold, etc." (J 271) with *Ratnagotravibhāga*: "Supposing that gold belonging to a man on his travels had fallen into a place full of stinking dirt. As it is indestructible by nature, it would stay there for many hundreds of years", etc. up to verse 110 (*Buddhist Texts*, 1954, pp. 128–3),—and in both cases this is a simile for the divine spark in man.

(17) Hyppolytos' *Philosophumena* (ca 250) refer to a Bactrian (= Bamian, Serae Parthorum) gnostic doctrine according to which the son of God was not incarnated (born) for the first time in Bethlehem, but was incarnated before and will be incarnated again in the future (A. Lloyd, *Mitteilungen*, p. 396).

A few further points concern the *Manicheans* in particular, e.g.:

(18) There is strong resemblance between the descriptions of a messenger (J 108, 230) and a Mahāyāna Bodhisattva.

(19) The loving contemplation of the repulsiveness of the body (J 227–8) surely owes something to the Buddhist, meditations on *aśubha* (see E. Conze, *Buddhist Meditation*, 1956, 95–107).

(20) The emphasis on Peace, self-sacrifice and *ahiṃsā* (J 215–6, 232; *Buddhist Texts*, p. 169) unites them both.

(21) Jonas (232) says of the "Elect" that they "must have led a monastic life of extraordinary asceticism, perhaps modelled on Buddhist monasticism".

(22) The Pentads of the Manicheans (J 217–8) are closely analogous to those of the Vajrayāna (H. Hoffmann, *Die Religionen Tibets*, 1956, pp. 40–2).

(23) The Buddha's triple body corresponds to the triple Jesus of Mani. The three forms of Jesus are: (1) transcendental, corresponding to the *dharmakāya*; (2) historical, who only apparently underwent the Passion, corresponding to the *nirmāṇakāya*; (3) *Jesus patibilis* (P 82–3, J 228–9), who is not at all dissimilar to the Buddha's intermediary body (*saṃbhogakāya*, etc.) in its more cosmic interpretations: *iti kāritra-vaipulyād buddho vyāpī nirucyate* (*Abhisamayālankāra* VIII 11). "From the abundance of his activity the Buddha is thus described as "all-pervading'." It is true that the Buddhists speak of the Buddha's "activity" and the Manicheans of the "passion" of Jesus, but on closer consideration this difference will be found to be mainly a verbal one.

These are some of the points which may be worth following up.

How then can we account for the facts? There are, as far as I can see, only three hypotheses, all equally unattractive:

(1) The kinship may be due to *mutual borrowing*. We now have abundant evidence of the close contact between the Buddhist and the Hellenistic world,[1] and many instances of

[1] See e.g. H. de Lubac, *La rencontre du Bouddhisme et de l'occident* 1952, pp. 9–32 (période hellénistique). S. Radhakrishnan, *Eastern religions and Western thought*, 1940. E. Lamotte, *Les premières relations entre l' Inde et l'Occident*, in *La Nouvelle Clio*, V, 1953, 83–118. M. Wheeler, *Rome beyond the imperial frontiers*, 1955, pp. 141–202.

borrowing by one or the other side have come to light.[1] Nevertheless, even if there was a large-scale exchange of ideas, the mode of their transmission remains obscure. It is a fact that both the Mahāyāna and the Tantras developed in the border regions of India which were exposed to the impact of Roman-Hellenistic, Iranian and Chinese civilizations,[2] and we also know that the Buddhists were in contact with the Thomas Christians in South India and the Manicheans in Central Asia. But that is about all. And it is indeed remarkable that Gnostic texts often invoke Jewish, Babylonian, Iranian, Egyptian, etc. authorities, but very rarely Buddhist ones.[3]

Alternatively we may have to deal with either a (2) *joint* or a (3) *parallel* development. (2) In the first case one may assume that both Asia and Europe form one unit in which a parallel rhythm assures a fairly uniform development from age to age. This hypothesis works better for some periods than for others, and somewhat lacks in a respectable rational foundation.[4] (3) In the second case one may assume that Gnosticism is one of the basic types of human religiosity and therefore likely to reproduce itself at any period. Its self-consistent theoretical statements would then spring from a common mentality and from common spiritual experiences, and occur whenever certain men feel not only totally alienated from the world around them[5] but also in contact with a living spiritual

[1] See e.g. M. Eliade, *Yoga*, 1958, pp. 202, 431–2. E. Conze in BLSOAS, xiv, 1952, pp. 252–3 (= *S* 170–172).

[2] E. Conze, in *The Concise Encyclopedia of Living Faiths*, ed. R. C. Zaehner, 1959, pp. 296–7 (= *S* 49–50). G. Tucci, pp. 210, 212–6.

[3] An exception is, of course, Mani. See P 23, 31, 44, 59, 61, 144–5, 147 n. 249, 149. The references to "Nirvāṇa" in the Central Asian documents (P 86, n. 359), as well as the designation of Mani as a "Buddha (P 28, 45, n. 250) are, however, later accommodations to a largely Buddhist environment.

[4] I have discussed it in some detail in *Oriental Art*, I 3, 1948, pp. 148–9.

[5] J 49–50, 65–8, 237, 251; P pp. 70–1, nn., 273, 278.—The rather startling paper of G. Lanczkowski about the gnostic elements in ancient American religions (pp. 676–687) has led me to think of a *fourth* possibility. Perhaps the basic ideas were thought out in some prehistoric period as a kind of *philosophia perennis*, at a time before Europeans, Asians and Americans dispersed into their respective continents. In the same way we infer from the similarities between the various Indo-European languages that the ancestors of those who now use them once lived together in the same part of the world.

tradition.[1] In that case one would still have to explain why it reached such prominence just when it did, both in India and the Mediterranean at the same time.

All I can say is that there is here a definite problem, but as yet no definite solution. And what, of course, still remains to be seen is whether my alleged parallels will stand up to the scrutiny of the experts!

[1] This is what differentiates the Buddhists and Gnostics from most modern existentialists. H. Jonas in his otherwise very instructive article on *Gnosis und moderner Nihilismus*, in *Kerygma und Dogma*, 1960, pp. 155–171 seems to overlook this vital point, and I cannot agree with his thesis that the Gnostics, and for that matter the Buddhists, are "nihilistic" in the sense in which our post-Nietzschean existentialists are. At one point (p. 167) Jonas concedes that "Ein entscheidender Unterschied allerdings zu den modernen Parallelen ist der: obwohl geworfen in die Zeitlichkeit haben wir der gnostischen Formel gemäß unseren Ursprung in der Ewigkeit. Dies stellt den innerweltlichen Nihilismus in einen metaphysischen Horizont, der dem modernen Gegenstück fehlt". I would suggest that it is more than a matter of "metaphysical horizon", that the *spiritual practices* which correspond to the conviction that "we had an origin in eternity, and so also have an aim in eternity" (so the English version at J 335) make life far from meaningless, that to describe the renunciation of the world by mystics and ascetics as "innerweltlichen Nihilismus" is a misuse of words, and that Jonas (J 239) is wrong in emphasizing the "non-traditional" character of Gnosticism. It is true that without the "Beyond" "we should have nothing but a hopeless worldly pessimism" (J 261). But it is precisely this Beyond which is the lifeblood of both Gnosis and the Mahāyāna. As I put it ten years ago: "What then is the subject matter" of the *Prajnā-pāramitā* Sutras? It is just the Unconditioned, nothing but the Absolute, over and over again". "Out of the abundance of the heart the mouth speaketh. The lengthy writings on Perfect Wisdom are one long declamation in praise of the Absolute" (*Selected Sayings from the Perfection of Wisdom*, 1955, pp. 18–9). For a fuller discussion of this important topic see also what I have said in "Philosophy East and West", xiii, 1963, 111–3 (=*S* 237–239) and in the Suzuki Commemorative Volume pp. 38–9 (=*S* 139–140). My point is, I think, very well borne out by R. Crahay's paper on p. 330. In modern existentialism we find plenty about la séparation, la descente, la chute, l'exil, l'obscurcissement, la captivité, la souillure, la peur. But when ever do we hear about le rappel, la confiance, la purification, la libération, l'illumination, le repatriement, la remontée, l'union?

3
LOVE, COMPASSION AND SYMPATHETIC JOY

1. Love

Christian apologists have often attacked Buddhism as a religion without God and without Love. Since we live in an environment which is either still Christian, or at least strewn with the debris of the Christian tradition, it might not be without some interest to try to define our position with regard to "love" considered as a virtue. In addition there is, in Seng-ts'an's poem "On Trust in the Heart" the verse which says of the Way: "Only when freed from hate and love, It reveals itself fully and without disguise." Many readers stumble when they come to this line, and I have for a long time wanted to explain it and to render it plausible.

The first thing to note about the word "love" is its intolerable vagueness. Religion is the science of the spiritual life. Its teachings will be unintelligible, its precepts ambiguous and its adherents an easy prey to self-deception, unless all words are scrupulously avoided which are incapable of a precise definition. And what could be more vague and ambiguous than this word "love"? First of all, it is used of a great variety of *objects*. We "love" food, dogs, children, parents, women, our fellow men, England, painting, God, and I do not know what else. All these attitudes may in some way be similar, but the similarity is extremely slight and approaches the vanishing point. Then there are different *modalities* of love. I will mention only a few of the most outstanding. There is (1) "Fondness", a desire for someone's presence and company, but without desire for physical contact. (2) "Tenderness", a desire for skin contact, but without excitement or possessiveness. (3) "Infatuation" also called "cardiac-respiratory" love, because disturbance of breathing and blood circulation is an important factor in it.

It is a short-lived phenomenon, more frequent in adolescence than later. (4) Sexual love, on all its many levels—oral, anal, genital, homosexual, heterosexual, etc. (5) "Narcissistic" love which is diffused over one's own body, and which usually combines with (3) and (4). (6) "Romantic love", which is a combination of (3) with a set of philosophical ideas which originated in the South of France at the time of the Troubadours. Mate love is idealised, and held to make life worth while, an infatuation is expected to last a life-time, and two persons of the opposite sex are believed to be specially and exclusively "made for each other". "Romantic love" is again subject to many gradations of refinement, ranging roughly from Dante to Hollywood, and it is either combined with marriage or held to be incompatible with it. In many cultures it is completely unknown. Finally we have (7) "spiritual" love, or "charity", which is directed to a quite unworldly spiritual essence, and which is equally intense in respect of all.

The common denominator between these seven kinds of "love" is merely verbal. In the interest of mental clarity, instead of speaking about "love" in general, one should make an effort to state precisely which one of its modalities one has in mind. As it is, the ambiguities of the word "love" help to bemuse and confuse the marital relations of modern man. Recently I saw a play by Somerset Maugham in which two people complained about lack of "love" in the other. It was entirely based on the wife, after fifteen years of marriage, wanting a mixture of (3) and (4) from her husband, whereas the husband was content to offer a mixture of (1) and (2).

In view of all this I contend that the word "love" is quite useless for descriptive purposes, and that the less we hear of it the better it is. If we now turn to the Buddhist Scriptures, we find that they are without an equivalent to the word "love" in its bewildering variety. On the one hand there is *maitrī*, or *mettā*, a virtue. Although *maitrī* is sometimes carelessly translated as "love", it is more properly "friendliness', as it is derived from *mitra*, "a friend". *Maitrī* "is so called because it is found in a friend, or because it proceeds with regard to a friend".[1] Loving-kindness" would be a possible rendering, but not "love". On the other hand, words like *anunaya*, or

[1] Buddhaghosa, *The Path of Purity*, p. 318.

sneha, describe "love" in the sense of "affection", which is condemned as a vice and a fetter.

"Love cometh from companionship;
In wake of love upsurges ill.
Seeing the bane that comes of love,
Fare lonely as rhinoceros".[1]

In this verse of the *Suttanipāta*, *sneha* is spoken of. We are also warned that, when friendliness is cultivated, it may lead to the strengthening of its "near enemy", which is worldly greed, and degenerate into passionate or sensuous love (*rāga*), or exclusive, particular affection, which makes distinctions, and tries to find a privileged place for some rather than others. Finally, there is also *bhakti*, "loving devotion", a term which occurs only very rarely.

What is usually called "love" is a strange blend of different factors which are, spiritually, of very unequal value, and which include sensuous titillation (more precisely "skin pleasure"), possessiveness, desire for security, self-aggrandisement and self-effacement. Something is, I suggest, to be said for the Buddhist practice of keeping the different factors terminologically apart.

But this is not all. In Buddhism, "friendliness" is a virtue, but a subordinate one. Wisdom alone can set us free. "Friendliness' is not one of the steps of the holy Eightfold Path, does not figure among the seven "limbs of enlightenment" or the thirty-seven "wings to enlightenment", and is not reckoned as one of the five cardinal virtues, or one of the six perfections. The *Anguttaranikāya* (v. 342) enumerates eleven advantages of the practice of friendliness. Nirvāṇa is not one of them. In order to justify this relegation of friendliness to a secondary position, I must be content here to briefly indicate four reasons which suggest that a religion does well not to put too much stress on the love aspect of the spiritual life.

1. First of all, there seems to be a *law of compensation*, by which much talk about a virtue indicates less an abundance than a lack of it. Ordinary experience shows that someone who always assures you of his honesty is likely to cheat you. Someone who praises his truthfulness is likely to be a liar.

[1] E. M. Hare, *Woven Cadences*, p. 6.

Someone who speaks much of humility is likely to be very conceited. Someone who always talks about the slaying of the self will present a veritable mountain of selfhood to the outside world, though he may not perceive it himself. Someone who makes much of wisdom is probably a singularly foolish person. The reason is not far to seek. A virtue is emphasized, by praise or by the condemnation of its opposite, to the extent that it seems personally important to us, and it is personally important to us to the extent that we are in need of it, and to the extent that its opposite is a temptation to us. I have in my life met many people who told me that religion means that "love is all". Invariably I have found them to be either cold-hearted people, or full of hatred and hidden malice, or, alternatively, bursting with unused libido. When Professor Suzuki was recently in London, we noticed that he spoke not once in praise of "love", or even of loving-kindness. This may have been because kindness had become so natural to him that he no longer needed to whip himself up about it.

2. There is the psychological *law of ambivalence*, by which love and hatred belong inseparably together. It applies to sex love, and to all love to the extent that it is intense, sensuous and self-seeking. When one strengthens love, one automatically strengthens hate at the same time, if only unconsciously. It is true that ambivalence is not recognized by psychologists who reject the whole concept of the "unconscious", and that the general public is not well aware of the numerous facts which support it. In this brief article I cannot argue the point. I take it for granted that love and hate are inseparable, like two sides of a coin, so that in actual fact there is really neither love nor hate, but a third factor, which appears respectively as either love or hate, just as the circumstances demand. One would then expect that religions which stress love should also manifest more hatred than those which do not. Observation seems to bear this out. Love is for ever on the lips of the Christians. They are also the people who have enriched history by crusades, pogroms and the Holy Inquisition, and they never tire of blessing guns, tanks and warplanes, and of fomenting 'righteous wars". In addition they tell us "to hate evil", when I would have thought that to hate evil is nearly as bad as to do it, and in its effects it usually comes to the same thing.

3. The stress on love must involve a stress on the *personal aspects of the deity* who otherwise would be devoid of attributes which render it lovable. On certain levels of spiritual development it is certainly significant and fruitful to describe the Absolute as a father, a mother, a friend, a sweetheart, etc. But, strictly speaking, such statements are inaccurate and untrue. In consequence, wherever *bhakti* is placed above wisdom, a religion is in danger of throwing up dogmas which are ultimately untrue. They have then to be defended with the intolerance with which we guard against incipient doubts in ourselves, for it is well known that just the most dubious statements evoke the greatest fanaticism. The true character of the Absolute can be revealed only to wisdom, and that is even-minded, beyond hate and beyond love.

4. If *self-extinction* is the *supreme goal* of the spiritual life, then "love" is not the means by which it can be achieved. In Buddhism, friendliness is taught as an antidote, not to self-infatuation but to ill-will and malice. This is its purpose, and that circumscribes its possibilities. In recent times it has become habitual to oppose "love" to "selfishness", and to believe that a growth in love will *ipso facto* promote unselfishness. Nothing could be further from the truth. Self-seeking is a most conspicuous element in most of what is currently regarded as "love". In mother love, for instance, the child is as often as not a mere extension of the mother's self, which is not weakened, but immensely strengthened by this identification with something outside it. To some extent at least she loves the child because it is "her" child, because it is a piece of herself, which makes her more important to herself. In mate love, likewise, the narcissistic component is easy to observe. One cannot make love successfully unless one builds up the self-esteem of one's partners, and makes them feel "wanted" and "precious". Or, let us consider G. Gorer's excellent account of "The Americans" (1948). If the average American believes passionately and deeply in love, if, unable to tolerate loneliness, he craves insatiably for the signs of love, and measures his success by how much he is loved, and is worthy of love, then all this has nothing to do with unselfishness. It is clearly a bolstering up of the ego, and not a diminution of it. We can go further, and say that even acts of self-sacrifice are no sure

indication of unselfishness. They are often accompanied by sad musings about the ingratitude of those who do not appreciate what is being done for them, they may spring from self-hate, or from hatred for what is sacrificed, or they may just transfer property from one part of the self to another. For whenever we consider this matter of selfishness and unselfishness scientifically, we must bear in mind the elastic boundaries of the "self", which is the sum total of all the parts of the universe we claim as our own. It is certainly not the whole truth about love that it "seeketh only Self to please". But this is an important element in it. The eradication of attachment to self is therefore unlikely to be achieved by the cultivation of "love" as such. It is claimed that by loving someone else, one forgets oneself. The same effect is produced by alcohol, hard work, rapt gazing and many other activities. It requires, however, little subtlety of mind to see that this kind of self-forgetting leaves the self substantially intact.

Love is an important raw material of the spiritual life. Just as iron ore will not by itself turn into steel, without the help of much fuel, acids and labour, so also the emotion of love must be changed out of all recognition if it is to become a weapon in the fight against self. And this process of refinement, sublimation and spiritualisation demands the intervention, not of emotional, but of intellectual forces, which deprive love of all those features which make it dear to us. Wisdom alone allows us to see the self for what it really is, and discloses both its nature, boundaries and ultimate inanity, and the workings of the unseen, impersonal, actually real cosmic forces which pervade the universe. When transformed by wisdom love becomes impartial, and thus nearly unrecognizable.

2. *Friendliness and Compassion*

(1) There has never been any controversy about the definitions of friendliness and compassion, and they have remained the same throughout Buddhist history, from the Nikayas to the Tantras. So it will be sufficient to put down here what Buddhaghosa says in his *Path of Purity* (p. 318): "Friendliness consists in that one bestows benefits on others, it is based on the ability to see their pleasant side, and it results in the stilling of ill-will

and malice. Compassion consists in that, unable to bear the sufferings of others, one strives to lead them away from ill, it is based on seeing the helplessness of those overcome by suffering, and it results in abstention from harming others." So far Buddhaghosa.

Both friendliness and compassion are necessary antidotes to the hatred which plays such a crucial part in our mental economy. Hatred is the result of the frustration which we feel when we do not get what we want. We usually expect and demand very much more from life than it is willing to grant us. Each frustration generates a corresponding impulse of hatred or "aggressiveness" in us, which is not only all the time on the look-out for opportunities to hurt others, but also effectively impedes and stifles our own spiritual growth. The latent hatred which is in us as a result of our manifold disappointments sets up a process of self-poisoning, both mental and physical. It also blinds us, and we fail to see the virtues of our fellow men and their lovable qualities, as well as the weight of suffering they have to endure. The cultivation of friendliness and compassion can bring about a reorientation of our attitude to others, open our eyes to their virtues and problems, induce us to be tender to all that lives, and direct our hatred away from other people. But the root of all this hatred is the belief that we are separate individuals, and this cannot be eradicated by the cultivation of the social emotions. Left to themselves they can do no more than replace private egoism by tribal egoism, and that is not the way to peace.

It is fairly easy to make edifying remarks about friendliness and compassion. As soon, however, as one gets down to actually doing something about them, the problems and difficulties begin to crowd in. There are two sides to friendliness—absence of hatred and active benevolence. As to the first, the evils of hate are obvious, but to actually dispose of one's hatred is hard. The impulse of hatred cannot be annihilated by a mere act of will, because the attempt to suppress malevolence merely drives it underground, and forces it to seek expression in all sorts of indirect, stealthy and often nearly unrecognizable forms. A genuine and wholehearted benevolence can be gained only if we learn what to do with our hatred, if we can find for it an outlet which is both harmless to others and spiritually fruitful to ourselves. In this context ascetic practices are greatly to be recommended, because in making ourselves uncomfortable we turn a part of our hatred on ourselves and use it up that way. It is rare to find someone who loves both his own comfort and his fellow men.

But this problem of using up the hatred generated by the frustrations of life is as nothing compared with the difficulties attending the desire to do good to others, and to provide them with what is useful. As soon as we get down to actual details, we find it hard to decide what is good for others, and what is of real benefit to them. Is it, for instance, an act of friendliness to kill an animal in pain, or to give whisky to a tramp? But, leaving quite aside these comparatively trifling problems pertaining to the casuistry of love, do we not all know that one good thing can be the foe of another? The highest good is said to be the gift of the Dharma. In that case the gift of anything else in so far as it increases peoples' worldly welfare, may militate against the development of their spiritual potentialities, because it binds them still further to this world and increases their worries and anxieties. This is not at all a trivial problem, since on its solution will depend the ability of Buddhism to be a social force in this generation, and probably some of those to come as well. In other words, does Buddhist friendliness wish to increase the material welfare of the people, or does it not? In the past, there has been a great deal of rhetoric about this in Mahayana texts, but the actual achievements of Buddhist countries fell far short of it. This is not surprising because social services are not only a matter of good will, but of the productivity of labour. Before the advent of modern technical development there simply did not exist the means to raise what is nowadays called the "standard of living" of the common people to any appreciable extent. Now, for the first time in history, there is a possibility of doing so, and everywhere the average person has come to regard this as the most burning issue of social life. Our attitude to this development is not easy to determine. On the one side our compassion would probably make us glad to see that people are becoming less poor, that they live longer, that their sickness is treated with some care and skill, that justice is dispensed with greater humanity, and so on. On the other hand all these benefits depend on the technical organisation of modern society, which makes a spiritual life next to impossible. How do we stand in this dilemma? I am afraid I do not know, but I feel that the issue deserves some thought, although the solution may quite possibly not be found in Europe at all, but in Tibet where the two ideals now have come face to face.

Not only the effects, but also the motives of doing good to others present serious problems. Charity has so much fallen into disrepute because too often it was motivated by a sense of guilt, by the desire to humiliate the poor, or to buy them off with a few crumbs. If others are so often ungrateful for what we have done to them, if they hate us for the help we gave, they are in most cases quite justified because somehow they divine that we considered ourselves first in what we did, and them only in the second place, degrading them into a mere means or material of our desire to do good. Generosity as such is praiseworthy because, and in so far as it is an act of renunciation by which we give up parts of our property and thus become more free. Its benefits to ourselves are not in doubt. It is the benefit to others which is in question. It seems to me that it requires a very high degree of sanctity in order to do good to others without harming or irritating them. Only the pure in heart have the vision necessary to decide what is really beneficial to others, only they have the purity of motive, and only they. Everyone else should do good in an apologetic frame of mind, as one who pursues his own welfare probably at the expense of others, in fear and trembling lest he harm those weaker than himself.

In the Scriptures the ability to benefit others is called "skill in means", and it is regarded as a very high and rare virtue, the last and most sublime flowering of a mature development of perfect wisdom. Eight hundred years ago Milarepa, the great Tibetan saint, was asked by his disciples "if they could engage in worldly duties, in a small way, for the benefit of others". Milarepa replied,[1] "If there be not the least self-interest attached to such duties, it is permissible. But such detachment is indeed rare; and works performed for the good of others seldom succeed if not wholly freed from self-interest. Even without seeking to benefit others, it is with difficulty

[1] W. Y. Evans-Wentz, *Tibet's Great Yogi Milarepa*, 1928, p. 271.

that works done even in one's own interest are successful. It is as if a man helplessly drowning were to try to save another man in the same predicament. One should not be over-anxious and hasty in setting out to serve others before one has oneself realized Truth in its fulness; to be so, would be like the blind leading the blind. As long as the sky endureth, so long will there be no end of sentient beings for one to serve; and to every one cometh the opportunity for such service. Till the opportunity come, I exhort each of you to have but the one resolve, namely to attain Buddhahood for the good of all living things."

(2) Leaving behind the perplexities of the world of action, we now turn to the greater certainties of meditation. Buddhist tradition knows a set of four meditations, which are called the "Unlimited" because they aim at extending to an unlimited number of beings the attitudes of friendliness, compassion, sympathetic joy and impartiality. They should be practised in the spirit of the mother who watches over her child, her only child, but without the usual exclusiveness.

The recommended procedure consists in the direction first of friendliness successively on four different kinds of persons: oneself, a very dear person, an indifferent person and an enemy. A knowledge of these practices must have reached the early Christians, probably by way of Alexandria, for we find them clearly described in S. Augustine. He writes that the right kind of love (*ordinata dilectio*) begins with oneself, and then widens itself by being extended first to our nearest friends, then to strangers, then to enemies. "First extend your love to those near to you, but do not call that a real extension. For you really love yourself when you love those that are close to you. Then extend it to strangers, who have done you no harm. Go beyond those even, and arrive at loving also your enemies."[1]

At the beginning of the meditation one must think of different persons, and apply to them the traditional formula expressing good will, i.e. "May all beings be without enmity, without fear, and at their ease!" (In Pali: *sabbe sattā averino hontu khemino hontu sukhino hontu*). In more modern language one might say that we wish them to be "mentally healthy". For the sake of greater emphasis one may prefer a more extensive formula which runs as follows:

[1] *In ep. Jn. ad Parthos*, tract, VIII 4.

"May (I, or X) be happy and at his (my, her) ease,
Free from pain, fear, distress or enmity,
Untroubled, well, unharmed, in peace."

Before one can get very much further, one must first of all become proficient in calling up an image of other people, in generating some degree of friendliness towards them, in recognizing and to some extent dispelling the aversion felt for them. It is in this context useful not to take people quite haphazard, but to trace out the four directions of space, and to go methodically round them, picking out the people who are situated in the East, then in the South, and so on.

In any case, after some initial practices of this kind, we are bidden to equalize the affection we feel for all or any of these people, to "abolish the dividing line" between them, and even to make no distinction between ourselves and other beings. And this, again according to Buddhaghosa (p. 307) is how one can recognize that one has broken down the barriers, and won an even and impartial attitude of mind to all the four kinds of persons: "Suppose someone were together with a loved one, a neutral person, and an enemy. Robbers would come along, and demand a monk, so that they can cut his throat and offer his blood in sacrifice. Now if that monk thinks, 'let them take this one or that one', he has not accomplished the breaking down of the boundaries, and also not if he thinks, 'let them take me and not those three'. For he does not seek the benefit of him whose capture he desires, but of the others only. But when he sees none among the four whom he would give to the robbers, then his mind proceeds just evenly towards himself and the other three, and he has broken down the barriers."

It must be admitted that it is surely not an easy task to equalize one's friendliness in the way here described. As a matter of fact, the normal mind is quite incapable of doing so. Success is possible only with the help of the virtue of meditative trance, and, as I have explained elsewhere,[1] cannot therefore be achieved by those who are afraid to leave the world. My own very limited experience fully bears out what I have read in the scriptures. I have devoted much time and effort to the cultiva-

[1] *The Middle Way*, XXVIII 3 (1953) pp. 95–96.

tion of friendliness. My exercises have, I think, greatly softened the innate ferocity of my disposition. But, because the meditations have not reached the level of trance, I still love myself very much more than I love anyone else, and when it is a question of pain, misfortune or disease, I still hope most fervently that they will descend somewhere else rather than on me. Scriptural tradition, personal experience and the observation of others all combine to show that no amount of cultivation of the social emotions can uproot our deep-grained attachment to ourselves. Only four factors have the power to bring about selfless love—trance, wisdom, ritual and unmerited grace. But this, of course, is no reason to discontinue our more elementary meditations on friendliness, because they render us so much more fit to develop the self-destroying forces of trance and wisdom.

3. *On Selfless Love*

The great Christian precept that "you should love your neighbour as yourself" has its exact parallel in our own religion. In the process of making friendliness unlimited, one should think, "as I myself wish to be happy and have an aversion to suffering, as I wish to live and do not wish to die, so also do other beings wish for the same", and one should desire exactly the same happiness for others as one desires for oneself.[1] The canonical formula of "unlimited friendliness" contains the statement that one should suffuse friendliness wholeheartedly and with all one's self (*sabbattatāya*), and Buddhaghosa[2] interprets this as meaning that a man should "identify himself (*attayā*) with all (*sabbesu*), be they inferior, middling or superior, be they friends, foes, or indifferent, etc.", that he "should identify them all with his own self, without making the distinction that they are other beings".

Love for oneself is thus held to indicate the level to which the love of others should be raised, and to constitute the measure and pattern of our love for others. It follows, paradoxically as it may seem, that to love others one ought to love oneself also. The natural man is often far from wishing well to himself.

[1] *Visuddhimagga* p. 297.

[2] *Visuddhimagga* p. 308.

I read in a book about the Christian conception of love that S. Augustine thought self-love to be so natural to us that a special commandment about it was unnecessary. If he actually did so, he was greatly inferior in psychological insight to his contemporary Buddaghosa who deems it necessary, during the practice of the meditation on *mettā*, that we should develop friendliness also towards ourselves, and fervently think, "May I be happy and free from ill," "May I be free from hatred, oppression and any kind of disturbance, may I myself lead a happy life!" For people may easily hate themselves, and much of our hatred of others is known to be a mere deflection or projection of self-hate. People may love, and even hug, their hates, and not at all wish to be rid of them. They may wish to die, because life is so disappointing, or because their destructive impulses are excessively strong, or because their "death instinct" is at work. They may not dare to want to be happy, because they suffer from a sense of guilt, and feel that they have not deserved happiness, but that, on the contrary, punishment is due for the deeds of the past. If a neurotic is a person who is both discontented with himself and unable to have satisfactory relations with others, then he can be made to live at peace with others only by first learning to endure himself. We must therefore agree with Aristotle when he said that only the wise man can love himself, and he alone, just because he is wise. "Such friendship for oneself can exist only in the good man; for in him alone the parts of the soul, being nowise at variance, are well disposed towards one another. The bad man, on the other hand, being ever at strife with himself, can never be his own friend".[1] And here we come to our first paradox: Self-love can be achieved only by losing its intensity and exclusiveness, i.e., by becoming detached and impartial, a mere acceptance of the contents of one's own self. For, the more possessive it becomes, the more ambivalent it will be, the more charged with latent hate.

So then it is really our duty to love ourselves, since our ability to love others depends on it? What then happens to the demand that we should be indifferent to ourselves? This difficulty is not a serious one. On the lower stages of spiritual development self-love is one of the decisive motives for the

[1] *Magna Moralia* 1211a.

love of others, and only on the very highest is it extinguished.

True self-interest should induce us to be friendly to others, because to do so is advantageous to ourselves. The *Anguttara Nikāya* (v. 342) enumerates eleven advantages of *mettā*, and promises that as a reward of friendliness we will be happy, die at ease, have no bad dreams, win a good rebirth, etc. The friendly man wishes other people to be happy, and that is clearly to his own advantage since it makes them so much more pleasant to live with. He impedes the anger that is rising in his throat by reflecting that a man's enemies are his best friends, and deserve his gratitude. For they deprive him of the dangerous impediments of wealth, fame and worldly happiness, and give him an opportunity to exhibit the virtue of forbearance. They threaten that which is dear to us, without being really our own—because otherwise it could not be threatened. Hostile pressure thus strengthens our resolution to renounce these things, and so to become less vulnerable and more free. Both in the Christian and the Buddhist tradition, friendliness is taught as an intelligent method of self-seeking, for the simple reason that spiritual virtues remain empty words unless actually effective motives are mobilized on their behalf, and in the spiritually undeveloped self-interest is the only motive they really appreciate. So "let the self-lover harm no other man".

On the other hand, both Buddhist and Christian tradition equally teach that in the spiritually fully developed man friendliness is quite selfless and "seeketh not its own". No Buddhist could find fault with Thomas a Kempis when he says (I, ch. 15): "One who possesses the true and perfect charity does not seek himself in anything, but it is his unique desire that the glory of God should operate in all things. Oh, if you had a spark of that true charity, how vain all earthly things would instantly appear to you!" But all those who have really thought out the implications of such self-extinction, and who have tried to realize it in themselves, have come to see how nearly impossible, how truly miraculous such an achievement is. It is not so much the result of dogmatic considerations, as the fruit of experience and observation, when the more thoughtful Christian theologians despair of the possibility of achieving selflessness without the intervention of some supernatural agency. On the highest levels the Christian conception of charity, or *agapé*, does not essentially differ from that of the Buddhists, and I rejoice to note the close parallel which exists between Christian and Buddhist ideas on this point. They are both at one in the belief that the inherent selfishness of human beings cannot be broken by a cult of the emotions, or by good deeds, but only by contact with spiritual reality. In other words, we can never find ourselves through our relations with others, but only through contact with a Reality which is extra-individual or supra-individual.

Only four factors, as I said before, have the power to bring about selfless love, and they are trance, wisdom, ritual and unmerited grace. I will now briefly consider these four factors one by one.

To begin with the last two, *ritual* and *grace* belong, as much to Buddhism as they do to Christianity. It is quite easy to understand that Christians should believe that unselfishness is so contrary to our natural endowment that it can be induced in our unwilling frame only by either the influence of the ritual of holy communion, or the miraculous intervention of the grace of God. But where have Buddhists been known to teach the same thing? The Tantras expect salvation from a ritual which relies on contact with supernatural forces, and the Zen doctrine of "sudden enlightenment" is the Buddhist counterpart to the Protestant doctrine of the grace of God. Protestants teach that our self-will can be removed only by the power of God's unmotivated love, freely given when he sent us his Son. This gift we receive by grace, because it is given for nothing, irrespective of our merit, whether it consists in good works, good resolutions, or a good will, and therefore this saving love on the part of God is an incomprehensible miracle, which defies all explanation and motivation. In a non-Theistic form the Zen Buddhist teach the same thing. Enlightenment, and with it self-extinction, is the result of the Absolute suddenly bursting in on this world of relativity, irrespective of what has preceded it in this conditioned world.

With *meditation* and *wisdom* we are, of course, on much firmer ground, and no one would wish to deny them their place in the Buddhist scheme of salvation. Their mode of operation is, however, not easy to explain.

The alchemy of the *dhyānas* is said to cleanse friendliness and compassion of their exclusiveness, and to make them "unlimited." Unable to show here in detail how this effect is produced, I must be content with pointing out that it is the close connection with the practice of trance which gives to Buddhist friendliness the detachment and aloofness which baffles so many observers. Love of a more hearty, but less spiritual, type is often nothing but an excuse to satisfy the social instincts, and to drown anxiety by merging with the herd. The fear of loneliness is the icy core of much that passes as "human warmth". True love can be found only in contact with the truth, and the truth can be found only in solitude. The ability to bear solitude, and to spend long stretches of time alone by oneself, is therefore one of the more elementary qualifications for those who aspire for a selfless love, which owes its spiritual character to the agency of trance and wisdom. In passing I must also draw the reader's attention to the large dose of misanthropy which spices Buddhist loving-kindness, and I recommend him to read up what Śāntideva says on pages 82 to 86 of his "Path of Light"[1] about the state of mind of those who practise transic meditation.

But enough of this. We must now turn to the links between wisdom and selfless love. Spiritual love is non-sensuous, and therefore must have for its object something which transcends the senses. In Christianity this is God, and to him correspond the dharmas in the wisdom-form of Buddhism. Since the Christian doctrine is quite analogous to the Buddhist, I will first describe it in a few words:

To Christians spiritual love for people is entirely dependent on the love for God, and secondary to it. Since we are bidden to love all people equally, we can do so only by loving them in the one respect in which they are equal, and that is their relation to God, in that they are children of God. The love of God is therefore the necessary antecedent to the love of others in its more spiritual form. The love of the neighbour is only a special instance of the love of and for God. God alone is truly worthy of our love. The neighbour is not strictly loved for himself, and, in himself, he is quite unworthy of such love. "He who in a spiritual way loves his neighbour, what does he

[1] Translated in *G* 110–113 and *L* 100–102.

love in him but God?"[1] We must love God with all our heart, soul and mind, and all the other things because they are made by him, and because they are the means of returning to him, as the ultimate aim. But they must not be loved for themselves and there must be no enjoyment of what they have to offer. The quality of our love for God, in its turn, will depend largely on our knowledge of him, and it will grown in proportion to our understanding. And it is wisdom that will give us a true idea of God.

Similarly, in Buddhism: Normally we live in a world of false appearance, where I myself seem surrounded by other persons. In actual truth, I have no self, and they have no selves, either; there is nothing but an incessant flow of impersonal dharmas. True, spiritual, selfless love therefore must operate on the plane of true reality, and, selfless within, it must transcend also the false appearance of a self in others, and must be directed towards that which is really there, i.e., to the dharmas. But wisdom is the ability to contemplate dharmas, and therefore selfless love is dependent on wisdom.

It is quite inevitable that Buddhists should try to combine friendliness and compassion with impartiality, and with a belief in the emptiness of all things. The ordinary person cannot see how impartiality, which, in the list of the "Unlimited", is placed above friendliness and compassion, can fail to destroy compassion, because, as he says, if you are impartial you must be indifferent, and your compassion will dry up. He also fails to see how the perfect can claim to practise compassion without a belief in the reality of the persons whom they love and pity, in what seems to him a mere vacuum created by the absence of concrete individuals, who are ultimately unreal.

These doubts cannot be stilled by argument, but only experience can lay them to rest. It is foolish to expect too much advance information about spiritual states which are perceived only from a distance, and to think too much about what is above one's head. If, however, such advance information is given, then one must bear in mind that paradox and contradiction are inseparable from all statements that can be made about selfless behaviour and the state of self-extinction. The saints "practise compassion, but are not given to petty

[1] S. Augustine, *In ev. Jo. tract* LXV, 2.

kindnesses; they practise loving kindness, but are not given up to attachments; they are joyous in heart but ever grieved over the sight of suffering beings; they practise indifference but never cease benefiting others". These paradoxes cannot possibly be translated into the ordinary logic of common sense, because common sense is based on self-centred experiences which are here transcended. No service is done to the mysteries of the spiritual world by trying to flatten them out into the appearance of commonplace events.

It is largely a waste of time to concern oneself with the apparent inconsistencies of the transcendental world of self-extinction. What is the use of worrying about whether the impartial are compassionate or not, if one has oneself no distinct experience of impartiality, and often even no clear notion of what it is? What good can come from reflecting about the loss of compassion in emptiness, as long as "emptiness" is no more than a word? In these questions the decisive factor is not what is said, but who speaks, and to whom. And so we better leave it at that. No one can be made perfect in a day.

4. *Sympathetic Joy*

A system of religious training must regulate our attitude to at least four fields of experience: to the unwholesome passions which tie us to the world and prevent us from reaching the freedom of the spirit; to the occult forces which pervade the universe everywhere and on all sides; to the spiritual reality to which we want to gain access; and, finally, to other living beings, be they men, animals or supernatural beings. In our present age we can observe a certain tendency to shift the weight of the emphasis to our relationship with other men. Many Christians, both inside and outside the churches, seem far more concerned with their neighbour than with God, even among the Quakers philanthropy has superseded mystical contemplation, and nowadays one often gains the impression that kindness to individuals and social work among the afflicted constitute the sum total of religious aspiration. Few outside the Communist fold would probably go so far as to deliberately restrict all selfless endeavour within the context of visible human society, but quite in general the importance of good works is readily understood, whereas faith, ascetic practices, devotion and wisdom are suspected as manifestations of a cloistered and unprofitable virtue. This absorption in our social duties is a modification which religion has undergone during the last century. It can, I think, be explained partly as a result of the fact that modern civilization, by atomising society, has thrown the relations of people to each other into a profound disorder from which only conscious and sustained effort can rescue it, and partly as a result of the fact that technical progress and the belief in science have dimmed the immediate awareness of the spiritual world, which seems more remote than ever. One must, however, remember that traditional religion saw these things quite differently. There the soul of man is regarded as essentially solitary, the true struggle takes place in a condition of withdrawal from society, and the decisive victories are won in solitude, face to face with the deepest forces of reality itself, "where men and mountains meet", and not at all by jostling in the street. By comparison with the secret life of the spirit our life in society seems secondary, though not entirely irrelevant, of course. It is just one of the outer wings of the temple we raise to the almighty, but by no means the inner sanctum itself. The Buddha is regarded as the Buddha because he won enlightenment under the Bodhi-tree, alone, except for a retinue of Devas in the distant heavens. And while he became enlightened, his mind was occupied with metaphysical and not with social questions.

Nevertheless, Buddhism does not believe that our relations to others can be safely left to either chance or metaphysical insight. If they were left to chance, the weeds of our natural malice would soon choke the frail wheat of our benevolence. If they were governed by metaphysical insight, then in the case of Buddhism that would lead to a complete aloofness from others. For according to Buddhist theory it is ultimately, as far as true reality is concerned, quite impossible to enter into a relation with other individuals, because separate selves, separate individuals as such do not really exist. Among the meditations prescribed to Buddhists we therefore find a set of four, called somewhat mysteriously the "Stations of Brahma", which regulate our attitude to other people. They aim at the development of friendliness (*mettā*), compassion, sympathetic joy (*muditā*) and impartiality. They do not constitute the core of the Buddhist effort, and are relatively subordinate, though important. They are not specifically Buddhistic, occur also in the *Yoga Sutras* of Patañjali, and were perhaps borrowed from other Indian religious systems. In this article I ignore the first and the fourth of the "Stations of Brahma", and concentrate on compassion and sympathetic joy.

The two obviously belong together. In compassion we participate in the sufferings of others, in sympathetic joy in their happiness. Compassion makes the heart tremble and quiver at the sight and thought of the sufferings of other beings, and that for Buddhism includes animals and ghosts as well as men. We suffer with them, and, unable to endure their suffering, make efforts to lead them to greater happiness. Compassion is regarded as a virtue which kills out in us the desire to do harm to others. We become so sensitive to the sufferings of people, make them so much our own that we do not wish further to increase them. We feel that the harm done to them is harm done to ourselves. And that we naturally avoid. Left to itself, however, the virtue of compassion would degenerate into the vice of gloom. To contemplate so much pain and affliction is apt to depress the mind. To remove this vast mass of sufferings seems quite a hopeless task, and one is tempted to sink into helpless despair. We are indeed threatened with irretrievable melancholia once we start identifying ourselves with all the pain which this world contains, all its frustrations, misery, calamities and horrors.

Nevertheless, compassion is placed before sympathetic joy because it is much easier to call forth. The suffering of his fellow creatures is not altogether repellent to the natural man. It seems, as a matter of fact, as if to some extent, he was positively attracted by it. The popular newspapers would not devote so much space to calamities if their readers did not really like to read about earthquakes, wars, murders, traffic accidents, atrocity stories, etc. Psychologically speaking, compassion is closely allied to cruelty—which can be defined as the pleasure one derives from contemplating the sufferings of others. The two are the reverse and obverse of the same medal. In both cases one is sensitive to the sufferings of others, and avid to watch it. In compassion one derives pain, in cruelty pleasure from watching it. But it is well known to modern psychology that the division between pleasure and pain is by no means a clear and unambiguous one, that in masochistic pleasure the two are inextricably interwoven, and that in addition we are endowed with so striking a capacity for self-deception that our true motives can rarely be ascertained with any degree of certainty. It is, as a matter of fact, possible for a man to be secretly drawn to the calamities of the world, and to derive, to some extent unknown to himself, a hidden satisfaction from gloating over them, while he himself is convinced that he is actuated by pity. That is one of the reasons why Buddhism insists that the practice of friendliness should precede the development of compassion, because it is the function of friendliness to purify the heart of hatred and ill-will, both manifest and latent.

But it must really be left to the practice of sympathetic joy to overcome the negative sides of compassion, i.e. despondency and cruelty. Sympathetic joy consists in that one sees the prosperous condition of others, is glad about it, and shares in their happiness. Logically speaking one might expect that the happiness of others should be emotionally more welcome to us than their misery. In fact, nothing is farther from our natural inclinations, which are distinctly misanthropic. Homo homini lupus. Language is one clue to our true feelings. In his recently published *Social Psychology and Individual Values* Prof. D. W. Harding points out that "the Oxford English Dictionary shows that we have never managed to fix linguistically the concept of generous admiration for good fortune or achievement that goes beyond our own; any word used for this purpose seems at some point in its history to convey the sense of a grudge or ill-will against the superiority of others" (p. 150). To some extent this is perhaps a mere linguistic accident, and other languages are better placed in this respect. In war time propagandists did not tire to point out that the Germans have the word *Schadenfreude* for the happiness felt at the misfortune of others, and that this throws a rather sinister light on the German national character. In fairness one must however add that the Germans can also express the joy felt at the happiness of others in the simple word *Mitfreude*, which contrasts directly with *Mitleid* (for "compassion"), whereas we must make do with "sympathetic joy", a rather clumsy circumlocution.

But quite apart from these linguistic considerations, we have a definite aversion to dwelling on the happiness of others, particularly in the deeper layers of our mind. Envy and jealousy are strong, deep-seated, though rarely admitted, counterforces. All the time we jealously compare our lot with that of others, and we grudge others the good fortune which eludes us. The very fact that we are concentrating, or are believed to be concentrating, on spiritual values may militate against our sympathy with the happiness of others. Happiness can be of two kinds: worldly or spiritual. For the overwhelming number of people success means material prosperity. When they are elated by having made some money, or having got a better job, or a new house, or because their children get on in the world, the spiritually minded are easily tempted to respond to this elation with a mixture of derision and pity. To those trained in the laws of the spiritual life it seems a sign of great foolishness to be happy about things like that, and wisdom seems to prompt the reflection that this kind of prosperity cannot possibly last, is often bought at the price of spiritual enslavement, and is likely to lead to great sufferings in the future. To rejoice with the children of the world in what they value as successes requires a spiritual perfection greater than most of us possess. It demands a complete and total indifference to material things, because only then is the spirit of rivalry over them quite dead in us, and only then can we ungrudgingly approve of the joy over them. Just as a grown up person rejoices with a baby who has just learnt to walk or with the athletic prowess of a young boy, or with the beautiful sand castles built by children at the sea shore. Because all that lies quite outside the field in which we compete and in which our self-esteem is at stake.

But it is of course not only material but also spiritual happiness which is the sphere of sympathetic joy in the Buddhist sense. It is regarded as a praiseworthy exercise to dwell lovingly in detail in one's mind on the great achievements of the spiritual heroes of the past, Buddhas, Bodhisattvas and saints, and to reflect that such achievements are taking place even to-day and will take place in the future. The world and its misery is a fact, and in our compassion we suffer with it. The overcoming of the world and the conquest of the absolute happiness of the Beyond are, however, also a fact, and in the practice of sympathetic joy we share to some extent in this victory and its fruits. When we can be happy with the world in its intervals of worldly happiness, then this is a test by which we can know that we have overcome in our hearts the cruelty which may so easily mask itself as pity. When the despondency over the seemingly endless misery and stupidity of this world threatens to paralyze us, then we regain our hope from the contemplation of the bliss which spiritual endeavour can manifestly confer. In addition, sympathetic joy with the spiritual world-conquerors will also root out the self-pity which so easily attaches itself to the pursuit of a spiritual life. The textbooks of Buddhist meditation point out that it is one of the chief rewards of the practise of sympathetic joy that one loses the discontent engendered by the privations of a secluded life, and by the mental aridity which accompanies some of the more advanced spiritual states. A life of renunciation brings many inconveniences in its train, and the threat of being engulfed by the world is ever present. Only at the end of a long journey there arises the reward of the happiness which is greater than the world can confer. By sympathetic joy with the happiness of the saints we anticipate to some extent this final stage of bliss, and regain zest and the courage to persevere. Compassion can be so wearying to the mind because suffering is easily felt to be a contagious force. When we witness disaster or deformity, we are inclined to feel that we might have to endure the same, that it is really only by a quite incomprehensible privilege that we are spared the same kind of fate. So there is always the fear that the misfortune will jump over into us, if this state of luck or privilege should cease. But when we practise sympathetic joy we feel tangibly that we are indeed privileged, that we somehow belong to the community of the saints, and that the day is drawing near when the world can no longer touch us.

The best and surest way of finding out about the manifold and subtle laws which govern the growth of compassion and sympathetic joy is of course the actual practice of the meditations prescribed for developing them. The most suitable introduction to them is the ninth chapter of Buddhagosa's *Path of Purity* to which I must refer the curious reader.

II. THE PHILOSOPHICAL BACKGROUND

I

THE OBJECTIVE VALIDITY OF THE PRINCIPLE OF CONTRADICTION[1]

I. The Problem and its Justification

The present essay is intended as a contribution to the investigation of the relations between the theoretical and the practical life of man. It makes the attempt to show that our assumption or rejection of even the highest and most abstract law of thought and reality is based on and rooted in our practical attitude towards the world. It tries to show that even the principle of contradiction (P.C.) owes its validity or non-validity to decisions made by the practical and emotional part of man, and that the objective validity of the P.C. is not absolute, but relative to the practical and emotional attitude you choose to assume.

First leaving on one side the question, what the P.C. exactly means and in which sense we speak of its "validity," we must show at the very outset in what sense it can be at all a subject-matter for discussion. How can the P.C. be a matter of any serious discussion, since it is generally considered to be beyond all discussion? In what sense can it afford a problem, since it seems to be an indubitable truth? But, on the other hand, whether the P.C. *can* be denied or not, it *has* been denied in the course of the history of human thought. Aristotle, in his still unsurpassed and valid discussion of the P.C. in the third book of the *Metaphysics* maintains that practically *all* his predecessors *denied* it. Later on we find that eminent thinkers like Nicholas of Cusa, Hegel, Bostroem, Bradley, and others in Europe, the Taoists in China, the Madhyamikas in India denied the validity of the P.C. in one way or another. Lévy-Bruhl

[1] Throughout this article for "principle of contradiction" the abbreviation "P.C." is used.

made at least an attempt to show that the P.C. is not observed by "primitive" mentality. Svend Ranulf demonstrated the same for the Eleatic methods of thinking. How can these historical facts be reconciled with the assumption of logicians that the P.C. is beyond all doubt and dispute? Is it possible to account for these deviators from the P.C. with an impatient wave of the hand, assuming that these thinkers have been utterly wrong, unable to grasp the fundamental condition of all thinking about realities? Or how is this radical difference of opinion to be reconciled?

Perhaps it may be useful in this dilemma to examine the reasons on which Aristotle and all his direct or indirect disciples based their claim that the P.C. must be considered as a principle standing high above all dispute.

First it has been said that the P.C. can neither be proved nor refuted because it is *self-evident*. A truth is considered to be self-evident if it is immediately, that is without the intervention of any proof or deduction, perceived by reason to be indubitably true and known by itself. It is not difficult to see that no mere psychic state of belief, be it as unshaken as it may, can be sufficient to assure us of the fact that we are in immediate touch with truth and reality as such. Unfortunately a wrong idea may be as self-evident as a true one. So many "self-evident" propositions have been shattered in the history of human thought that alleged "self-evidence" cannot be considered to be any ultimate guarantee of truth. Recourse to it cannot exclude the discussion of a problem. "Self-evidence" of a proposition can never exclude the possibility that a more satisfactory self-evident proposition about the same object may arise. Just the *substitution* of self-evident propositions for each other forms one of the main elements of the development of human thought.

More serious is the second contention: the P.C. cannot be proved or refuted, being the unspoken *condition* of all proof, in this sense, that if it is denied, all proof is denied. Even those who deny the P.C. confirm it by denying it, for they assume denial not to be the same as affirmation, else they would take no pains to deny it. This argumentation in fact excludes the possibility of a complete denial of the P.C. But it leaves open the possibility of *limiting* the *extent* of its validity. The possibility is left open that not *all* objects may be on the same level as regards the P.C. Let us now call A the class of things for which the P.C. is valid and let us call B the class of things for which it is not valid. Then A may be *subordinated* to B. Under the assumption of different degrees of truth the lower degrees may observe the P.C., but not the higher. The P.C. would be the necessary condition of all arguments concerning A, but it would be abolished at the threshold of B, although leading to it. So for the German romantics (Novalis, Schlegel, etc.), for Schelling and Hegel the P.C. is observed only by the lower logic of the *Verstand*, whereas the higher logic of speculative reason rejects it. In a similar spirit, Nicholas of Cusa declared four hundred years earlier that the P.C. is the first principle only of the lower discursive reason, "limited by the contradictories," i.e. of the first step towards truth, but it has no validity for the higher, truer, and infinite faculty, for the "most simple and detached" faculty of the *docta ignorantia*, of the *intellectio videntium*. Besides, there exists another possibility: A and B can be *co-ordinated*; for one part of the world the P.C. may be valid, but not for another; human thought, which surveys them both, may then belong to that part of which the P.C. is valid.

The two lines of argument mentioned above attempted simply to exclude any discussion about the validity of the P.C. This is not the case with other more modern forms of argument, which regard the P.C. either as an outcome of the generalization of the data of *experience* or as the necessary condition of all fruitful *practical* behaviour. This nominalistic and pragmatistic "proof" of the P.C. can never exclude *a priori* the possibility of the emergence of either new data of experience or of a new fruitful attitude which would exclude the P.C.

II. The Formulation of the P.C.

The P.C. may be stated as the psychological fact that mind or consciousness, owing to their nature and constitution, *cannot* actually judge at the same time that a thing is, and that the same thing is not. But logical theory is not concerned with the question, whether in fact the P.C. is thoroughly observed in actual thinking, or whether there are exceptions to it. The logician, in case he should find contradictions in the actual thinking-process, would point out that these are cases of wrong thinking, that they are instances of a thinking which is not quite clear and distinct, that they are cases in which reason has not been able to overcome the obstacles of irrational tendencies, etc. Logical theory assumes the P.C. to be not the principle of all judgment, but of all *true* judgment only.

But what reason can be given for this assumption? *Why* can we call true only reasoning processes which observe the P.C.? I can see only one satisfactory reason for this, namely that the P.C. is also the principle of the *objects* of judgment and reasoning. The P.C. is a principle of true judgment, because it is a principle of objects, of reality. The laws of reality are the foundations of the laws of the logical mind. We cannot *judge* that the same man is learned and is also not learned at the same time and in relation to the same group of facts, *because* in fact he *is* learned and cannot *be* not learned at the same time and in relation to the same group of facts. The P.C. may be a postulate, as Schiller has put it; but it is a postulate demanded by reality. Else it would be gratuitous and would not concern reality, would not help the mind in its proper task, the reflection of reality.[1]

Now, each general law and principle is always concerned only with *one* feature or property common to a class of things. So also the P.C. is not immediately concerned with all the manifold aspects and qualities of things, i.e. their colour, shape, etc. Being the most general of all laws, covering everything, it must be concerned with a property which is common to everything, which is a common factor in all reality. But this is the property of being as being. We may apply to the P.C. the method of Baconian induction and ask for the reason of its validity. Then the reason for the P.C. must be wherever the P.C. is, must be nowhere where it is not, and must be present always in the degree in which the P.C. is fulfilled. Only being as being accomplishes these three conditions.

Being as being is the primary object of the P.C. So the ultimate statement of the P.C. would be: "Being is not and cannot

[1] It is, of course, impossible to discuss here in full the very controversial relations between thinking and being. The assumption that being is at the basis of thinking, although I personally am inclined to deem it correct, need be accepted by the reader only as a convenient working hypothesis.

be non-being"; or "contradictory being, i.e. being which is also non-being, is nothing". All the other formulations which can be given of the P.C., and which I need not enumerate and discuss here in detail, are secondary to, are special cases of this one, for all other "objects" obey the P.C. only because and in so far as they participate in this one identical property, in being. Thus the P.C. can be stated of *real things* and their *attributes*, and it is with this aspect of the P.C. that we are especially concerned in this article. But when we say, e.g.: "a 'thing' cannot at the same time be and not be", or "contradictory attributes exclude each other and cannot coincide in one and the same identical part of a 'thing'," we apply the categories of being to "things". The same is true for the different ways in which we may state the P.C. for our *judgments* and *thoughts*. They all are valid, because logical thinking participates in and reflects "being." In the case of *human consciousness* it can be shown *in detail* that it observes the P.C. only as far as it assumes the categories of being.[1]

To assume the P.C. to be a principle of general validity means to say that being is the *dominating idea* of all thinking. This statement, which is the starting-point of my further investigations, was first suggested to me by the admirable analysis Rosmini has given of the P.C. It means that being is present as an indispensable element in the interior of all objects of thought and is reflected in all logical judgment. Only the presence of and the implicit relation to the idea of being makes judgment and thinking possible. The data of sensation are transformed into thoughts only when touched by the idea of being. But what is "being"? We can give the definition of "being" only by pointing to its law (the P.C.) and to its *categories*. It may happen that another name is given to this complex of properties, which we called "being", e.g. the name of "spirit." It is essential for the P.C. only that the *categories* of being are an element of the dominating idea, be this called "being" or "spirit".

[1] See E. Conze, *Der Satz vom Widerspruch*, 1932, 4–77.

III. The Concept of Being and the Conditions of the Destruction of the P.C.

(1) *General Survey*

The fundamental property of being, as expressed in the P.C., is not an isolated one. It is connected with other properties, as with its conditions. We now must ask: which properties must "being" communicate to a thing that it may be subject to the P.C.? Which are the chief properties of being, i.e. the chief ontological conditions of the working of the P.C.?

First, as a matter of course, the contradictory attributes, in order to be really contradictory, and to annihilate each other, must have one and the same subject. They must not only be "somehow united", but the two properties must concern the *same* identical object, seen at the *same* time and in relation to the *same* part.

Secondly, being and the things which participate in being are *determinate*, i.e. they are different, they are distinguished from everything that is not themselves. To be determinate, to be different, to be separated from all other objects, to be itself and nothing else, these all are one and the same. For it is just by its definite characteristics that a thing is marked off and distinguished from all others. This excludes all *ambiguity* from the reality of things. Each object, at a certain time and in a certain relation has only one attribute and not more than one in one relation. Reality in itself is supposed to be unequivocal.

The P.C. cannot be applied to indeterminate objects, in so far as and in the respect in which they are indeterminate. In particular propositions, affirmation and negation are compatible with each other: "Some A are B; some A are non-B." These two judgments are not contradictory: both can be true. There is an element of indeterminativeness in them, and that is in the word "some" (which either means "at least some" or "only some"). By abolishing this indeterminate element in "some", by saying: "All these some A are B" and "all these same some A are non-B," we obtain a real contradiction. The case is similar with the indefinite judgments. The P.C. is the law of things and judgments only in so far as they are determinate.

It is a condition of the P.C. that diversity cannot at the same time be unity, non-diversity. In our world everything suffers from a dearth of properties, it has not at its disposal an infinite wealth of attributes, it is excluded from a great amount of properties and qualities; in this world things are repelled from each other, they collide and they cannot penetrate each other indefinitely. This *finiteness* of things and their *hard exclusiveness* against each other is a condition of the P.C.

Now the P.C. can be inadequate to express the fundamental law of reality either in the sense that it is *meaningless* in regard to this reality or in the sense that it is *violated* by it. The principle of contradiction becomes meaningless in regard to a reality if this does not show or contain the categories implied in contradiction, if there is no object to which the P.C. can be applied. The P.C. is violated by a reality, if contradictions do actually appear in it, if contradictory attributes actually coincide in one and the same thing.

A further distinction must be drawn: We may distinguish two aspects of reality, one initial, unsatisfactory, only "apparent" and untrue, the other final and true. Then the P.C. can be abolished for either one or the other. Kant, Herbart, Bostroem and Bradley abolish the P.C. in some sense or other for the initial world only. Heracleitism, Nicholas of Cusa, Hegel, etc., abolish it for the final and true world. It is only with the latter view that we are concerned here.

We first investigate the question, under which conditions the P.C. becomes *meaningless* for ultimate reality. We saw that the P.C. presupposes the existence of *identity* and of determinate and sharply defined *distinctions* in reality. Where one of these two is denied to be a character of ultimate reality, the P.C. does not express and render a characteristic of ultimate and real reality.

Now these two aspects of reality seem to be strongly guaranteed by the necessities of practical life. But the attitude of philosophers towards everyday practical life is very often a critical one: they do not accept the data of everyday experience as ultimate data: they try to go behind and beyond them. Most philosophy is concerned with a world which appears to the philosopher to be qualitatively different from and more real than the world of the average man in the street. The denial of the practical world may in some cases go so far as to imply even the P.C.-character of this world. It is with these cases that we are now concerned. We shall now consider first the case that the category of *identity* disappears from the real world, and secondly the case that the category of *distinction* disappears.

(2) *The P.C. is Meaningless in Reality*

(*a*) *Because there is no identity in the real world.* The insistence on the fact of change in the universe which goes so far as to exclude from the image of the real world all elements of rest, stability, permanence, identity and being, has been propounded at different times for different motives. We find it in the school of Heracleitus, in the doctrines of *Protagoras* and *Cratylos*. The humanistic system of Protagoras tends to exclude all definite and determinate properties from the reality of things in order to transfer them into man, into his sensations and aspirations. Recently *Bergson* developed a similar theory. It is a common feature of both theories that stability, rest, etc., are considered as illusions created by the considerations and needs of an everyday life, which appears equally inferior to the aristocratic and esoteric haughtiness of an Heracleitus, as to the prophet of the rich, spiritual, irrational, and vigorously antimechanic *élan vital*.

In the case of Heracleitism, Plato and Aristotle have conclusively shown the destructive effect on the P.C. of any doctrine which interprets movement as a mere becoming, as the absolute negative of rest, and as the only real feature and aspect of things.[1] Movement, conceived by Heracleitism as excluding all elements of being, is devoid of all identity and sameness. There is movement and becoming, but there *is* nothing which moves or is moved, or which becomes. There is a perpetual, uninterrupted, and complete flux, and nothing lasts or remains in it. Without interruption one change follows the other. There is no halting-point at which the P.C. might be applied. Nothing substantial outlasts the perpetual change of events.

[1] The following description of the relation of the Heracleitean world to the P.C. and its conditions is taken from Plato's *Theaitetos* and *Cratylos*, and from different passages of Aristotle, Alexander of Aphrodisias, and Asclepius. For the exact references, see E. Conze, *Der Satz vom Widerspruch*, 1932, n. 29.

There is no self-identical nature, which unites several "states" or "aspects" of one thing". Everything is in a perpetual flux, without a constant relation to one another, unconnected, incoherent like flame or fire, without cause, permanent order, or immobile law, without definite distinctions. It is just because for Heracleitism no lawful connection exists between events that it is distinguished from the modern dynamic theory of matter and from the Buddhist doctrine of universal impermanence and change; for these doctrines assume the persistence of a physical or moral law above the perpetual change. "Things" are for Heracleitism neither determinate nor determinable, because they do not even for a fraction of a moment persist in a definite identity, because everything loses its properties or qualities in the very moment in which it got them. Everything *is* and also *is not*. There is only a becoming which neither is nor is not. In fact, as Plato says, "there *is* neither anyone to know, nor anything to be known" in this world.

(*b*) *Because there are no distinctions in the real world.* The school of thought, which we may—somewhat inadequately—call the school of "*mystical pantheism*", tends to make the P.C. meaningless by abolishing the differences and distinctions in the real world.

The culminating point of all mystical experience is the state of *ecstasy*, of complete union with God, with the One. In mystical ecstasy one and only one idea, one and only one object fills the whole mind, binds all attention and *is* the whole of reality. *Mysticism* develops into *mystical pantheism* under two conditions, namely, that the state of ecstasy is considered to give a true, the *only* true image of reality, and further that the one object of ecstasy is expressly stated to *include all* reality. If distinctions and oppositions are, although different in ordinary practical life, but one in the object of ecstasy, if a contact with true reality is attained only in ecstasy, and if the object of ecstasy comprehends all reality, then the unreality and vanity of the distinctions and opposites in the object of ecstasy renders also the P.C. meaningless. Mysticism shows a strong tendency towards mystical pantheism especially in the Indian Upanishads, in Chinese Taoism, in Mahāyāna Buddhism, in Mahometan Sufism, in German Metaphysics (Master Eckehart, Nicholas of Cusa, Jakob Boehme,

Hamann, Hegel), and occasionally in England (e.g. Brook).

Generally mystical pantheists do not devote much attention to the consequences of their ideas on logical thinking, its categories and laws. As far as I know, the German cardinal *Nicholas* of *Cusa* has, at least in his *De docta ignorantia* and his other writings between 1440 and 1450, clearest of all elaborated this aspect of mystical pantheism. In his philosophy the infinite totality, the absolute infinite, the maximum *quo majus esse non potest* is the "dominating idea". There is only one true reality, the one infinite totality which has the fundamental property to comprehend everything. This conception affects the P.C. in a double sense:

On the one hand, the mystical pantheist can assume that in fact nothing except the One and infinite Absolute does exist. All differences are then absolutely reduced to nought. Since contradictions are not possible without differences, the P.C. is meaningless and inapplicable.

On the other hand, a more dynamic and somewhat complicated theory can be given, and was in fact given, by Nicholas of Cusa: Reality appears as a complete and undivided unity in the experience of *mystical ecstasy*. It is the attitude of *everyday practical life* which acknowledges the differences and divisions in reality. Now, man does not begin his conscious life with mystical experience, but, before he reaches it, he first has to go through the experience of everyday life. In the theory of Cusanus the everyday aspect of reality has not entirely vanished away even on the highest summit of truth; it is preserved, but seen and interpreted against the background of the reality of mystical experience. Cusanus does mention the differences, distinctions, and divisions. He first predicates them of the Absolute, and only after that he shows their unreality and vanity. Therefore in his philosophy the P.C. is *actually violated*.

It is violated first with respect to the one and absolute reality itself. For in the everyday world the incompatible attributes are distributed among different and mutually exclusive things and aspects. Now this difference between things has gone, they are all united in one reality and the contradictory attributes are all united in the one infinite reality. The totality is the one and identical subject of all contradictory, incompatible, and mutually exclusive attributes. As Cusanus has put it: "Since nothing is opposed to the Greatest, also the Smallest coincides with it." Cusanus explains that in this one totality distinctiveness is the same as indistinctiveness, plurality the same as unity, identity the same as diversity, particularity coincides with unversality, posteriority and priority do not exclude each other, etc. The trend of the whole argument demands and the texts show clearly[1] that Cusanus, like the other mystical pantheists, does not maintain a mere *unity* of *opposites*, but an *identity* of *differences*, which is a *contradiction* in itself and of which the *identity* of *opposites* is a special case.

The logical mind will try to evade this conception by assuming that of mutually exclusive properties one is predicated in this, the other in another relation, that they are all attributes of the same thing, but of different and particular aspects of it. But this interpretation is excluded by the consideration that also the parts and the whole must coincide, must be the same in the totality. It is *one* totality; it has no proper parts; it is present as a *whole* and *undivided* in whatever we may consider as one of its "parts". Each predicate is without any restriction or limitation affirmed of the totality, and so is the attribute, which is different from and incompatible with it. For in the absolute totality there is one relation only for everything, the relation to the totality itself—since there is nothing outside it—and the relation to the totality wholly and undivided—since it has no parts.

There is a further aspect of the Absolute which excludes the P.C. Cusanus says: "Since the absolutely Greatest is really everything, which can be, and is so far removed from all opposition that the Smallest coincides with it, it is above affirmation and negation." But since the P.C. speaks of the relation between affirmative and negative judgments, it cannot be applied here.

The P.C. is also violated with respect to the world of different things. For the unity and identity of things in the maximum

[1] See E. Conze, *Der Satz vom Widerspruch*, 1932, 368–70. Robert Grenville (Lord Brook), *The Nature of Truth*, 1640, p. 100: "I fully conclude with Aristotle's Adversaries, Anaxagoras, Democritus, etc. That Contradictories may be simul and semel in the same Subject, same Instant, same Notion (not only in two distinct respects or notions, as one thing may be causa and effectum, Pater and Filius, respectu diversi; but even in the same respect, under one and the same Notion)."

devours and *annihilates* the differences they had in the ordinary world, but at the same time the differences are *maintained* and preserved in the maximum. So the differences *are* and they *are not*, first successively, but also in some sense simultaneously, since even on the stage of absolute truth a semblance of difference still clings and adheres to the identity of things in the Absolute.

(3) *The P.C. is Violated by the Dialectic Nature of Reality*

Thus there is an element of dialectics in the theory of Nicholas of Cusa, which later on was developed by *Hegel*. Various considerations and motives have formed Hegel's rejection of the P.C. We may distinguish *three* main currents which contributed to it: First it is often forgotten that Hegel was not only a great logician, but also a great mystic. It is from *mystical pantheism* that he takes the fundamental assumption of his Logic that all categories are attributes of the one Absolute, are 'definitions of God". We have just discussed the consequences of this assumption for the P.C. But Hegel combined this idea of one all-comprehending totality with a certain form of *Heracleitism*. The Hegelian Absolute is in constant movement, and so is everything which forms a "part" or an "aspect" of it. But the movement of the Absolute is not the perpetual and lawless flux of Heracleitus. It is a change governed by definitive laws. Hegel's Absolute develops through a long history. One of the fundamental laws of this historical movement is the law of *dialectics*.

Dialectics, as conceived by Hegel and his school, maintains a connection between movement and change on the one side, and contradiction on the other. At least two explanations of movement are possible: The one explains each movement and each change by the influence of some external cause which *pushes* a thing out of the state in which it is, out of a state in which it would rest and remain, unless an external cause acted upon it. But Hegel, without denying the effects of the exterior cause, attributes change and movement also to an interior cause. He sees all things against the background, and in some sense as parts of the perfect Absolute, and believes that a changing thing shows by the mere fact of its change and alteration that it was an unsatisfactory, incomplete, unfinished, imperfect reality. *In itself* the thing has a tendency to destroy *itself*, to move *itself*, change *itself*, as a sign of its inherent imperfection. Everything thus contains its own negative, and is driven out of its state by this inherent contradiction. Contradiction is the impulse of movement, it is the actual power which drives it on. Contradiction is real; but it is impossible for reality to be content in contradiction and to remain in it. According to formal logic the contradiction is dissolved into zero, into an abstract nought. The "result" of a contradictory being is the not-being of this being. Also in Hegelian dialectics a thing cannot acquiesce in contradiction; but the contradictory thing or process is dissolved into the negation, not of everything, but of this particular thing or process. The contradiction is solved by the thing moving out of its present state into another one. Movement and change are the solution of the contradiction.

It is not possible to discuss here the many problems connected with this conception. I will only illustrate it by one famous example, by the dialectic interpretation of *local movement*: Local movement can be accomplished only because a body is at the very same moment in one place and also in another place, because it is in one and the same place and also is not there. Local movement is the continual positing and the simultaneous solution of this contradiction. The body moves *because* it had come into a contradictory situation and wants to come out of it, out of a situation which makes incompatible demands upon it. *Because* the body cannot *be* at the same time at A and B, it *moves* from A to B.

This theory is of course open to many objections. But we are in the present essay not concerned with defending or refuting the theories which reject the objective validity of the P.C. Our only task is to expound them as clearly as possible and then show their emotional and practical basis, to which they owe their existence.

IV. The Practical and Emotional Basis of the Differences of Opinion about the P.C.

We now make the attempt to show that it was through entertaining certain types of practical and emotional attitude towards the world that the objective value of the P.C. was destroyed. At the basis of Heracleitism is a sad and melancholy feeling that all things instantaneously give way to fate and dissolution and nothing remains. Heracleitus himself was not as consistent in his theory of flux as some of his disciples; besides the irrational flux he acknowledged the assistance of a certain law, of a certain Logos, in the world. But the case of *Buddhism* shows that, whereas pessimism only *tends* to destroy the P.C., radical pessimism, i.e. *radical* negation of the practice of self-preservation, destroys it *in fact*: The doctrine of the "impermanence" of things, as expressed in the religious formula "all things are evanescent", is at the very root of Buddhism. Buddhist philosophers elaborated this idea. For *Vasubandhu*, e.g. things perish in the very same moment in which they come to existence, and it is important to note that they perish without any cause, but simply in consequence of their own constitution; in them, as we would say, affirmation and negation, being and non-being, coincide simultaneously and thus they perish instantaneously. This doctrine is clearly the theoretical counterpart of the annihilation of the world through meditation and wisdom. The *Madhyamika*-theory of the universal "emptiness" of things expresses the same intention: The Madhyamikas look at the universe from the standpoint of "absolute truth", i.e. from the standpoint of Nirvana. Then things are "void" of all properties; all properties and categories can be affirmed and equally well denied of them, being inapplicable to a reality which is without plurality, properties, and differences. Things neither are, nor are they not; nor have they being and non-being at once; nor have they not non-being and being at once. The wise clings not even in thought to any attribute, for this clinging will involve a desire and thus lead him astray. The same can be shown from the German pessimistic philosopher, Julius *Bahnsen*, a follower of Schopenhauer. He describes a world, as it appears and corresponds to a person who does not want to preserve, but who wants to annihilate himself. The person he has in view is so disgusted with life that he annihilates all he does. He simultaneously affirms and denies his self-preservation, he is interested at the same time in his own destruction and in his own preservation. This contradictory attitude of the tragical and radically pessimistic man is then projected into the outward reality according to the idea of Schopenhauer that the real essence of the world, the noumenal world, can be found only in the interior of man himself. So the volition of the utterly pessimistic man, turned as it is against itself, becomes the dominating idea of Bahnsen's philosophy. He says: "The metaphysical Ens is a Volition which has the only desire not to be a Volition". This volition is a never-ending contradiction in itself. It is rent and divided into two contradictory tendencies, and it is also the unity of these contradictory tendencies. It is an *ens volens idemque nolens.* All the contradictory acts of this tragic Volition are simultaneous, since, according to Schopenhauer's theory, there is no time in the noumenal world, and so everything is in the same absolute simultaneity, succession appearing only in the phenomenal world. So radical pessimism destroys the objective validity of the P.C.

We likewise saw that the P.C. is destroyed, if man, as *Protagoras* did, gets the proud conviction that his sensory and sensuous activities are the measure of all things, of the things being that they are, and of the things not being that they are not. We further suggested the emotional background of *Bergson's* irrationalism. We still have to describe the practical and emotional attitude which is at the basis of *mystical pantheism.* We described the *object* of the mystical pantheist and its law. We must now say some words about the *subject* to whom the world presents itself in this manner and whose attitude produces the particular features of this world: Man has abolished all action, has become indifferent to the differences between things, after having felt that all earthly things are equally valueless as compared with the absolute Value, God. Man has destroyed, has annihilated the Ego and *all* his aspirations. As Chuang Tsu has said about the true aim and attitude of man: "To embrace all things equally, without preference, without favour, that is infinity: all things considered equally, what then is short, what then is long?" Where not one thing is preferred to another, where not one thing is valued higher than another, where all action and impulse have died away, there also the difference between the one and the other dies away; everything becomes one and undifferentiated for him who has found rest. As Angelus Silesius has put it:

No man can ever know perfect felicity
Till Otherness be swallowed up in Unity.

If we further ask for the emotional and practical background of *dialectics*, we must not overlook the Christian element in *Hegel's* theory. He measures all things by the standard of the absolute, perfect, and infinite God. Some Christian thinkers of the Middle Ages, like Anselm of Canterbury, Petrus Damiani, and also Nicholas of Cusa were led by the same comparison of all things with God to the conclusion that the things of this world properly are more "not existing", than they "are existing". All things were polluted by sin, and sin had made them vain and fragile. In the Hegelian theory not sin, but contradiction is the sign of the imperfection and finiteness of things, and by the contradiction in things each thing is more "not existing" than it "exists", or, more exactly, it exists and equally does not exist. Owing to the contradiction it contains, no thing has a full and complete reality, no thing can rest content in the state in which it is, all things "must go to their judgment".

Now, I think, we can draw the following conclusions as a result of our investigations: A phenomenal world, a world as it appears to us, consists of two factors: On the one hand, the "noumenal" world; on the other, a strong subjective factor. The image of our phenomenal world is largely influenced and formed by our emotions, aspirations, and interests. These in their turn are not the outcome of pure reasoning, but the result of our character and of the actual situation we occupy in the world of nature and society. We can speak of the objective validity of a law only in relation to one of the many phenomenal worlds, which, as long as we do not know the noumenal world, must all be regarded as having the same theoretical value. Now, we have shown that the question whether we consider the P.C. to be a law of objective validity or not depends on the question whether we decide for optimism or for pessimism, for quietism or for activism, whether we feel as sensuous or as rational beings, whether we decide for or against a mechanical control of the environment, whether we are inclined to experience ourselves as perfect or as imperfect, as complete or as incomplete beings, as creatures of a God or as masters of the world. But decision in all that does not depend primarily on rational and theoretical considerations, but on our practical outlook. It is also this practical outlook which ultimately decides whether we regard "Being"—as it was described above—as the dominating idea or whether we choose another dominating idea, as, for example, the Heracleitean flux, the mystic Absolute, etc. Certain types of practical attitude have been proved to destroy the P.C. in the world which corresponds to them. Practical decisions penetrate and influence the validity even of the most abstract law of thought. The P.C. is in fact not an absolute law, but relative to the practical attitude you choose to assume.

2

SOCIAL IMPLICATIONS OF LOGICAL THINKING

1. The Problem and its Division

Were it not for the affection with which we cherish our own views, it would be easier for all of us to agree more readily about the historical character, the social origin and meaning of our ideas. In this paper I want to point out some aspects of the connection between the structure of logical thinking and social life. I want to show that without this connection with social life the principles and categories of logical thinking could neither exist nor have any sense.

We to-day think of man more and more as essentially working in society. All his faculties and actions are derived from his work in society. This would be a truism were it not for traditional idealistic philosophy which regards logical thinking, its laws and properties, as being rooted in and originating from *reason*. The traditional theory is based on the view that man is primarily a thinking and reasonable being and that from the very outset, owing to his very nature, he could not help being a logical thinker. As La Bruyère expresses this well-known theory: "Reason is universal, and its reign acknowledged wherever there are human beings." We are able to think logically because we are reasonable beings. Thc first principles of logic are self-evident and need no further proof as being rooted in reason itself. There is no incentive in this theory to go beyond "reason" for the explanation of logic and this may account to a certain extent for the recent origin of the sociological approach to logic which has reached a certain maturity only in the course of the last 30 years. However, after the latter has been once constituted on the basis of the *homo faber* theory of human nature, the adherents of the traditional view may also be interested to see the connection between these two fundamental activities of man, the rational and the social.

The attempt at a sociological treatment of logical thinking will meet with the objection that it is not "philosophy", but "psychology" and "sociology". Those who raise an objection of this kind have divided the world into watertight compartments and have lost sight of the unity of truth. They appear to infer the objective validity of these compartments from the usefulness of departments for our Universities. It is possible and useful to regard logical thinking abstractly and by itself. It is the legitimate method of scientific approach to isolate and to abstract. But this isolation and abstraction cannot be the last word of science, and philosophy can never legitimately refuse in the name of philosophical dignity to reset its abstractions and isolations into the concrete context in which they exist. It can never refuse to view logical thinking concretely, in all its implications.

For the purpose of this paper we must distinguish between ordinary logical thinking, the science of logic and theoretical thinking.

Ordinary logical thinking manifests itself partly as a form of verbal behaviour (forming sentences and drawing conclusions) and partly in rational and consistent active behaviour to our world. I leave aside the almost insoluble question as to the extent to which processes of logical thinking actually exist. I only try to show that, wherever logical thinking may exist, by its very nature and definition it is closely connected with social life and conditions. I shall show this in its connection with language, in its presupposition of a "common world", in its desire for "control of thought" and in its two fundamental principles, the principles of contradiction and identity.

Logical thinking yields in some sense the "raw material" for the science of logic. I shall try to show that the science of logic arose in special historical conditions and maintains itself only while and where the same social conditions persist.

Finally, out of the interactions of logical thinking with the new science of logic and its new demands on thought may arise a new type of logical thinking which we will call "theoretical thinking". Theoretical thinking seeks for truth, claims universal validity for its results and believes in deciding questions by arguments. The sociological basis of theoretical thinking will be the subject of the last part of this paper.

2. Logical Thinking

Language as such

If we examine the connection of logical thinking with society, we find, of course, that its connection with the social fact of language and speech is the most obvious of all.

Logical thinking is not possible without the help of language. There can indeed be intelligent behaviour without the accompaniment of language. There exists, to be sure, in many animals an organic intelligence which dispenses with it. No human thinking can, however, be logically mature without some language, without symbols which express ideas and represent things. We cannot think distinctly without the help of words or other spoken or written symbols. It may quite well be that from the standpoint of ultimate truth our mind is corrupted by symbols and that our intellect is darkened by words. It may be that personal intuition or mystical knowledge carry us further in the perception of truth. But from the standpoint of logical thinking the depth of the merely individual is the depth of the dream and the charm of the nameless is beyond its reach.

Words serve to fix and define attentions and intentions. They serve to hold a problem distinctly in the mind and to make possible the conscious differentiation and relation between objects. The capacity to experiment intellectually with situations not immediately perceived achieves a high development and extension only through symbols. Of all signs, the auditory and written signs alone yield the variety of expression and denotation we need.

What is thought logically can be fully and unambiguously communicated from intellect to intellect by articulate language and written signs. That is the essential difference from states of feeling which can be transmitted—as fully and unambiguously—from man to man only by sympathy and antipathy. This faculty must have died out to make logic desirable. Reason is, according to F. Lorimer, thought controlled by explicit statement, rather than by merely intuitive sensory, motor and visceral responses.

Speech is a social fact. It arose out of social conditions, out of the need of communicating with one another. This need was felt in common work, in the talk round the fire in the cave, in drama, song and dance. Speech involves a reference to other persons and arises out of social contact. All linguistic symbols imply a reference to society by being based on social custom. Speech is one of the institutions which are forced on the individual by social pressure and coercion (ridicule, etc.). Languages are peculiar to peculiar social groups. There are as many different languages as there are social groups. All symbols—as different from signs—are public, are socially and institutionally established as instruments of communication. There are none which are private and yet used to express logical thought. It is conceivable that logicians might have a language and symbols understood by nobody but themselves. But this is not the phenomenon we mean when we speak of logical thinking. The symbols of logistics are a case of artificial language, like the morse code. These artificial languages are based entirely on conscious convention and agreement and are essentially confined to small social groups.

Only articulate language can denote things in a manner which is common to all individuals of a group. When we denote something by the impersonal word and represent it in a concept we take away from it everything which has a singular relation to us and its entire singularity.

The Common World

Logical thinking is concerned with the objective world. The distinction between an objective and a subjective world is best defined as the difference between public and private worlds. The world denoted in language is a public world. Both language and logical thinking refer to a public world. The concepts and words used and the objects referred to must be common to thinker and listener or reader.

Certain data escape logical thinking and can as such never become its objects. Things which are essentially intimate and private will bear inspection only by certain subjects and not by others. If viewed by strangers, they change their nature and do not appear the same. They are the objects of an autistic thinking. Moreover, the absolutely singular, "das dieses da", the "this here", as Hegel calls it, is only given in being shown and pointed out and is accessible as such to neither thought nor to language.

The public world is experienced in society and is limited by the extent of our social relations. There is not one public world common to all. But each social group has a world, an environment of its own. Discussion and communication of thought is only possible where and in so far as social environments coincide. Different social groups do not understand each other and rarely a logos has been found to bridge the gulf between them. Each individual is the member of several social groups at a time and this determines the range of his possible contacts.

The Control of Thought

Logical thinking is controlled thinking. Demonstration is essential to it. No mental activity can exist without a drive or impulse behind it. The desire for verification and justification has partly a social origin. Until they are 7 or 8 years of age, children scarcely know any difference between fact and fantasy. Play and quasi-hallucinatory imagination allow them to regard their desires, scarcely born, as already realized. This reign of the "pleasure principle" is abolished only in the degree in which children grow up and merge into the society of adults. Only gradually are the categories of reality and objectivity used.

Verification is necessary partly for the adjustment to the hard reality of the world, in order that we may survive. In this sense it is for ourselves that we verify. But at least as important is a second factor. It is the clash of our thought with that of other people which produces in us doubt and the need for proof. Else the disappointment of experience would lead us to an overcompensation by illusions. The need of communicating and convincing is at the root of the need for verification. Proof is born from discussion and has no sense except in a social world. Verification further becomes valuable only through cooperation, which alone goes beyond the tiny futility of the merely individual existence.

The Principle of Contradiction

Contradictions annihilate the effect of activity. The law of contradiction is fundamentally a law of all efficient and successful activity, being a universal law of all being. The distinction between affirmation and negation is found originally in the distinction between positive and negative reactions, between yes-responses and no-responses which is common to all living beings and visible already in the most simple forms of life, in *Amœba proteus* and in *Paramecium caudatum*. Organisms react differently to differences before they think about them. The principle of contradiction is a fundamental principle of all activity which does not annihilate, destroy and defeat itself. In logic it is merely reformulated for a special branch of human activity, for the symbolic organization of thought.

The principle of contradiction has its origin far back in the history of organic life. In our social life its application is extended and reinforced. Its application is extended in the degree in which socially organized work is discovering new incompatible properties in things and new, incompatible attitudes to them. Its application is strengthened through social pressure. Inconsistency leads to maladjustment and, for social beings, also to maladjustment to the social environment which is instantaneously punished by society. Inconsistency is rebuffed because we prefer in our social relations persons whom we can rely upon and on whose reactions we can count. People exhibiting habitually contradictory reactions are not "taken seriously". Only the absence of contradictions makes success possible. The desire for success is reinforced in society. Finally most people do not stand alone, but are engaged in some more or less useful work. Social pressure compels them to avoid contradictions which would nullify their own actions and destroy their usefulness.

The Principle of Identity

This principle is concerned both with logical objects and with the objects of logic, both with concepts and propositions and with the "being" of which they are supposed to be valid. Identity has three aspects. It means permanence, independence and definiteness.

1. A symbol or proposition must have the same constant reference within any set of related symbolic processes. Things

must have lasting aspects, either a permanent substance or a constant law.

2. In order to maintain their permanence in varying surroundings and circumstances, logical symbols and objects must be to a certain degree independent from and superior to their context and environment. The logical symbol or proposition remains the same wherever it occurs, in different persons, is independent of the character, motives, etc., of these persons, and remains the same in any connections with other symbols and propositions, in any language and in all logical operations. An object of logic remains the same in different environments, it is not completely altered by coming into relation with other objects and is not modified by being brought into the sphere of a rational subject.

3. Logical symbols and objects of logical thinking are unambiguous, definite, and each of them is different from all other symbols and objects.

The data of experience assume this identity only if we assume a certain attitude towards them. This attitude has its basis in our organic constitution.[1] But it has developed in society. I want to draw your attention to a curious parallelism between logos and ethos, between logical things and ethical man.

Logical objects can be identical only if the logical subject has identity. Where man loses his identity with himself, the objects of his thought also lose their identity. The different shades and manifestations of this parallelism are outside the scope of this paper. I only refer to an extreme case, to the "flight of ideas". Persons who suffer from "flight of ideas" lose simultaneously the identity of their personality and that of the objects of their thinking. These persons have lost the autarchy and relative independence of their mind and the trend of their ideas is continually diverted by the immediate impressions from their environment, which have them in their power.

[1] I cannot deal here with the fascinating problems of the organic basis of logical thinking. I must refer to my book *Der Satz vom Widerspruch*, 1932, where I deal with the importance of organic identity, of upright posture, of brain and hand for the development of logical thinking. Terminologically I must note that I call "identity" not only the relation of a thing to itself, but also that which remains identical.

They are incapable of any continuity in uniform activity. They are also unable to dwell on the same thing for any length of time and to recognize things in their identity. Only with an identical constitution of our personality do we get at the identity of things, perform logical activities and handle the logos properly. At the present time, logical science and thinking are frequently regarded as matters of a mere intellectual routine. We have, in general, lost sight of their ethical basis. Philosophical tradition at its best has, however, been always quite conscious of the intimate connection between logical and ethical activity.

The virtuous man, by living up to his ethical demands and principles, assumes the triple aspect of the identity of logical things and concepts:

1. Ethical value and behaviour are permanent. Aristotle observed that the good man always remains the same and does not change his ethos, whereas bad and stupid people are always unequal to themselves. We become as permanent as are the logical objects when we practise the virtues of perseverance, constancy, persistency, reliability and faithfulness. The same desire for permanence is expressed in the striving for immortality, fame and stability.

2. The independence and superiority of man is one of the fundamental assumptions of his ethical behaviour. It is reached in the undisturbed active rest of the soul, in the faculty of decision, and self-control, in the perseverance and patience in facing and overcoming difficulties. We say of a person that he has character when he vigorously resists all influences alien to him. We find this independence in the steadiness and equanimity with which he rejects influences of the environment which are pushing him this way and that way. We find it in the ideal of the upright man and of the steadfastness of the soul.

3. Man must be definite. The unambiguity of a person is of value. Virtue is unambiguous and ὡδισμὲνη λὸγω. Freedom is the self-determination of the independent identical part of man against external things.

It is not possible to do more than indicate the parallelism between the structure of logical objects and that of ethical man. The principle of identity is a postulate. Because I have identity or should have it, also the things I think about must have it. We demand in logic that things and in ethics that persons should be identical because identity is something socially valuable. Identical things and persons are necessary for social work and co-operation. The moral virtues in which we reach identity are social virtues which are demanded and enforced by society in the interest of the preservation of society and which can be gained only in society.

3. The Science of Logic

The Historical Origin of Logic

We can easily date for Europe the historical beginning of logical science. The preliminary discussions began in the Greek colonies of Asia Minor and Sicily about 500 B.C. After 450 B.C. Athens began to take part in them. Logic itself emerged in the years between 390 and 340 B.C., between the writing of Plato's early dialogues and the completion by Aristotle of his logical writings and the third book of the Metaphysics. In India and China logic, curiously enough, developed at about the same time; but exact dates are not available.

For tens of thousands of years magical methods had been as effective in adapting man to his environment as was logical science later on in some parts of the world. The psychological processes which lead to these results are—mainly through the unbounded arrogance of the modern civilized European—as unknown to us as are the processes which lead to adaptation by "instinct" in plants and animals. But there can be no doubt about the results themselves. Magical knowledge disclosed many facts about the world, made a high degree of technical and artistic skill possible, and led to a high degree of control of nature and society. Rain magic and primitive healing arts work with the same degree of certainty as do modern meteorology and medicine. Modern medicine frequently rediscovers in its own way healing methods, which magic had discovered before. The deep knowledge of plants attained by the North American Indians in cultivating maize has not been reached again by their more scientific successors. The method of cultivating cotton traditional with the fellahin remained 30 per cent superior to the scientific system of the Americans who finally adopted it. The English system of irrigation in India has never reached the perfection of the old Indian system. Aurignacian art reached a high level of achievement with magical procedures. And, what counts most, the adaptation as a whole of these tribal communities compares favourably with our own.

But this magical knowledge is indissolubly bound up with the tribal system. With the tribal community also this knowledge of the world through primary sympathetic and intuitive understanding is disintegrated. Magic works only in the tribal community. At the present time we witness the joint disintegration of the tribal community and of magic in those vast areas which are being colonized by industrialized countries. The agrarian population adapts itself through magical knowledge and lacks logical science, not through want of intelligence but through absence of interest. It was only after the old instrument was broken up together with its social basis, through economical changes, that logic became something desirable and that science became necessary as a new means of adaptation. In some parts of the world the tribal community was and is displaced by the introduction of a monetary economy and the establishment of larger cities which can lead a life of their own and are more than a casual meeting place for country people. In Greece logic and science developed at a time when a monetary, commercial, and urban community had gradually grown since the seventh century under the pressure of the increase of the population, and had undermined the old tribal community.

Magic and logic are irreconcilable, and unintelligible in terms of one another. For magic, science is either sacrilege or absurdity. For science, magic is nonsense. Magic is so foreign to logic that, in terms of logic, it is merely an agglomeration of logical mistakes, as many authors have shown with great complacency. This mutual hostility between them makes it impossible to regard magic as a form of logic or logic as a form of magic. They are radically different.

Logical thinking is a form of verbal behaviour. It is therefore the magical and tribal attitude to language and words which must be scrapped before logic becomes possible.

Avoiding Ambiguity

Logic demands that we avoid ambiguity. This is one of the main conditions of the critical adaptation of language to thought. It means in the interest of the new value of accuracy the reduction of the wide margin of vagueness and the breaking up of the meaning which the word owes to the thought of a long tradition. For ages philosophers have deplored the imperfection and the defects of the existing language. They are striving for a logically satisfactory and accurate language which avoids ambiguities and confusions and in which each linguistic symbol has a single, clear, precise and constant function.

A standard outside language is introduced, the standard of meaning of which is relatively independent. Logicians discover that words express propositions but that they are not propositions. They discover that the same set of words can have more than one meaning and that the same meaning can be expressed in more than one set of words.

These ideas appear to us to be a matter of course. There was a time, however, when they seemed an enormity. When conceived in China and Greece, between 500 and 450 B.C., they constituted a revolutionary change.

In China the change was brought about by Teng Hsi and Confucius, in the time of the decay of feudalism. Teng Hsi stressed the importance of a correct terminology in legal texts and discussions. Confucius wanted to correct life by correcting the names of things. He composed about 480 B.C. a chronicle of the state of Lu which treated of the events between 722 and 480 B.C. These *Ch'un Ch'iu* (spring and autumn annals) to-day appear quite trivial, meaningless and futile. At that time, however, they created a very great impression. Meng Tse reports: "Confucius finished the *Ch'un Ch'iu* and rebellious ministers and depraved sons were struck with terror." This book, quite colourless for us, was composed for the express purpose "of reforming a depraved age and leading it back to righteousness". Confucius said: "For the *Ch'un Ch'iu* the ages will love me; for it they will also detest me." What was the new thing in the book that created this astounding effect? It was nothing else than that Confucius for the first time attempted accuracy of linguistic expression and a distinction of homonyms. "Each fact and each idea should have a distinct proper name; if the name is confusing the fact and the idea will also be confused; right will appear as wrong, etc." (*Li Chi*, XXIV, ch. 7). The new attitude aroused strong protest. As an attack against tradition and the common people's usage it appeared to Hsuentsu as "the greatest evil".

In Greece the new attitude to words had a similar reception. Men like Prodikos and Protagoras aroused considerable enthusiasm in the towns. Prodikos saw his main task in exposing the ambiguity of words (*ὀνοματα διαιρειν*). Eudemos, pupil of Aristotle, who was still near this time, reports that at the time of Parmenides nobody had as yet heard of the ambiguity of words and the method of their solution. Still the "eleatic logic",[1] as practised by the Eleatic philosophers and Sophists (Megarics and Antisthenes) kept all the ambiguities with which tradition had loaded language.

It is socially impossible to reshape language for the needs of logical thought where all members of a society are convinced that language is given by nature, adapted to nature and one of the forces of nature. For magical thinking speech has a greater power than anything else; it can perform the greatest things; it can kill and revive, protect against death, quench fire, smooth storms and tear chains. To know the name of a thing means to hold it in one's power. "O fever, thou shalt not escape me; I know thy name," said the witch doctors of the *Atharva Veda* in their conjurations. This magical speech is separated by a whole world from that of the logician, which is used for the communication of theoretical knowledge. We find coupled with the magical beliefs the conviction of the correctness of one's own language. Vendryes[2] reports from France: "Listen to a peasant discussing the patois of a neighbouring village; he will proudly affirm that himself and the people of his village alone speak properly and correctly and that the correct method of speech ends with the brook which bounds his own side of the valley." Primitive tribes are inclined to think that other "barbarian" tribes speak no proper language but babble like

[1] For a detailed proof of the existence of a specific eleatic logic which was first discovered by the Danish philosopher Svend Ranulf, I must refer to my book *Der Satz vom Widerspruch*, 1932, n. 483.

[2] *Language*, 1931, 242.

children or animals. We see the Pythagoreans rejecting the distinction of homonyms on the basis of the old *φύσει* theory; since "words are by nature and not by convention, one word is always said by nature with regard to one thing".[1] Words in themselves are a guide to truth. To each word corresponds an entity. "Meaning" can rule only after the word itself does no longer express the essence of things. It can develop its own laws only after the word has appeared to certain strata of society as a largely arbitrary convention, being of no account on its own.

The development of logic was preceded in Greece by long discussions on the nature of language. A stage in the dissolution of the magical (*φύσει*) theory is the archaic theory which we find in China with Confucius and with which Plato deals in his "Cratylos". The archaic theory assumes that names represent the truth of things but that these names are not necessarily those of the traditional domestic language. It was the necessary condition for logic that language should be regarded as brought about by convention. Aristotle expressly rejects the *φύσει* theory in "*Περὶ Ἑρμενείας*".

The attitude of the logician gained its victory through social forces and not through the power of arguments. We have not refuted the magical theory but it has died out socially in town populations. In Greece the magical theory was dissolved through the development of trade and travel. The development of the city economy was there closely bound up with the development of external and international trade. A more extensive knowledge of foreign countries must shake the belief in the superior correctness also of one's own language. The mere contact with foreign groups does not lead necessarily to the annihilation of the faith in the exclusive correctness of the mother tongue. De Morgan reports the saying of the English sailor: "The French call a cabbage a shoe (*choux*); the fools! Why can't they call it a cabbage when they must know that it is one." The contact must be a continual and living one. In Greece rapine and piracy were originally linked up indissolubly with trade and prevented mutual understanding. Very gradually trade itself, peaceful trade, developed with certain

[1] Simplicius *in cat.* 40, 6.

common rights between homelanders and foreigners and a certain equality between them in the harbours, etc.

The tendency towards accuracy of language is reinforced where written laws replace customary traditions. Fixed and unambiguous laws are indispensable for commercial calculation. They are introduced in most Greek towns in the sixth century as a result of the rebellion of the lower and commercial classes against the big feudal proprietors, and, according to tradition, through the operation of individual and specially inspired legislators.

These are some of the reasons why scientific philosophy could develop only in the commercial towns of Asia Minor, Sicily and Central Greece. Sparta, the tribal state of rough warriors, did everything to discourage and suppress money economy, industry and trade, it isolated its citizens from foreigners, had no written laws and at the same time prohibited philosophy.

Tradition had co-ordinated word and thing in a certain way. Now this co-ordination is loosened and broken. This is possible only if a group of audacious and daring individuals detaches itself to a certain degree from tradition. Where tradition appears beyond criticism, logical science is inconceivable. *Why* did Confucius think that he might be detested for his work? Because it was he who as an ordinary individual praised and blamed historical actions, a privilege reserved to the son of heaven in whom Nature itself spoke. It was he who added personal judgments to the annalist and that gave his work its unique importance.

We cannot dwell here on the numerous signs of rising "individualism" in all fields of activity in the Greek commercial towns since the sixth century. The independence of individuals critical towards tradition reaches the degree necessary for logic only in unstable societies. Only where societies need adapt themselves to continually changing circumstances is the freedom of personal opinions tolerated to a certain degree and later on even encouraged. Freedom of personal thought is generally proportional to the instability of a society. We see both grow together in our own civilization. In the fifteenth century innovations and originality in science were *eo ipso* suspect; now, on the contrary, we reproach a scientist for saying nothing new and original. Only under this social condition is the tyranny of tradition diminished in comparison with the initiative of individuals, in the interest of the preservation of society. The initiative of the individuals then represents the new interests of the group compared with tradition which represents the sum of correct answers to the former situations.

The social character of the new attitude to tradition is also visible in the reaction of the social group which it provoked. Philosophers are tried and persecuted only for the social implications of their ideas. By breaking the magical conception of words logical philosophy lent itself to prosecutions for impiety, for rebellion against the traditional attitude to the Gods and the country. In this way, Protagoras and Prodikos were prosecuted in Greece and Teng Hsi executed in China. The attempt of the first logician, of Socrates, to intellectualize Athenian social life met with the same reaction. By regarding the *νοῦς* as the essence of divinity Socrates replaced its magical power by intellectual superiority. In place of the common prayer of magical coercion he put a refined intellectual prayer. The aristocracy of blood and soil he wanted replaced by that of reason. His doctrines were detrimental to ancient custom and education by shifting the emphasis from organic custom to anarchic thought. Socrates' teaching either removes people from economical and political action; or, what is worse, the Socratic innovators show the apatriotic character of their logos by being friends of every country except their own: Alkibiades starts the Decelian war against his own country for the arch enemy, for Sparta; Critias rules Athens, as one of the Thirty Tyrants, for Sparta, betrays the holy places to the enemy and pulls down the walls of his own city; Xenophon fights in the army of Cyros against Athens. No wonder that Athens, at the same time the most prosperous and the most pious town, occasionally reacted violently against this undermining of traditionalism.

We may add that logic, as it arose only in money economies, could also only maintain itself in its subsequent history in money economies and town civilizations.

Grammar

The same free, detached and reflective attitude to language which we need for the distinctions of homonyms, is necessary for the grammatical treatment of language. The grammatical treatment of language of necessity everywhere, at least in India and Greece, preceded the logical treatment of thought. In Greece grammar was developed by the Sophists and by Demokritos. Plato (*Soph.* 261d) distinguished parts of speech in order to find out whether they "fit together" (*ξυναρμόττει*). He was thus led to the distinction between verbs and nouns, between words which are capable of being respectively predicates and subjects. It is well known that Aristotle's logic owes much to the structure of the Greek language. Where his logic was transposed into the Syrian language, in which the verb *precedes* the subject as a rule, it could never become a living thing. The logical categories are first taken from language. The logical structure of the proposition is, at least at the beginning, not entirely independent of the grammatical structure of the sentence and is partly derived from it. Later on the logician may emancipate himself more and more from it. But logic has first to go through this stage. In China logic was stifled from the very outset by the Chinese language which has no grammar proper "but whose entire morphology is contained in the less tangible processes of combining isolated words". (Vendryes.)

The grammarian stands somehow outside language, is superior to it, masters it and is not entirely absorbed in it. Grammar can arise only under social conditions which favour a strong degree of individualism. It is at once combined with the attempt to rectify and to standardize language. *'Ορτῶς λὲγειν* became the slogan of the Sophists. Protagoras called his work *Περὶ ὀρότητος των ὀνομάτων*. His attitude aroused the ridicule of the conservative public (Aristoph. *Clouds* 659–92).

4. Theoretical Thinking

Truth as a Value

Through the interaction between logical thinking and the science of logic a new type of thinking can be formed which we will call "theoretical thinking". Theoretical thinking is directed by a new value, by the value of theoretical truth, by the desire to attain and to convey disinterested truth. It approaches objects with a disinterested attitude. F. Lorimer observes that there are objects and facts which are so charged with intense love and fear that they are immune to critical discussion and intellectual organization. Such were, to give well-known instances, the Germans in Europe during the war, the bolsheviks and the Nazis in post-war times. There are people who think that anything to be worth while must be full of these emotional charges. The logician thinks differently. He demands that the objects of thought should be completely stripped of all emotions and from all immediate reference to practical interests. This demand is reflected in formal logic which, as Dr. Schiller remarks, leaves out in its analysis of thought such obviously irrelevant matters as meaning and its communication, understanding, context, truth, error, relevance, selection, risk, interest and purpose.

People who devote their life to the discovery of truth for truth's sake provoke the contempt and laughter of the man in the street. As Plato said, the pure theoreticians are regarded as "poor mad fools" ever since the girls laughed at Thales dropping into the well and Socrates "was for the most part despised and laughed at" (Diogenes Laertius). No individual can bear alone this weight of social disapproval. The theoreticians have therefore united and fomred a social group of their own.[1] This social group has the function to compensate the theoretical individual for the loss of social respect by creating an adequate group ideology.

This ideology praises the theoretician and inclines him to disregard the ordinary person. It is fond of praising the superior value of intellectual and mental activities and tends to produce in the members of this group a somewhat exaggerated estimate of the part which reason, theories and books play in the world.

[1] This group does, by the way, not comprise everybody who is engaged in scientific research. Many of these research workers are not interested in the discovery of truth, but in that of a new marketable commodity. They are despised by the real theoreticians. The extensive social use to which theories have lent themselves during the last two centuries has brought new complications into the ideology of the theoretician. I must refer to my book *Der Satz vom Widerspruch*, 1932, 417–54.

On the other hand, the theoreticians confirm one another in the belief that they are above everyday society and do not properly belong to it. Contempt for the "mob", for those people who are engaged in everyday activities and who do not care for truth or wisdom, is a strong tendency in this group. Contemptuousness for the masses is bound up with the very existence of pure theoreticians. The theoretician claims that by a disinterested approach he can get at the truth about things, at the things as they are in themselves. In order to arrive at disinterested truth he must leave behind the aspirations and interests of the everyday person who is entangled in everyday society. He must become detached from the interests of everyday society. He must feel superior to it; else he could not regard his truth as a better truth than that which the man in the street perceives with the sharp eyes of his material interest.

Theoreticians can form a social group only under certain economic conditions. As we saw already, the old tribal community must be broken up through a money economy and cities, and intelligent research must have taken the place of instinctive knowledge. Further, a high development of the productive forces of society and a very developed division of labour are obviously necessary conditions for the existence of this group.

Universal Validity

The validity of thoughts has a social origin and meaning. In a society statements are universally valid if they are universally believed in. The only ultimate proof we have for validity is by the testing of the assertion in society and the attempt to gain the confirmation of others. In modern science an experiment is regarded as conclusive only if it can be repeated and has been repeated by others.

Some theoreticians do not accept this interpretation of general validity. They imagine that statements are universally valid quite independently of the question whether they are recognized by anybody—except themselves.

The flaw in this theory is that its proponents show by their behaviour that they do not believe in it. All theoreticians are, in actual fact, striving for social recognition. A truth is precarious until it is recognized by many. It is secured, fully also in the view of the theoretician, only after having become common property. Their thinking is felt to be incomplete and they have a sense of insecurity about their conclusions as long as these are confined to themselves. The recognition of others increases their own conviction, and for them too it is of the greatest importance that other people should also think as they do. "All solitary experience is imperfectly realized, baulked and frustrated in the realization of its own nature" (MacMurray).

The delusion that a supersocial validity can be reached has its social roots. These theoreticians represent social groups which are not aware of their limitations owing to the firm conviction that they represent the interests of the entire society. At the same time this attitude is another instance of the overcompensation we find in theoreticians. The "mihi cano et musis" is the expression of misjudged and angry theoretical foxes for whom the grapes of social recognition are too sour, but which they strive for all the more ardently, as experience proves.

Discussion and Arguments

In Greece, India and China logic obviously was invented for the regulation of a social activity, i.e. discussion. The widespread interest in discussions created the social conditions under which man turned his attention to the mechanism of reasoning which otherwise does not much interest him. Monological thought grew out of a dialectical thinking which was controlled by an audience. Plato's logic is still the art of him "who knows to ask questions and to answer them" (*Crat.* 390).

In India logic never lost the traces of this origin. We find for instance enumerated as an essential part of their syllogism up to the latest times the "example" which does not strengthen the proof itself but which, according to the statements of Indian logicians, has the aim of making the statement more intelligible and impressive to the partner in discussion. The regard for others remains visibly essential to thought. But also in the West monological thought keeps this social character. It is a talking of man to himself, a self-dialogue, a self-control. A conflict of views is at the root of theoretical thought. This conflict is almost always embodied in concrete persons. We, internally, discuss with Aristotle, Kant, Mr. Smith, etc. And, as has been pointed out, since the lonely thinker wants also to convince, he finishes up again in social relations.

Theoreticians assume that arguments and proofs mean and decide something. This conviction is not shared by all strata of society. It is not the natural thing to have an argumentative mind. People argue only if they have no power to compel or command. This is one of the reasons why the theories of revolutionary lower classes are so frequently superior to those of established ruling classes who do not take the trouble to argue. Powerful men are too proud to argue. Also in good society arguing is regarded as bad manners. As Nietzsche says: "Honest things like honest men do not carry their reasons on their sleeve in such a fashion. It is not good form to make a show of everything. That which needs to be proved cannot be worth much." These facts, without invalidating the use of arguments and discussions (of which I personally approve) are an indication that argumentative thought as such must be treated sociologically. Lack of space prevents me from continuing the rather complicated study of this aspect of logical thought.

Conclusion

A fuller treatment of the subject of this paper would have required an analysis of the contribution of society to the formation of abstract ideas and general concepts, to the awakening of self consciousness, and to the development of those mental faculties like memory which are indispensable to logical thinking. It would further need a study of the effects of social isolation, in dreams and young children, on the structure of logical thought. But I hope that even as it is this paper will furnish ample material for discussion and argument.

3

SOCIAL ORIGINS OF NOMINALISM

I

In the older books on the history of philosophy Descartes marks the turning point from medieval to modern philosophy. Later on German historians began to date modern philosophy from Nicholas of Cusa. Both these estimates are now out of date. Ever since Duhem published his researches on Leonardo da Vinci and the origins of modern science, it has become each year more and more evident that the real turning point in European thought was the change from scholastic realism to Nominalism. The Nominalist philosophers of the fourteenth century were the pioneers of modern thought, the characteristic feature of which is the endeavour to control nature by mechanical means.[1]

In university circles the question has been hotly debated whether the economic structure of capitalism is responsible for the development of a capitalist mentality, or whether antecedent changes in the religious and philosophical convictions of men led to the growth of the economic structure of capitalism. It has been claimed that it was the re-interpretation of Christian religion at the time of the Reformation which led to the bourgeois mentality that created the capitalist economic system. Recent economic historians have, however, shown that the beginnings of capitalism lie in the fourteenth century. We are thus faced with the strange coincidence that a new (capitalist) economic system begins to arise simultaneously with a new (Nominalist) philosophical system. We have to ask ourselves whether this is more than a coincidence and whether, perhaps, the Nominalist philosophy expressed the needs of the economic structure that began to shape itself

[1] There is an almost complete agreement among recent historians of philosophy on that point. Ernest E. Moody, in *The Logic of William of Ockham*, has, however, challenged the current evaluation of Occam's philosophy. He represents Occam's logic as an attempt to return to pure Aristoteleanism. His arguments are far from convincing.

at that time. In the seventeenth and eighteenth centuries, Nominalism was at the basis of the philosophy of precisely those thinkers who most ardently and clearly fought for the realization of a bourgeois conception of society. Could Nominalism from the very start have been an expression of bourgeois mentality? I think that we must come to this conclusion. Naturally I cannot hope to give an adequate proof for my contention in a short article. All I can do is to try to render it plausible, and to refer the reader to the more detailed account I have given elsewhere.[1]

Bourgeoisie and Nominalist Intellectuals

A bourgeoisie existed already in the fourteenth century, in France, England, Northern Italy and some parts of Germany. It is a curious fact that the bourgeoisie at that time was strong precisely in those parts of Europe where Nominalism flourished. To be sure, the agrarian population and its mode of production still predominated. But the economic system was strongly tending toward capitalism and the production of commodities. The instruments of a money economy were emerging: calculation was simplified, bills of exchange and bookkeeping developed, the stability of monetary value established, weight, measure and money regulated uniformly, and new laws passed which encouraged trade.

A certain concentration of capital took place. In England the Lombards concentrated the wool trade in their hands. Trade grew. In vain did the guilds try to conserve the collapsing artisan production. Restrictions on the number of workers allowed in each workshop were either sabotaged or openly abolished (as in Paris in 1307 and in 1351). Rich people, mostly traders, advanced money to artisans, many of whom thus became mere wage-workers. This development was specially marked in the textile industries. In this way a considerable number of workers were placed under one command, the productivity of their labour increased, greater specialization, division of labour and quicker application of technical improvements achieved. The first machines were set up in Boulogne, Augsburg and England. In 1340, in Bristol, a manufacturer

[1] Edward Conze, *Der Satz vom Widerspruch* (1932), pp. 205–66.

was punished "for having caused various machines for weaving and making woollen clothes to be set up, and hired weavers and other workmen for this purpose". The liberation of the serfs created "free" workers everywhere. In Italy the serfs were set free very early, at the instigation of the bourgeois towns, and by about 1500 they are "free" almost everywhere. In Flanders feudal serfdom had been abolished in the thirteenth century, and in England it had almost disappeared at the end of the fourteenth century.[1] Since it proved more and more difficult for artisans to become masters, the number of skilled workers increased. Feudal retainers flooded the country, a pauperized mass of hirelings, beggars, criminals, prostitutes, creating a labour reserve which legislation and hunger soon placed at the disposal of capitalist production.

The growing bourgeoisie was conscious of its tasks and needs. It was a considerable political force. Under Edward III the towns sent 226 deputies to Parliament, compared with 76 from the countryside. In France the bourgeoisie of the towns became the main social force used by the King in his attempts to break the power of the feudal lords.[2] The bourgeoisie had started to act politically on its own. In 1306, in 1357, in 1382, in 1412, the *corps de métiers* of Paris, the artisans, tradesmen and workmen, revolted against the feudal powers. Etienne Marcel, their greatest leader, put forward demands for reform which retained their significance and power down to the time of the great French Revolution.[3] The Third Estate increasingly conquered administrative positions, and it played a dominant part in the States General which steadily gained influence during the fourteenth century, owing to their power to grant taxes. Between 1355 and 1358 the bourgeoisie had secured great influence in the French state. Thereafter the brutal and savage repression of the Jacquerie turned back the wheel of

[1] Karl Marx, *Das Kapital* (ed. Kautsky), v. I, p. 648.

[2] Louis the Saint writes in his Testament: "Especially maintain the good cities and commons of thy realm in the same estate and with the same franchises as they enjoyed under thy predecessors .... For because of the power and wealth of the great cities, thine own subjects, and especially thy peers and thy barons, and foreigners also, will fear to undertake aught against you."

[3] Thierry, *Essai sur l'histoire de la formation et des progrès du tiers état*, pp. 53, 58–63; J. M. Hyndman, *The Evolution of Revolution*, ch. 18.

history. The allies which the bourgeoisie had found in the countryside were either massacred or terrorized into submission. It took the French bourgeoisie 400 years and the English bourgeoisie 300 years to conquer political power.

The leading Nominalists were not at all "pure theoreticians". On the contrary, they took an active part in the political struggles of the bourgeoisie. To mention only some few points: Occam fought passionately for Louis of Bavaria who based his power and policy mainly on the town bourgeoisie and whose political aims were those of the bourgeoisie—a secular democratic state. For parliamentary democracy is, according to Engels, the normal form of bourgeois rule. In 1359 Occam wrote an apology for Edward III, that pioneer of capitalist economy in England. Nicholas of Oresme and Buridan influenced the French Court to introduce those monetary reforms which the new money economy required so badly.

Dominated by Nominalists the University of Paris exerted its considerable political influence in the direction of the bourgeois revolution. From 1353 to 1358 it led a violent movement against feudalism. It took part in the bourgeois revolution of Etienne Marcel, and in the rebellion of the butchers which occurred in 1413. It elaborated a plan for the administrative and legal reform of France which foreshadowed the France of the nineteenth century. The population backed the University's new constitution by conquering the Bastille; the King even recognized it for a time; but in the end the mass butcheries of the Jacquerie delayed everything for centuries.

If we now take for granted the fact that both the conditions for capitalist development and a powerful and class-conscious bourgeoisie existed already in the fourteenth century, we may ask what the rising bourgeoisie would expect of its theoreticians. In accordance with its social position it would require (1) arguments against feudalism, and especially against the Church, and (2) a strengthening of that attitude of mind and of those methodological instruments which are necessary for technical control over nature.

Church and Religion

Feudal aristocracy and the clergy were the two classes that opposed the rise of the bourgeoisie. The nobility was fought with guns and money. The clergy owed their power largely to the hold which their authoritarian philosophy of life exerted over the minds of the people, and especially over the educated classes. This hold could be broken only by the creation of an alternative philosophy of life. Here was a task for the theoreticians of the rising bourgeoisie.

The bourgeois, although often anti-clerical, was not directly anti-religious. He was even pious. What he objected to in the Church was its wealth and its political influence. The bourgeois supported the Emperor and the kings in their attempts to restrict the political influence of the Church. They resented the accumulation of wealth by the Church. Not only was this wealth withheld from capitalist accumulation, much of it was spent in a way which shocked the bourgeois conscience. The budget of Pope John XXII (1316–34), for instance, must have appeared to a merchant or an artisan as the budget of a wicked waster. The Pope spent on war 63.7 per cent, on salaries 12.7 per cent, on alms, church building and missions 7.16 per cent, on clothes 3.35 per cent, on meals, 2.5 per cent, etc.[1] What the bourgeois wanted was a cheap church, *une église a bon marché*. They demanded a simple organization of the Church which would eliminate the unproductive monks, clergymen and the Roman Court, in short all those clerical features which were the most expensive.[2] Finally, the new class further objected, rather inarticulately at first, to Church interference with the secular knowledge necessary to develop the forces of production.

The attitude of the Nominalists to Church and religion, social questions at that time as to-day, consistently reflected the attitude of the rising bourgeoisie. Occam and his followers, in their criticism of the Church, proposed concrete reforms the economic intent of which was obvious. They demanded a church pruned of over-elaborations, insisted on poverty of the clergy, and called for a return to the simple life of the *ecclesia primitiva* and to the poverty of Christ. They further

[1] Hermelinck, "Das Mittelalter", in *Handbuch der Kirchengeschichte* (1912), p. 174.

[2] Engels, *Bauernkrieg*, pp. 37, 38–28. Later on Helvetius held the same ideas, *Oeuvres*, v. V, pp. 63, 93.—The Basque deputy in the Cortes said on October 2, 1936: "We want a poor Church."

demanded that the activities of the Church should be restricted to the purely religious and spiritual field. The fraction of the Franciscans to which Occam belonged dreamt of an ideal Church, spiritual, virtuous and poor, in contrast to the Roman Church of the time, carnal, vicious and wealthy.[1]

The Nominalists further taught that the doctrines of Christianity could not be proved by reasoning; and that they were in fact contradictory to the principles of reason. They asserted that the existence of God, rationally speaking, can be established, at best, as probable only. God's essence cannot be understood by our reasoning power. Nothing can be rationally understood except on the basis of some intuition. But of God no intuition is possible. In the absence of empirical data one cannot even be sure about the immortality of the soul. It cannot be rationally demonstrated—as St. Thomas had attempted to do by studying the essence of man—that man has any aim that lies beyond himself. Nominalism left man without an essence, and in consequence led to interminable doubts about the meaning of life. Many doctrines of the Church were declared by the Nominalists to be in express opposition to reason.[2] Even the basic principle of logic, the principle of contradiction, is, according to Occam and R. Holkot, violated in the sphere of faith.

The relation of these Nominalist doctrines to the class tasks of the rising bourgeoisie can, I think, be shown in three respects:

1. By insisting on the doctrine that faith cannot be proved rationally, Nominalism prepared for the secularization of knowledge, and for an elimination of theological considerations from our knowledge of the world. As G. Ritter[3] has pointed out, Occam's radical division between faith and rational knowledge contributed considerably to the success of purely secular science in winning its independence from theological sentiments and ideas. At the same time, it is characteristic that Nicholas of Oresme worked consciously to break the clergy's

[1] Denzinger, *Enchiridion*, n. 494, 485.

[2] Pierre d'Ailly states that faith contains "nonnulla quae apparent manifeste contra rationem et quorum opposita sunt consona rationi", Denzinger, *ibid.*, n. 229.

[3] G. Ritter, "M. v. Inghen und die okkamistische Schule in Deutschland", *Stzb. d. Heidelb. Ak. d. Wiss. Phil-Hist.* (1921), p. 69.

monopoly of education. He writes for "tout homme qui est de franc condition et de noble engin", disseminates knowledge also among laymen and makes Aristotle accessible to the lay *conseillers du roi* through his French translation of the *Politics*.

2. By asserting the unreasonableness of the doctrines of faith, the Nominalists revealed how strange the feudal religious traditions appeared to the common sense of the new bourgeois class. The same emotional reaction to feudal religion is shown in the famous Nominalist doctrine that all commands of God are arbitrary. They must simply be accepted, and we need not think that they are really justified.

3. Many writers assume that it was out of mainly religious motives that the Nominalists attempted to increase the gap between knowledge and faith. This may be the case as far as the motives of individual Nominalists are concerned. But these are sociologically unimportant compared with the social results of increasing the gap between knowledge and faith. Weak and not yet quite conscious of themselves, the Nominalists could not openly throw feudal religion overboard. They could only bow it politely out of the room. This explains, I think, those curious Nominalist doctrines which *indirectly* rendered religion superfluous in scientific research. Since the activity of the *causa prima* cannot be understood in detail, rational research will have to deal exclusively with empirical causes, with the *causae secundae*. As regards psychology and ethics, Occam and Pierre d'Ailly taught that one cannot prove rationally the necessity of the supernatural *habitus* (Faith, Hope and Charity) since it is possible to derive all their effects from the natural *habitus*. The modern Roman Catholic writer H. Denifle[1] admits that this doctrine cannot escape the conclusion that the supernatural *habitus* can be dispensed with in a rational account of the activities of the human soul.

To be sure, many mystics out of religious motives have claimed that God is too high and too sublime to be grasped by our natural reasoning powers. But the mystics coupled this thesis with a contempt for the natural faculties of man. This is, however, emphatically not the case among Nominalists. They deprive the Christian doctrine of any support it was supposed

[1] H. Denifle, *Luther und Luthertum in der ersten Entwicklung* (2nd ed. 1906), vol. I, p. 592.

to have in the natural gifts and aptitudes of man, but at the same time they attribute a high value to those natural gifts and aptitudes. The result of necessity is damaging to the cause of religion and it required only a little time for the Church to experience it. The Nominalist teachings on the relation between knowledge and faith, worked out to their logical end, contributed in no small measure to the decline of religious convictions, and consequently, of the power of the Church. But in the fourteenth century, the Church was socially still very powerful: it could be opposed only by those who at the same time kneeled before its majesty.

Knowledge and the World

Members of different social groups acquire knowledge for different reasons and motives. The studies of medieval scholastics aimed at saving the individual soul and at increasing the power of the clerical hierarchy. The Nominalists deliberately and consciously turn away from many of those questions which agitated the scholastic mind, but which appeared to them as *magis subtiles quam utiles*. Nicholas of Oresme shows a marked contempt for pure speculation, for a "philosophe speculatif qui n'estoit pas expert en vie politique, pratique et active". Everywhere he looks for practical applications. The increase of man's practical control over his environment more and more becomes the goal of knowledge. The cultivation of pure reason is deemed an impossible chimera. For Occam, in accordance with Franciscan tradition, the will is superior to the intellect. Pure reason does not exist. "*Omnis actus intellectus est actus voluntatis*."

For St. Thomas, for instance, the "essence," the object of pure theoretical speculation, had been the aim of thought. In its search for truth the intellect must leave aside the particular and contingent things.[1] Now, for the Nominalists, the particular, the concrete thing becomes the object of thought. The "essences" of scholasticism become accessible only when we discard our practical attitude towards things. The leisure classes of Greece had studied only those sciences which were connected with beauty and perfection. The Third Estate,

[1] St. Thomas, in 6. Eth 1, 2–3.

earning its living by work, turned to those sciences which deal with the necessities of life, despised by Aristotle and the scholastics, who for all their intellectual power were the ideological representatives of economically parasitical classes. Mechanics, as is well known, appeared degrading to Plato. It corrupted geometry by making it go "like a runaway slave from the study of incorporeal, intelligible things to that of objects which come under the senses and by using, in addition to reasoning, bodies which have been fashioned, slowly and slavishly, by manual labor". St. Thomas shared those sentiments[1] the denial of which is the very starting point of Nominalism.

Knowledge, as conceived by the Nominalists, aims at the control of events, and not at a knowledge of essential being. Questions concerning the nature of being *qua* being, discussions about *forma* and *substantia*, become purely verbal and uninteresting. Ontology as a rational discipline begins to lose ground rapidly. Not the things themselves but their signs and symbols become the true objects of science. Jean de Jeandun, fellow combatant of Occam, states quite openly that astronomy has merely the task of giving an account of appearances (*salvare apparentias*). The astronomer is not interested in knowing whether those orbits, epicycles, etc. which are hypothetically postulated for the purposes of calculation have an existence in *esse et secundum rem*. He is interested in the calculation, not in the real cause of events.[2] This theory opened the way to the Copernican revolution which rendered calculation of the movements of the stars easier without claiming to come nearer than Ptolemy to "the reality" of things. For Jean de Jeandun it does not matter whether the hypotheses are true if only they are useful, if only they work. Other

[1] "Artes liberales sunt excellentiores quam artes mechanicae. Sed, sicut artes mechanicae sunt practicae; ita artes liberales sunt speculativae . . ." Those arts which are not "liberales", "ordinantur ad opera per corpus exercita, quae sunt quodammodo serviles". St. Thomas, I, II, q. 57, a. 3.

[2] Duhem, *Leonardo da Vinci*, v. IV, pp. 101–03. Schelling (11th lecture): "Es ist wahr, dass man durch Anwending der Mathematik die Abstaende der Planeten, die Zeit ihrer Umlaeufe und Wiedererscheinungen mit Genauigkeit vorherbestimmen gelernt hat, aber ueber das Wesen oder An-sich dieser Bewegungen is dadurch nicht der mindeste Aufschluss gegeben worden."

hypotheses, which no one has as yet thought of, may perhaps perform the same service; we therefore can never be certain of having truly contacted "reality" itself.

Reality of Universals and the World as Chaos

The central thesis of Nominalism, viz., that universals are not real, is familiar to everyone. For the Nominalists things lose their *substantia essentialis* which, according to Aristotle and the scholastics, constituted the inner core of their being and the object of true scientific thought. In the Aristotelean tradition the essence of things was invested with quite a number of important functions. By denying reality to the essence of things the Nominalists developed the new conception of scientific method which rendered possible the machine age. They also evolved a picture of the universe which has remained basic for the bourgeois mind.

In this context it is interesting to note that the "principle of parsimony" is for Occam one of the main arguments against the reality of universals.[1] The assumption that nature is organized along the simplest and most economical lines, that *entia non sunt multiplicanda sine necessitate*, was not made for the first time in 1350. But the emphasis laid on this principle ever since, the fact that in subsequent periods it has been invoked to decide innumerable theoretical questions, and that in no previous age was it regarded so seriously as during the last six centuries, seems to suggest that in some way it made a particular appeal to the bourgeois mind by suggesting a close affinity between the workings of nature and those social and mental processes which characterized early bourgeois activity. It is indifferent to feudal mentality how much one spends or wastes, but the argument for economy finds a ready echo in bourgeois hearts. If the principle of parsimony were denied, not one of the results of modern thought would remain untouched.[2] The principle is patently an arbitrary one. Why

[1] Occam: "Dico quod species neutro modo dicta est ponenda in intellectu, quia nunquam ponenda est pluralitas sine necessitate. Sed sicut alias ostendetur, quicquid potest salvari per talem speciem, potest salvari sine ea aeque faciliter. Ergo talis species non est ponenda."

[2] The best way of exploding a doctrine is to drag its tacit assumptions into the light of day. It would be a useful task for a Marxist to trace the history of the law of parsimony throughout the history of bourgeois

should nature be governed by the needs or limitations of the human mind? Its unquestioned acceptance can be explained only by the natural bourgeois desire to project his own aims into his picture of the world. In the cosmos as in society, there is no need for fripperies, extravaganza, hierarchies of principles, laws or prelates.

The Nominalists teach that things by themselves have no relation to one another. Man has to establish relations between them. Before man operates upon them things are an unrelated and unorganized chaos. Universals are organizing principles which alone bring order into things. But Occam denies any objective existence to universals and to the relations between things. Only our mind establishes these relations.[1] The world of nature is not the *locus* of relations but our mind and the words of our language. The order of the Thomistic cosmos has become a heap of *inconnexa*.

That the world should appear to be a chaos to the bourgeoisie and its theoreticians is a natural consequence of its social position. The capitalist producer is confronted by a chaos of commodities. He finds himself involved in an unplanned economy in which production is affected by the perturbations of an unregulated market. Nowhere does he find any order which might govern his actions. Where there is some order in society, laws, codes, agreements and contracts it is *he* who has brought it about. The structure of the world always appears to man to be in many ways a reflection of the structure of the society in which he lives. Just as the Church found its hierarchy reflected in and supported by the structure of nature, so the bourgeois mind enshrined the chaos of bourgeois society in the cosmos of which it was a part.

Since the rise of Nominalism, bourgeois thought has never ceased to feel that the world, ontologically, is a chaos before man brings order into it by his thoughts and by his actions.[2]

thought, and to show how many of the tenets of modern thought rest on that extraordinary assumption.

[1] Occam: "In re nihil est imaginabile nisi absolutum vel absoluta." "Relatio tantum intentio vel conceptus in anima importans plura absoluta." "Nihil sciture nisi complexum; complexum autem non est extra animam, nisi forte in voce vel in consimili signo."

[2] In *Der Satz vom Widerspruch*, n. 241, I have given a long list of pertinent statements from bourgeois philosophers.

Feudal scholasticism found order in the world as it is. Post-bourgeois Marxism regards the world not as a chaos but as a "net-work of natural phenomena".[1]

Conclusion

A more detailed investigation of Nominalism would have to go further, and show that the law of inertia which, although clearly formulated only about 1650, is the very foundation of all mechanical (i.e. bourgeois) thought, is the automatic consequence of the Nominalistic denial of the reality of universals. It would have to show how the bourgeoisie in its very attempt to extend the power of an anarchic society over nature, feels more and more like a stranger in the world around it and therefore continually discusses whether it can really understand or reach it. It must show why the bourgeois mind can never lose the feeling of being strange and lost in the world, why it will always be subject to the illusion that there is an unknowable reality behind appearances. One would further have to meet obvious objections by showing, for instance, that the mentality of the so-called "Nominalists" of the eleventh century was radically and profoundly different from that of the Nominalists of the fourteenth century. A survey of the last six centuries would have to show that class-conscious bourgeois thinkers have always taken Nominalism for granted, and that all deviations from Nominalism in modern philosophy are due to non-bourgeois tendencies caused by the necessity of effecting a compromise with the Church and nobility. In that way, it might be possible to prove that the Nominalist philosophy and the bourgeoisie not only arose together, but that they remained indissolubly bound together during the entire course of their respective histories. This article is a small contribution to a study of the bourgeois mind and preparatory to a clarification of the relation between Nominalism and dialectical materialism, or what is the same thing, of the relation between the mechanical and dialectical method.

[1] From Lenin's commentary on Hegel's *Logic*, quoted in Luppol, *Lenin und die Philosophie* (1927), p. 86.

II

In his communication to the *Marxist Quarterly* (April–June 1937), James Feibleman raises, on the whole, seven objections to my treatment of nominalism. Owing to reasons of space I can deal with two of them only at some length. As regards the other five, although they would deserve a fuller treatment, I can merely hint at what would be my answer.

1. First of all we must get our definitions clear. Feibleman defines *nominalism* as the thesis that "universals are fictions of the mind, a proposition which renders particular things ultimate and real, and denies the mental interpretation of these real things."[1]

(a) Now, if Occam was a nominalist—and I think we can take that for granted in this discussion—Feibleman's definition is not correct, although it can claim the authority of some dictionaries. Occam expressly *denies* that universals are fictions of the mind, because that would destroy the objective validity of universals and the practical value of experimental science.[2] Universals are not purely imaginary, they have a basis in reality. What is characteristic of modern nominalism is not a clear-cut theory as to the relation of universals to reality but a wavering uncertainty about what corresponds to universals in reality, an uncertainty which has never left the nominalists to this very day, being of the very essence of the theory.

On the one side we hear that the commonness which the universals express is based on an objective *conventia* of things in *reality*.[3] It is based on an aptitude, a "gentle force," as Hume called it later on, in the particulars. The universal is even called a *similitudo rei*.[4] On the other hand, by denying reality to relations, Occam reduces the objective world to a chaos of isolated individuals, for the uniformity of and the similarity between individual things is a relation. Universals are symbols which stand for (*supponunt*) individual things,

[1] The part after "and" I fail to understand.

[2] A good collection of the passages appear in N. Abbagnano, *Guglielmo di Ockham* (1931), p. 91 *et seq.*

[3] Ritter, *M. von Inghen und die okhamistiche Schule in Deutschland* (1921), pp. 60, 118; Hume, *A Treatise* etc., vol. 1, pp. 1, 5; E. Hochstetter, *Studien* (1927), p. 82 note.

[4] Hochstetter, *op. cit.*, pp. 82, 103–108.

that is Occam's final formula. In this way universals have an objective validity, although the exact nature of their relation to reality remains rather obscure.[1]

(b) Nor is the thesis that "only particular things are ultimate and real" in any way characteristic of nominalism only. There is, indeed, one type of "realism" which regards universals as self-subsistent entities that can exist independently of individual substances, and are prior to them (*Universalia ante rem*). But this Platonic form of realism, which was very widespread in the early Middle Ages, was opposed by a host of Aristotelean realists who claimed that only particular or individual things could exist independently, or separately. Universals only exist together with an individual substance, but they are nevertheless real. Abelard tried to define the kind of reality of these universals by calling them "*status*", something which is neither a thing (*res*) nor nothing (*nihilum*).[2] (*Universalia in re*). The Aristotelean realists thus share with the nominalists the conviction that only individual things have a *separate existence* (*subsistentia*), but they ascribe *objective reality* to universals, while the nominalists spoke of *objective validity* only. This distinction may sound a bit subtle. Without it, however, we cannot understand the difference between the so-called "nominalist" doctrines before Occam and nominalism proper, to which we shall turn soon.

(c) The *bourgeoisie* is "defined as the trading and mercantile class". While there have been traders in many periods of history the traders developed into a new class, into a bourgeoisie proper, in the fourteenth century, when they turned to *manufacturing*. The trader who turned manufacturer at that time steadily increased the productivity of labour by increasing the number of workers in each unit of production, by developing the division of labor and by introducing technical improvements and even machines. He more and more employed "free"

[1] Elsewhere (in *Der Satz Widerspruch*, n. 237) I have attempted to show that this insecurity of nominalists about the relation of universals to reality is connected with a general estrangement from reality which is a consequence of the social position and social aspirations of the bourgeoisie.

[2] I have noticed that some dull-witted writers—mostlyProtestant theologians—call this Aristotelean realist with Platonic leanings a "nominalist".

workers. The manufacturer—far more than the trader—is interested in that control over nature which experimental science gradually rendered possible. A trader is a trader. He becomes a bourgeois only in that capitalist system of producing and manufacturing which gradually developed from the fourteenth century onward.

2. If it could be shown that Porphyry, Pyrrhon, Boethius and Roscellinus were nominalists, I would be wrong in asserting that nominalism has always been the doctrine of the bourgeoisie. We would in that case have nominalists who do not represent bourgeois aspirations. The point is vital for my theory. It also serves to illustrate the superiority of the concreteness of the Marxist approach to that unhistorical treatment of philosophical tendencies which prevails in our textbooks. A Marxist would indeed be surprised to find that fundamentally identical doctrines should have arisen in fundamentally different historical circumstances. He therefore keeps his eyes open for differences which escape the friends of unhistorical definitions.

Porphyry, who in his *Eisagoge* "first raised the question of nominalism explicitly", gave evidence of logical acumen but not of a nominalist bias. *Pyrrho* is usually regarded as a skeptic who would not commit himself to any theory as regards universals, and for whom a nominalist doctrine would have been clearly incompatible with his desire for suspension of judgment.[1] *Boethius*, in his discussion of Porphyry, emphatically and unambiguously comes out for Aristotelean realism.[2] I therefore agree that "it has not yet been determined" whether Pyrrho and Boethius "were themselves members of the bourgeois class". I would add that it has equally not been determined whether they were nominalists.

The real problem lies with Roscellinus (1050 to 1120), and with the "nominalism" of the eleventh and twelfth century. I gladly take the opportunity to supplement my former article "by showing that the mentality of the so-called 'Nominalists'

[1] Pyrrho and his followers "were constantly engaged in overthrowing the dogmas of all schools, but enunciated none themselves." Diogenes Laertius IV, 74.

[2] *In Isagogen Porphyrii Commenta* (ed. S. Brand 1906), especially pp. 159 to 176. Boethius says of universals, of the genera and species, "*non est dubium quin vere sint*"; "*ista vere subsistant*" (p. 26); "*sensibilibus juncta subsistunt in sensibilibus*" (p. 176).

of the eleventh century was radically and profoundly different from that of the Nominalists of the fourteenth century".

In connection with Roscellin, we have first to bear in mind that he was not a person of great importance. The materialist conception of history is concerned with socially successful and representative ideas and not with the freaks. At any time one can find one writer or another who has said almost anything. Before he decides about the social basis of a doctrine a Marxist will want to know whether it was a typical doctrine in any way representative of anything or of anybody. As a matter of fact, Roscellin was an individual with few followers. John of Salisbury[1] reports that his doctrine "almost entirely disappeared with him" and "vanished with its originator." Similarly Abelard has little to say of Roscellin's (his teacher's) doctrines, and passages in his *Dialectica* make it plain that he considered it little worthy of attention.[2] What notoriety Roscellin possessed at the time he did not derive from his teachings on universals but from his unorthodox interpretation of the doctrine of the Trinity which was attacked by Anselm of Canterbury, and condemned by the Council of Soissons in 1092.

Now, what about Roscellin's "nominalism"? The prevalent doctrine of the time was a realism of the Platonic type. Roscellin, indeed, was an opponent of that realism. But that in itself does not make him a nominalist.

De Wulf, a first-rate authority, states expressly that "it must be borne in mind that this twelfth century nominalism has a very special sense. It is different from the nominalism of the fourteenth century."[3] Roscellin's views are known to us only second-hand, from the writings of his opponents. According to these very scanty reports Roscellin indulged in the somewhat paradoxical statement that, far from being the

[1] *Metalogicus* II, 17; *Policraticus* VII, 12.

[2] J. G. Sikes, *Peter Abailard* (1932), p. 90.

[3] *History of Mediaeval Philosophy* (1935), vol. I, p. 179. When discussing Occam the same author states: "We need only compare the doctrines of Occam and of Roscellin to see how utterly misleading it is to label both these philosophers as nominalists. The two systems have nothing in common save the denial of extreme realism." (*History*, pp. 425–26).

real realities in the world, the universals were *flatus vocis*, vocal emissions, composed of letters and syllables. By using the word "*vox*" he referred to the spoken word as to a physical sound, as distinct from its meaning (*sermo*). This is a way of opposing "Platonic" realism by a striking formula. But it is not nominalism. There is no evidence that Roscellin denied the reality of universals. "That is a question with which he does not deal."[1] Occam expressly rejected the opinion that the universal might be a *flatus vocis*.[2]

By reducing a doctrine to a bald statement one too easily tears it out of its context. The philosophical initiative, from Remigius of Auxerre (841–908) to Abelard (*c.a.* 1140), rested with "Platonic" realism. According to this doctrine universals, e.g. humanity, have an independent existence, and the individual things, e.g. individual men, have their existence only as a modification of the universal substance, by participating in it. This doctrine was extremely popular at the time, not only, among writers and teachers but also among men of action, for reasons into which I cannot go here.[3] It created a reaction, the representatives of which all agreed that only individual things could exist separately and independently or "substantially", and that universals are not things (*res*). They, however, did not conclude that universals had no reality in connection with individual substances. The opponents of "Platonic" realism therefore all inclined towards some form of Aristotelean realism which cannot be confused with modern nominalism. For the "universale in re" stands even though the "universale *ut* res" is denied.

We have thus re-placed Roscellin's thesis into its context. In addition we may further look at its fruits. It is not only what a man says that matters but also whereto his doctrine

[1] De Wulf, vol. I, p. 149. Similarly Ueberweg-Geyer, *Geschichte der Philosophie*, p. 209.

[2] *In sent.* I d. 2 q. 8. He describes the universal as a *terminus* or an *intentio*.

[3] One of its motives was the interest in original sin which could easily be rendered plausible that way. For if what really exists is the human race as a specific reality, which is then scattered amongst its many individual representatives, the entire substance was infected by Adam's sin and by participating in that vitiated substance we all suffer from the consequences.

leads him and others. The radicals of the anti-realist reaction of the twelfth century were led to *skepticism* and *sophistry*, the nominalists of the fourteenth century to *empiricism*, to experiment and observation. The former formulated their doctrines with an eye on "Platonic" realism, Occam with an eye on observed reality.

Occam argued that, if only singulars are real objects and if only in perception we have immediate access to them, experience and observation become the test of true knowledge. In this way he laid the foundation of experimental science. His positive achievement in logic, the interpretation of concepts as symbols, openly contradicts the theory of the *flatus vocis*.

In the eleventh century the Church had reached a degree of corruption unusual even in the history of that body. In consequence new sects and heresies sprang up everywhere, and the doctrines of the Church became the object of destructive argument. Many clerics amused themselves as best they could. Some of them, with more intellectual tastes, spent some of their time in argument for its own sake and basked in the frivolity of their argumentations. They discussed whether a pig led to market is held by the rope or by the one holding it. They turned Roscellin's doctrine to good use by forming syllogisms like this one: "Mouse is a syllable; a syllable does not gnaw cheese; therefore a mouse does not gnaw cheese." This sort of thing was an intellectual by-product of clerical decay which was then, temporarily, brought to an end by the monastic reforms and the crusades. Not only sociologically but also in their spirit these early skeptics and the nominalists are miles apart.

3. When he states that nominalism "gave rise to the middle classes", Feibleman raises the question of the importance of intellectuals. This is a very vast problem, and I can only restate my conviction that the philosophers owe more to the people than the people owe to the philosophers. Making Occam into a sort of father of the bourgeoisie reminds me of a Nazi who argued that Adam Smith was the father of the industrial revolution. It seems to me that intellectuals should not be as conceited as all that. But, naturally, I cannot argue the point *here*.

4. While separating faith from reason, St. Thomas' theology

is far more rational—in intention—than Occam's. According to him the articles of faith, like the doctrine of the Trinity, of original sin, of the sacraments, etc., could not be justified by reason but are compatible with it. According to Occam and the nominalists they are incompatible. According to St. Thomas the articles of revealed faith are above reason but not against it. Reason can justify them negatively, by showing that the objections of opponents are unfounded. In my argument I stressed not the point that the nominalists *separate* faith and reason—that is what St. Thomas does, too—but that they regard the doctrines of the Church "to be in express opposition to reason".

5. Far from ignoring the history of science, I quoted Duhem, one of the leading authorities on the subject, in support of what I said about Jean de Jeandun and astronomy. If Nicholas Oresme wrote against the black arts, he did not do so because they were practical but because he was against magical, as opposed to rational, practice. He clearly voiced his contempt for pure theoreticians, and I must refer to my quotation in the original article.

Copernicus, as far as I know, was interested in obtaining accurate astronomical tables. Whether we can call this a "practical application of results" is largely a matter of opinion. It is also besides the point. What the Marxist claims is that a careful study of the history of modern science has shown more and more clearly that, whatever may have been the conscious motives of scientists (who like most people easily deceive themselves), their researches were very closely connected with the practical aspirations of the bourgeoisie.

6. As regards the principle of parsimony I must admit a weakness in my argumentation. I showed that it is a product of bourgeois mentality and that it is emphasized by nominalists. Assuming that no bourgeois philosopher can fail to be a nominalist, I believe I have shown indirectly that it is a nominalist principle. I should have given more direct proof. But I feel that Feibleman takes the word "realism" here in a very loose sense. As the word is used in modern philosophy, in England and the United States, it is often perfectly compatible with nominalism.

7. I believe, indeed, that Marxists cannot be nominalists.

But I do not conclude that they must be realists. The world consists of *concrete* objects which are in themselves neither universals nor particulars. In certain situations we determine the concrete objects as universals *or* as particulars, but in most situations this question of universality or particularity does not arise, being irrelevant to our purpose. In this way, as I see it,[1] Marxism transcends both nominalism and realism.

The dialectic, tracing, as it does, the impulse behind movements and changes to material contradictions, seems on the surface to involve a realism of the Aristotelean type. For a material contradiction is the conflict between the *essential* features of a process. But the "essential features of a process", as Marx e.g. understood them in his discussion of the contradictions of capitalism, while they are incompatible with nominalist assumptions, should not be confused with Aristotle's "essence". But that is clearly another story.

[1] I must refer the reader to *Der Satz vom Widerspruch*, pp. 243–66, where I have tried to justify this statement.

III. SHORTER ARTICLES

I

THE BUDDHA'S BODIES IN THE PRAJÑĀPARĀMITĀ

The *Abhisamayālaṅkāra* (ch. 8) distinguishes four "bodies" of the Buddha. 1. the *svābhāvikakāya*, 2. the *dharmakāya*, 3. the *sāmbhogakāya*, and 4. the *nirmāṇakāya*. Of these the first seems to be no more than a scholastic construction of the Yogācārins, and I shall not deal with it in this paper. In any case, the *Prajñāpāramitā* texts, as far as I can see, contain nothing corresponding to it.

This leaves us with three "bodies". Of these the *dharmakāya* and the *nirmāṇakāya* present no great difficulties. The distinction between the Buddha in so far as he is a channel for the spiritual force of the Dharma, and in so far as he is an historical individual, is of the very essence of a religion which lays claims to an objectively valid truth. The one is Gautama or Shākyamuni, the other the Buddha in the strict and proper sense, just as we have Gandhi and the Mahātma, Jesus and the Christ. The *Prajñāpāramitā* knows this as the distinction between *dharmakāya* and *rūpakāya*, which is, however, explicitly made relatively late. In the *Aṣṭasāhasrikā* it is found only in the later strata, and it is curious that its occurrence in *Vajracchedikā* 26b is not attested by Kumārajīva, or the old Central Asian manuscript. Must we conclude from this observation that the *dharmakāya* doctrine is a doctrinal innovation? I do not think that this is necessarily the case. It seems to me that such a teaching belongs to the very essence of Buddhism, and that it must have been taken for granted from the very beginning, although it was explicitly formulated only in the course of time, as and when misunderstandings became more and more widespread.

Be that as it may, the real problem lies with the *sāmbhogakāya*. At first sight it may appear that it is clearly mentioned in the *Prajñāpāramitā Sūtra*, for in the Nepalese Ms of the *Pañcaviṃśatisāhasrikā* at Cambridge (Abbreviated as P) we find a description of it on 523 b, where incidentally it is quite obviously understood as an "Enjoyment-body", because in it the Buddha is said to "demonstrate to the Bodhisattvas the supreme Dharma of the Mahāyāna which brings them unsurpassed delight and joy, happiness and ease". But a comparison with other, earlier, recensions, as e.g. the *Śatasāhasrikā* or *Aṣṭādaśasāhasrikā*, shows this passage to be interpolated by a follower of the *Abhisamayālaṅkāra*. In the *Abhisamayālaṅkāra* the *sāmbhogakāya* appears as the substratum of the 32 major and 80 minor of marks of the superman. The *Prajñāpāramitā* has indeed much to say about these marks (P 532–6), but of the *sāmbhogakāya* there is no trace at all in the actual text. The marks are there the last item in a list of factors constituting "the Bodhisattva's gift of the supramundane dharma" (P 530), which in turn is introduced in the course of a discussion of the fourfold "means of conversion" (*saṃgrahavastu*) of a Bodhisattva. So in the later part of the Sūtra, where the *Abhisamayālaṅkāra* asserts the occurrence of the *sāmbhogakāya*, the text contains nothing whatsoever about it.

It is, by contrast, at the beginning of the Sūtra, in its very first pages, that we hear of a "body" of the Buddha which in fact, though not in name, suggests the *sambhogakāya*. At P 11 we read of the Buddha's *āsecanakakāya*—or the word may also be *asecanaka*, we cannot decide that—of his "glorious" body, in which he appears when preaching this Sūtra. But if we read the whole of P 5–17 carefully, we find that this *āsecanakakāya* is not the same as the body which is marked with the 32 marks (see P 6), and it appears that the Sutra has in mind quite a number of "bodies" which are however, never described in definite detail. All we have are hints, and also Nāgārjuna's commentary avoids saying here anything definite and precise. Why should that be so?

The doctrine of the *mahāpuruṣalakṣaṇas* is, as also Raghavan has recently shown, even older than Buddhism itself. At the same time it is obvious that these marks are not attributes of the body visible to all, but adhere to some glorified body which is visible only to the eyes of faith, and manifests itself to the community of the saints. Why then, if the assumption of such a "glorified" body is inherent in the doctrine from the very start, should there be so much vagueness about it still in the first century of our era? Because, I suggest, this was a particularly holy and secret subject, which could be explained only orally to those few who were spiritually qualified to hear of it, while the remainder had to be contented with a few vague hints.

If this were so, we could draw the following tentative inference: The Buddhists themselves, as we know, view the history of their religion as one of continuous decline. In fact we observe, among other things, an increasing profanization of the doctrine. In early times a monk was even forbidden to recite the actual text of the Sūtras to laymen. Later on first the Sūtras ceased to be secret, and then other secret teachings were one by one divulged. It is easy to see that a considerable methodological difficulty at once confronts the historian of Buddhist thought. What seems to be doctrinal innovation may really be nothing but the gradual shifting of the line between esoteric and exoteric teachings. At first, even up to Aśoka, the bulk of the doctrine, except for some moral maxims, and so on, was esoteric. By the time of the Tantra even the most esoteric doctrines were written down, although the formulations still retained some of their mysteriousness. This process can be understood as one of compensation for the increasing admitted failure to achieve the spiritual goal aimed at. Unable to succeed inwardly in their self-realization, the monks indulged in the extraverted activity of spreading their doctrines among the general population. From the fact that a statement is attested only at a later date we cannot therefore conclude that it was invented at that time, but only that then it ceased to be the prerogative of the initiated and became more or less public property.

2

REMARKS ON A PĀLA MS. IN THE BODLEIAN LIBRARY

Among the problems raised by the eleventh century manuscript Sansk. a.7(R) of the *Ashtāsāhasrikā-prajñāpāramitā* (= Ashtā),[1] the apparent lack of connection between text and illustrations is of some weight. The illustrations do not illustrate the text itself. As a metaphysical treatise, the *Ashtā* lends itself as little to pictorial illustration as the *Metaphysics* of *Aristotle*, or as *Kant's Critique of Pure Reason*. Nowhere does the text refer to the scenes from the life of the Buddha which the manuscript illustrates—if we except the enlightenment under the Bodhi-tree. What is more, the majority of the deities depicted in the manuscript are not mentioned in the text, and a number of them were neither heard nor thought of when the book was originally composed, presumably between 200 B.C. and A.D. 100. In fact, the *Ashtā* is content to expound the *metaphysics* of the Mahāyāna. The extensive mythology of the Mahāyāna, with all its multiplicity of Buddhas, Bodhisattvas and minor deities is scarcely, if at all, touched upon.

Of the persons illustrated, the Bodhisattva *Maitreya*, and the Hindu Gods *Indra* and *Brahmā* are figures common to the scriptures of both Hīnayāna and Mahāyāna. They alone appear in the text of the *Ashtā*. *Maitreya*, illustrated in number 7, personifies friendliness, and he is the future Buddha who will appear on earth in a few thousand years, three thousand or five thousand years after *Gautama*. He is the only Bodhisattva known by name to the Hinayana. On two occasions he takes part in the discussions of the *Ashtā*.[2] The illustration shows him as holding in his left hand the flask of nectar (*amrita*), which contains the water of eternal life. While the figure of *Brahmā*

[1] Described by H. J. Stooke in *Oriental Art, I*, 1, 1948, 5–8.
[2] A, vi, 135–154; xix, 358 sq.

remains rather shadowy in the *Ashtā*, *Indra*, under the name of *Śakra* is the third most important person in that text, next to the Buddha himself, and to *Subhuti*, his disciple. In fourteen chapters out of thirty-two he appears as an interlocutor. The Buddhists did not deal with the gods of other religions by declaring them to be figments of the imagination. Their usual procedure was to "convert" them, and to incorporate them into their system. So we find Indra in the *Ashtā* expressing his admiration for the perfection of wisdom, for the Buddhas and Bodhisattvas. He preaches *dharma* to the Gods of the Thirty-Three, but the Buddhas and Bodhisattvas he regards as his superiors. On the illustrations he can easily be recognized by the eyes painted all over his body.

Apart from these three exceptions, the greater number of the illustrations have no direct counterpart in the text of the *Ashtā*. Nevertheless, they are not just an arbitrary embellishment. Though but loosely connected with the letter of the text, they emanate from the spirit behind it. This manuscript is not just a stray freak, but there are many more of the same kind. These manuscripts are, in fact, a faithful reflection of Buddhism in *Bengal* under the *Pāla* dynasty (750–1150).

The official Buddhism of that period was a mixture of *Prajñāpāramitā* and *Tantra*. *Tāranātha*[1] reports about King *Dharmapāla* (*ca.* 770–810) that "he made *Haribhadra* and *Buddhajñānapāda* his priests, filled all regions with *Prajñāpāramitā* and *Guhyasamajatantra*, and ordered that the scholars who knew *Guhyasamaja* and the *Pāramitas* should occupy the place of honour on the bench. . . . Immediately on ascending the throne, he invited all those who explained the *Prajñāpāramitā*, but he chiefly honoured the Acharya *Haribhadra*.[2] This king founded a total of fifty religious schools, of which thirty-five were devoted to the exposition of the *Prajñāpāramitā*. Beginning with this king, the *Prajñāpāramitā* spread more and more."[3] The monks who lived in *Nālanda*, and in the settlements founded by the *Pāla* kings—such as *Odantapurī*,

[1] *Geschichte des Buddhismus in Indien*, translated A. Schiefner, 1869, p. 217.

[2] Author of an extensive and authoritative commentary on the Ashtā.

[3] Already before that, King Rajabhata of Samatata, *ca.* 700, had shown great respect for the Prajñāpāramitā. *cf. History of Bengal* (Deccan University), I, 414.

Vikramaśīla, Jaggadala, Somarūpa, etc.—combined metaphysics and magic, almost like the *Gerbert of Rheims* and *Albert the Great* of mediaeval folklore. Their range of interest is well typified by *Vāgīśvarakīrti, ca.* A.D. 1000, about whom *Tāranātha* says:[1] "By constantly looking on the face of the holy Tārā, he resolved all his doubts. He erected eight religious schools for the *Prajñāpāramitā,* four for the exposition of the *Guyhasamaja,* one each for each one of the three kinds of Tantra—of *Sambara, Hevajra* and *Catuhshpīthī*—he also established many religious schools with provisions for teaching the *Madhyamika* logic. He conjured up quantities of the elixir of life, and distributed it to others, so that old people, 150 years old and more, became young again."

This combination of *Prajñāpāramitā* and *Tantra* has shown an astounding vitality. It was destroyed in *Bengal* by the *Muslims,* but it spread to *Java* and *Nepal,* and in *Tibet* it still continues as a living tradition. Logically speaking, magic and the metaphysics of emptiness do not seem to go too well together. But that need not deter us here. As a matter of historical development, the ideas represented in the illustrations of this manuscript have grown out of the teachings of the *Prajñāpāramitā* itself. I will now try in a few words to show that for a few of them.

We best begin with the central figure on the back cover. The *prajñāpāramitā* is (a) a perfection, (b) a book, (c) a deity, (d) an image, and (e) a mantra. There is no parallel to such multiformity in our Western traditions. The following explanation will try to make it intelligible. (a) In its origin, *prajñāpāramitā* was a term of what we might call religious psychology. It indicated the highest possible point, the climax of the development of wisdom. That is its meaning in the *Mahāvastu.* In an attempt to set out the principal qualifications of a Bodhisattva—i.e. of a person who strives to become a Buddha—the *Mahāyāna* enumerated a series of six perfections (*pāramitā*) —the perfections of giving, of moral conduct, of patience, of vigour, of meditation, of wisdom. The perfection of wisdom marked the culminating point of a Bodhisattva's career. It meant an attitude to the world in which one relies on nothing at all, is free from attachment, and from all belief in the inde-

[1] *Ibid.,* p. 236.

pendent reality of anything whatsoever, even-minded but compassionate. "All things are empty, and there is nothing desirable or to be sought after." Transcendental wisdom is the highest form of knowledge, in which subject and object become identical, and in which all dualism is transcended. Yes and no become the same.

(b) Secondly, by an easy transition, *Prajñāpāramitā* came to mean the *book* in which the virtue of transcendental wisdom was explained. Over a period of seven hundred years, from *ca.* 200 B.C. to *ca.* A.D. 500, a considerable number of treatises dealing with perfection of wisdom were composed. First came the *Ashtā*, in eight thousand lines of thirty-two syllables each, then many others, ranging between 100,000 lines and nine lines. But India has always been indifferent to the mere facts of history. To the believer, these sūtras were spoken by the Buddha himself, on the *Vulture Peak* in *Magadha*, and the various *prajñāpāramitā-sūtras* were considered as just abridgements of the original sermon on the perfection of wisdom. They were the word of the Buddha himself.

Now, because the *Prajñāpāramitā* was not only a treatise on metaphysics, but a sacred book, it was meant to be *worshipped* as well as read. In many places, the *Ashtā* recommends the writing, reading and reciting of this book as a powerful source of religious merit. What is more, in a stereotyped phrase, repeated again and again, the "sons or daughters of good family" are enjoined "to put up a copy of this *Prajñāpāramitā*, and to pay respect to it, to revere, worship and adore it, pay regard and reverence to it—with flowers, incense, scents, wreaths, unguents, aromatic powders, rags, umbrellas, banners, bells, flags, and with rows of lamps all round."[1] Also among non-Buddhists books of divine origin have tended to become objects of worship. The *Shefer Torah* is just one example. In this context the *Prajñāpāramitā* is then invested with a kind of magical power. It sanctifies the place where it is, makes it into a sacred, a holy place. "This perfection of wisdom makes a spot of earth into a holy place[2] for beings, worthy of being worshipped and revered. It makes it into a shelter for beings who come to it, a place of rest and refuge."[3]

(c) The *personification* of transcendental wisdom begins

[1] e.g. A III, 57. [2] lit. a caitya. [3] A iii, 57.

already in the *Ashtā* itself. There the *prajñāpāramitā* is described as "the mother of all the Buddhas".[1] What is the meaning of this phrase? Just as a child is born of the mother, so the full enlightenment of a Buddha comes forth from the perfection of wisdom. It is she who gives them their lives, and who shows them their way about in the world. In less metaphorical language: if you resort to the perfection of wisdom it means that you rely on nothing but emptiness, and, casting aside all sense of personal security, become pure compassion. But if you take your stand on emptiness and compassion alone, then you are enlightened. When speaking of "all the Buddhas", the *Ashtā* assumes that there is more than one Buddha. In fact, throughout the ages, Buddha upon Buddha appears in this world, to lighten it up, not only on this earth, but in other parts of the universe as well, which are also held to be inhabited. Because "all the Buddhas" are the sons of the perfection of wisdom, it is appropriate that they should appear in the illustrations. The clue to that picture lies in the *Ashtā*. There "all the Buddhas" are commonly referred to as "the Buddhas of the three periods of time", or "the Buddhas of the past, present and future". Here this conception is shown almost in the form of a diagram. It reminds the reader of the truly grandiose idea that this transcendental wisdom was taught by the Buddhas of the present period, and will be taught for ever and ever by the Buddhas to come. What is true must be true always and everywhere. The *Ashtā* claims that only a teaching based on transcendental wisdom—and which therefore does not maintain anything as true—can be said to be true in this sense.

Personification, together with worship of the book, was bound to make the perfection of wisdom into a *deity* as soon as a system of mythology developed into which she could be fitted. At the time when the *Ashtā* was written, such a system of Buddhist mythology did not yet exist. The *Ashtā* rejects a great deal of the ethics and metaphysics of the Hīnayāna. Its mythology is essentially that of the Hīnayāna. The few passages in which *Akshobhya*, one of the mythological Buddhas of the Mahāyāna pantheon, is mentioned can easily be proved to be later insertions.[2] The early date of the *Ashtā*, *ca.* 100 B.C.,

[1] A xii, 253 sq.

[2] A xix, 366–7; xxvii, 450–2; xxviii, 464–5, 474. See *S* 172–175.

can be surmised from the observation that it contains not a word about *Mañjuśrī*, *Amitābha* or *Avalokiteśvara*. Yet we know from *Fa Hsien* that about A.D. 400 the monks of *Mathura* worshipped the *Prajñāpāramitā* in conjunction with *Avalokiteśvara*, the Bodhisattva of compassion, and *Mañjuśrī*, the Bodhisattva of wisdom. What had taken place in the intervening five hundred years?

A movement of *Bhakti*, of loving personal devotion to adored deities conceived in human form, had *ca.* 200 B.C. impinged in its Vishnuite form upon Buddhism and altered it profoundly. In their move for popularity among laymen the Buddhists deified the Buddha, and at the same time humanized him, through the stories about his former births which we find in the Jatakas and Avadānas. Image worship was sanctioned, and throughout India the Jataka stories were represented in sculpture. The austere intellectuality of early Buddhism was mitigated by the admission that salvation through faith was possible. A great number of mythological Buddhas and Bodhisattvas were introduced, to serve as anchors to the faith of the faithful.

The illustrations in the Pāla manuscripts, however, belong to a still later development. They are not bhaktic, but *Tantric* deities. The mere fact that the *Prajñāpāramitā* is represented with four arms suggests the Tantric character of the image. The rosary also points to the same origin. The rosary became an essential tool among Tantric Buddhists, and served the purpose of counting the number of mantras murmured during a certain period. The Tantra developed from *ca.* A.D. 400 or A.D. 500 onwards, and after A.D. 750 it systematized the mythology which the bhaktic tendencies had thrown up. The pictures of Tantric deities were not at that time regarded as objects of aesthetic enjoyment. They were supports for a meditation which aimed ultimately at the full enlightenment of a Buddha. The significance of Tantric images can be understood only when they are put back into their religious context.

The spirit of the Tantra is very remote from our present habits of thought. It would be a fascinating task to show how the Tantra developed, almost inevitably, from a fusion of *Prajñāpāramitā* and *Bhakti*. A few hints must here suffice. The *Prajñāpāramitā* literature had shown that emptiness is the one ultimate reality. No particular fact could claim to be really real. The indifference to objective fact unfettered religious imagination. The Tantrists thought that, once one had extinguished one's individuality in emptiness, one could conjure up, out of the Void, with the help of certain sounds, called germ-mantras, a vast multiplicity of deities, all imaginary, but all conceived in visible form. One could then identify oneself with those deities, absorb the spiritual force which they represented, and in that way come nearer to enlightenment. Sculptures and paintings were meant to assist that process of creative imagination, and the identification which followed it.

Phantasy, as compared with logic and factual observation, has a certain indefiniteness. As in dreams, narrow rules of consistency are abrogated. I have examined seventy-seven images of the *Prajñāpāramitā*, and have been able to distinguish twenty-five distinct types among them.[1] The shape, colour and attributes of deities are described for us in the so-called *Sādhanas*. A *sādhana* is a procedure for conjuring up a certain deity. In our chief Sanskrit textbook, the *Sādhanamālā*, nine *sādhanas* for the worship of *Prajñāpāramitā* are preserved. Not one of them corresponds exactly to the image of the manuscript. Without an acquaintance with these sādhanas one cannot comprehend the religious background in which such images took shape. I therefore give here a translation of a part of the *sādhana* (no. 156) for the worship of another four-armed form of the *Prajñāpāramitā*.

"One should mentally pay homage to the three treasures, and worship them, confess one's sins, rejoice in sympathy with the merit gained by all creatures, proclaim one's faith in the Buddha, the Dharma, and the Samgha, aspire with all one's soul for full enlightenment, and transfer or dedicate one's own merit to the welfare of all creatures. One should also beg pardon for what one did wrong. After that one should develop friendliness, compassion, sympathetic joy, and impartiality. Then one should say: "I am, through the gnosis of emptiness, in my essential being of diamond nature." Thus one should develop emptiness. Thereupon, having in one's mind quickly seen, on a moon, the syllable DHĪH, one should imagine the Blessed *Prajñāpāramitā* as transformed from it,

[1] See *S* 243–68.

with a chignon, with four arms and one face—two hands in the gesture of teaching dharma—adorned with manifold jewels, luminous with a golden colour, her garments of variegated material. The left arm holds the *Prajñāpāramitā* book on a blue lotus. With her right hand she makes the gesture which reassures. Above a red lotus, on a moon as her seat, she sits in the diamond posture. Thereupon one should bring about a firm identification: 'What the Blessed *Prajñāpāramitā* is, that am I. What I am that is the Blessed *Prajñāpāramitā*.' Thereupon he should apply the mantra: In the throat OM DHĪH, in the tongue OM GĪH, in the ears OM JRĪH, etc."[1]

It is in the context of such practices that the *Prajñāpāramitā* became (*d*) an image, and (*e*) a mantra, i.e. an arrangement of sounds which brings forth the visual representation of the spiritual force of the transcendental virtue of supreme wisdom. As tradition describes many visual representations of the *Prajñāpāramitā* so it also records a number of different mantras corresponding to them.[2] The beginnings of these ideas go back many centuries, to the *Aṣṭasāhasrikā* itself. In that text[3] already the perfection of wisdom is taught as a spell which protects from dangers, and engenders peace of mind. And even in the *Niddesa*[4] *paññā* is equated with *mantā*, a statement which puzzled already the early Pali commentators.

The presence of *Vajrasattva* in a manuscript inspired by the ideas of the *Vajrayāna* is not really surprising. *Vajra*, literally the thunderbolt, was a synonym for the emptiness which is the true object of transcendental wisdom. "Emptiness is called *vajra*, because it is firm, sound in its core, and cannot be changed, pierced, penetrated, burnt or destroyed". The *Vajrayāna* maintained that deities often have feminine consorts. Its supreme being is called *Vajrasattva*, he whose essence is the thunderbolt. *Prajñāpāramitā* is the consort of *Vajrasattva* "who is without beginning and end".[5] *Vajrasattva* holds in one hand the *vajra*, which symbolizes indestructable

[1] The entire *sādhana* is translated by D. L. Snellgrove in *C* no. 191.

[2] e.g. *M* 24. Other forms in late Tantric Prajñāpāramitā Sutras such as *Kauśika* and *Svalpākṣarā*.

[3] A iii 54, 75.

[4] II n. 497.

[5] an-ādi-nidhana-sattvo. Jñānasiddhi, p. 84.

knowledge,[1] in the other the bell, which symbolizes the sound of Dharma, or "the wisdom which follows on the Word".[2,3]

[1] abhedya-jñāna-pratipadana JAs 225, p. 29.

[2] sarva-buddhānam prajñā ghoshānugā. JAs 225, p. 26.

[3] The remainder of this article has been omitted. It assumed that the attendants of the Prajñāpāramitā are Tārā's. This is not the case, as shown by Mlle de Mallmann in 1965; see *S* 257.

3

THE PRESENT STATE AND FUTURE PROSPECTS OF BUDDHISM IN ASIA

Slightly more than a century ago the great bastions of Buddhism first experienced the ruthless onslaught of modern civilization. The Buddhist religion, quiescent since about A.D. 1400, initiated nothing of its own between 1850 and 1960, remained on the defensive and constantly retreated before hostile forces. The societies in which it flourished, notably China, Tibet and Japan, had for a time sought safety in withdrawing upon themselves. The Buddhists have on the whole maintained the old behaviour pattern and prefer to ignore the new and unwelcome developments.

To appreciate their feelings we just have to look at the blows which this ancient religion has had to endure. In China, soon after the Opium War in 1842 forced the Manchus to admit the foreign invader, the "long-haired Christians" of the T'ai P'ing rebellion between 1850 and 1864 destroyed countless temples and monasteries, and Chinese Buddhism has been a shadow of its former self ever since. In Japan the threatened American invasion of 1853 was followed about 1870 by the disestablishment of the Buddhist Church and the burning or confiscation of innumerable temples, while the actual invasion of 1945 brought financial ruin through McArthur's "land reform" of 1947–50, and led to a "general trend towards profanity" and to an almost universal religious apathy. In Tibet the day of reckoning came only in 1950, and in 1959 the Dalai Lama was forced once more to flee the country. In Mongolia between 1935 and 1937 Soviet troops demolished the lamaseries and killed most of their inhabitants. Less openly brutal, the English in Ceylon and Burma did immense damage to the Buddhist Order. Unwilling to take over the ecclesiastical functions of the native kings they promoted indiscipline in the monasteries, drove monks into politics and disorganized monastic finances, while in addition the temple schools could no longer provide a socially advantageous education. These are only a few of the more dramatic blows which have reduced Buddhism to impotence. They are as nothing compared with the slow-working antagonistic forces which grind it down from day to day.

For there was little to attract Buddhists in the amalgam of ideas which the gunboats, soldiers, traders and missionaries from Europe and North America forced so assiduously upon Asian lands. Militarism, the backbone of the whole system and the only reason for the presence of these strangers in Asia, was extremely distasteful to them, as involving the deliberate, habitual and large-scale taking of life. Commercialism likewise displeased them because it increases greed and makes people discontented with what they have got. Modern medicine has its conveniences, but the wholesale multiplication of suffering and dissatisfied human beings is a doubtful boon. And to systematically increase the wants of the poor means to kindle an all-consuming furnace of discontent which is bound to destroy established authority everywhere beyond repair. Nor was the message of salvation through Jesus Christ presented to the Buddhists in a way likely to win their hearts. Missionaries remained profoundly ignorant of even the elementary tenets of the doctrine. To modern scholars their misconceptions seem almost grotesque, and yet they normally used the most offensive language when speaking of Buddhist beliefs and practices, or of monks and particularly nuns. To a Buddhist the way of life of these "Western barbarians" could only appear as a complete abomination, as a fulfilment of the worst prophecies about the Kali Yuga,—a mere lack of serenity and contentment, of beauty and charm, of manners and deportment, of peace and quiet, of respect for holy men and holy things.

The present situation of Buddhism is the outcome of the deadly and irreconcilable conflict between Buddhist traditions and the main forces of the modern age. The pressure of modern life is threefold, and affects: (1) monastic institutions; (2) doctrinal integrity; and (3) the co-operation between monks and laity.

(1) *Monastic institutions* are the powerhouses which generate

the thought-force that sustains the Buddhist community. In their absence the religion must die, as it has nearly done in Nepal. History has everywhere shown that congregations of contemplatives must first be suppressed before "Progress' can really begin. Once the "needs" of the "masses", as interpreted by their capitalist or bureaucratic sponsors, set the tone of society, monks must appear as mere idlers, "useful" in no way whatsoever. And monks are, of course, very vulnerable, and can be eliminated by removing either their physiological or their economic basis. In the USSR they were smashed by brute force. Of the 14,000 Buryat lamas who existed in 1917, 900 were left in 1935; by 1936 the number of Kalmuk monks was reduced to 70, and in Tuba 100 lamas survived by 1960. Direct slaughter was the method adopted in Mongolia and Tibet. In China and Japan economic pressure sufficed. China has preserved an unspecified number of monasteries as "living museums", or as "zoos of the past", to use Ivor Montague's charming phrase. In Japan many thousands of priests survive, but they could not protect their sanctuaries from invasion by the turmoil of the outside world. It is only in the Theravada countries that the state has taken concrete measures to further the dignity and security of the monks, and to assist the dissemination of their message among the population.

(2) The *doctrinal integrity* of the Buddhists is subjected to many pressures, of which it will be sufficient to mention four.

(a) Although Asian *nationalism* is an inevitable reaction to many years of humiliation and ill-treatment, it does not go very well with Buddhism. On closer consideration it must appear slightly ridiculous to compensate for one's own sense of inferiority by boasting about the achievements of one's ancestors. Nevertheless, in taking this detached point of view, Asian Buddhists would lose touch with their supporters. So we find them often buying survival by howling with the wolves, and in Ceylon, Burma and Japan they habitually recommend their religion for reasons of national pride. This is a departure which, if unchecked, must in due course degrade a universal religion into a conglomeration of frantic tribal cults.

(b) Basically the *cold war* is a matter of indifference to Buddhists. Nevertheless political issues seem at present in Asia to be so much more urgent than religious considerations that many Buddhists have become willing tools of the rival forces. The primacy of politics has nearly ruined the "World Fellowship of Buddhists". Thai monks sprinkle holy water on American tanks. After 1950 both the USSR and China have regularly sent high dignitaries on propaganda tours into Asia. Numerous prominent Buddhists have proclaimed the compatibility of Buddhism and Communism, while others have as vociferously demonstrated their incongruity. In other words, on these issues Buddhists have forgotten how to speak with a voice of their own.

(c) The corroding effects of *modern "science"* on the Buddhist faith have barely begun. Minor frictions have arisen from European geography, and Buddhist monks feel uneasy and embarrassed when asked to find Mount Sumeru or the land of Shambala on a modern globe. Likewise the prestige of science has undermined traditional beliefs by making a surprising number of Asian Buddhists ashamed of the magical elements in their religion. But up to now the deadly challenge has been so little understood that Asian Buddhists like to indulge in euphoric statements to the effect that Buddhism is the only religion which has nothing to fear from science. The future will bring a sad awakening.

(d) The concern for the *standard of living* and the urge to constantly increase the consumption of industrial commodities is also none too helpful to the Buddhist way of life. There is no more deadly poison to spiritual insight than bodily comfort. All this preoccupation with material possessions and social position must seem a complete mis-direction of energy which keeps people so busy that they have not much time left for religion. In consequence in all industrialized countries they eschew doctrinal complications, and prefer simple and "straight-forward" doctrines, such as that of the Jodo Shinshu in Japan.

3. The new age furthermore presents the monks with some *technical* problems. In the village communities their mass support was assured, but now they have to find it in the big cities. New institutions must therefore be evolved, such as the YMBA, and so on. Much more important, however, is the fact that the monks' *social ideals* are out of date. Religious bodies are

intensely conservative, and dislike it if one social system suddenly replaces another. Perfectly adjusted to feudalism, the Catholic Church has made gigantic intellectual and organizational efforts to adapt itself to an industrial society, and yet it has succeeded only imperfectly. For over two millenia Buddhism has subsisted within a relatively stable society, agricultural or nomadic, headed by an absolute ruler who was consecrated by the monks in return for his obedience to the Dharma and who established a harmony between society and the cosmic and spiritual forces on which its prosperity depended. None of this gives much sense in the modern world, and generally speaking the Buddhists have watched the change of events in a kind of stupor, without producing men like Lamennais or Marc Sangier, or documents like the encyclica *Rerum Novarum*. The one exception is U Nu, the one ruler who is also a sage, and who has tried to temper economic progress with an insistence on Buddhist values.

As to the future prospects of Buddhism, the short term outlook is extremely bad. Not one aspect of the present situation favours it as a religious force. If industrialization, militarization and national self-assertiveness are the three most powerful factors in Asian society at present, then the first two are uncompromisingly hostile to everything that Buddhists stand for, and the third favours them only on condition that they become untrue to themselves. Whether Buddhism be persecuted by the State or not, for quite a time to come increasing inanition will be its fate.

The long-term prospects are slightly better. And that for three reasons: 1. Modern communications have re-established contact between the various branches of Buddhism which had been separated for so long. Narrow sectarianism will therefore be slowly worn down, some cross-fertilization will take place, and a deeper understanding of the Buddha's message will thus emerge. 2. In the Communist countries Buddhism will in due course profit from the astounding similarities which exist between dialectical materialism and Mahayana philosophy. Many observers have commented on these analogies, and over the heads of both priests and commissars a new synthesis may well be created within the next century or so. 3. The glory of

Asia is bound up with Buddhism as a cultural force. Everywhere the finest periods were precisely those in which it was in the ascendant. Once the threat from the outside world is removed, once Asia is either united or tolerably secure, Buddhism may well recommend itself as the most suitable ideology. So many Asian empire-builders have in the past turned to it as the ideal cement of vast societies! A religion which has tamed the descendants of Jenghis Khan need not necessarily fail with the successors of Mao tse tung.

It must be borne in mind that Buddhism has never sought survival through self-assertive competitiveness. Though it has endured many persecutions, it has never resisted, and yet it is still there. Spiritual trends operate on levels too deep for historians to reach, and we must always be prepared for surprises. Some of them may be triggered off by something as intangible as the recent revival of Buddhist meditation.

READING LIST

South East Asia: Marxism in South East Asia, ed. F. N. Trager, 1960, Stanford U.P., Index s.v. Buddhism.

H. H. Wriggins, *Ceylon, Dilemmas of a New Nation.* (Princeton U.P., 1960), pp. 171–210.

A. Bareau, *La vie et l'organisation des communeautés bouddhiques modernes de Ceylan* (Pondichery, 1957).

O. H. de A. Wijesekera, *Buddhism and Society* (Colombo, Bauddha Sahitya Sabha, 1954).

D. C. Vijayavardhana, *Dharma-Vijaya or The Revolt in the Temple* (Colombo, 1953).

H. Tinker, *The Union of Burma* (OUP, 1957), pp. 165–77.

E. M. Mendelson, Religion and authority in modern Burma. *The World To-day* (OUP, 1960), pp. 110–18. A. Messianic Buddhist Association in Upper Burma, (*BSOAS*, 1961), pp. 560–80.

4

JUNGIAN PSYCHOLOGY AND THE DHARMA

The Great Mother, Erich Neumann, 1955. Routledge and Kegan Paul Ltd., 380 pp. and 185 plates. *The Mysteries*. Papers from the Eranos Yearbooks (by 13 authors). 1955. Routledge and Kegan Paul Ltd., 476 pp. *Journal of Analytical Psychology*. Vol. 1, no. 1. 1955. Tavistock Publications Ltd. 108 pp.

The above three "Jungian" publications have come in for review at short intervals, and it will be sufficient to say a few words about their respective value for the students of Buddhism. The first book, on the *Great Mother*, is quite indispensable for anyone who is at all interested in the psychology of religion. It also should go far to open the eyes of Buddhists who want to find their way through the variety of teachings which have been propounded as "Buddhist" at different times and in different places. Religions normally exist in either a matriarchal or a patriarchal form. The Protestant interpretation of Christianity centres round God the Father and God the Son, and views with considerable distaste the devotion to the "Mother of God" which is accorded so much prominence among Catholics. In Hinduism we have on the one side the male deities of the Vedas, and on the other the Mother-Goddesses of the Tantras. In some schools of Buddhism the central person is the Buddha himself, a Father figure, whereas in others the Buddha is subordinated to a feminine force, the Prajñāpāramitā, who is the "Mother of all the Buddhas". Likewise it can be observed that the discipline of Zen produces a masculine, that of the Nying-ma-pa an extremely feminine type of person. The psychological laws which govern our attitude to the masculine and feminine components of our personality are therefore of great interest to students of the religious life. During the last century there has been in Europe quite a reaction against the basically patriarchal assumptions of our civilisation. It began in the Catholic Church, which has step by step consistently increased the stature of the Virgin Mary, it was greatly strengthened by the discovery of matriarchal societies by Bachofen and Briffault, and in recent years the ardent devotion of Robert Graves to the Great Goddess is known to all who read books.

In Jung's system the "Great Mother" is, of course, one of the "archetypes", and it is convenient that the relevant material about her should now have been gathered into one book. It is true that Dr. Neumann shows none of the creative genius and depth of his master, and that his work is not always easy to read, partly because the translator has been content to retain the word-order of the German. But although Dr. Neumann's style is distinctly undistinguished, although he is imprisoned within the narrow horizon of the earnest and plodding specialist, and although he constantly irritates by calling assertions "unquestionable" and "without doubt" when they are well known to be extremely doubtful—nevertheless, in spite of all these discouragements, he has much to say that is interesting and important. It is quite impossible for me in a few words to sum up the wealth of material he has brought together, or the complications of his comprehensive divisions and subdivisions, relations, correlations and oppositions. The manifestations of the Mother are, indeed, most bewildering in their diversity, and they are traced here competently from the dim beginnings of the Stone Age to the sublimest and most spiritual form of femininity, which is Sophia, or Wisdom. This is a book worth buying, in spite of the price, not only for the information which it contains, but also for the wonderful collection of images of the Mother, which speaks with an eloquence denied, alas, to the author. The perusal of the 185 plates has given me many happy hours, and in addition there are still 74 drawings in the text. We must be deeply grateful to all those who have made this beautiful book possible. It is not so much a criticism of the book, as a contribution to the study of the relations between Jungianism and the Dharma, if we point out that in this book there are very few direct references to Buddhism, and that Dr. Neumann shows himself rather weak on the subject. On p. 236 he does not perceive that Padmasambhava is the name of a person, and on plate 183, as well as on pp. 332–3, the famous Leyden Prajñaparamitā is called a 'White Tara'. The statue is, however, golden-yellow, and not "white", and it is a Prajñāpāramitā, and not a "Tara". Neumann has here blindly followed Zimmer, who on this occasion was mistaken. And obviously nobody can know everything.

The second volume under review deals with the *mystery religions*, a singularly unpromising subject for scientific research. For these religions work on the assumption that spiritual truth should be reserved for the initiates who are ripe for it, and that, conversely, it should be concealed from the profane. This does not, of course, prevent the profane in academic circles from trying to puzzle out what was never meant for them, and this volume is filled with manifold learned speculations about the Greek mysteries of Eleusis, Orpheus, etc., the "mysteries" of ancient Egypt which turn out never to have existed, the mysteries of Mithras and the gnostics, and a great deal of space is given over to comparisons between the pagan mystery cults and the "hidden mystery" of the Christians. It is gratifying to find that the precautions which the ancient mystagogues took against the profanation of sacred things have proved fairly effective, and that the eager investigators of modern times are quite at sea. The authors never tire of complaining that the texts are "all too brief", that "many regrettable gaps remain to be filled", that "we have by far the most information concerning what interests us least", that "we shall never know" what the initiates saw, and in their zest for truth they also accuse their colleagues of "totally false assumptions", "scientific nonsense", "inventions based on no evidence whatever", and so on.

This is not an attitude conducive to spiritual rebirth. There is something both indecent and ridiculous about the public discussion of the esoteric in words which can be generally understood. The effect of these investigations is that of a prolonged strip-tease, with the vital difference, however, that the end-product is not the feminine body in all its glory, but a few tattered remains of some ancient stuffed doll. With rare exceptions, books which promise for a few shillings to reveal the secrets of this, or to disclose the mysteries of that, are not worth the paper on which they are printed. Just as some people who do not know what to do with their lives climb mountains for the sole reason that "they are there", so scientific historians must needs probe into everything just because it has happened. The academic mind can not, of course, be expected to appreciate the difference between forbidden and permitted knowledge, or even between fruitful and barren information. But at least it ought to be aware that some problems are soluble, and others are not. Here and there an occasional quotation in this book may well evoke a vague sense of edification, but on the whole it teaches us very little, and does not lift up the mind, or promote spiritual insight. To read it is a waste of time. The one exception is Prof. Jung's essay on the Catholic Mass (pp. 274–336), which has at least some substance to it, and is based on readily accessible public sources. The best documented of these mystery religions is, incidentally, the Buddhist Tantra. It is characteristic of the uneasy relationship which exists between Jungian Psychology and Buddhism that in this large symposium no room could be found for it.

The revival in recent years of religious interests and convictions in Britain has favoured the Jungians so much that now at last they can, like their Freudian rivals before them, issue their own journal. The first issue of *The Journal of Analytical Psychology*, their new biennial periodical, came out in October 1955, and it is certainly well done and full of stimulating contributions which elaborate some of the basic themes of this school. Here we can inform ourselves about "archetypal themes in depression", "the father archetype in feminine psychology", or "the function of counter-transference", and the article on "loathsome women" might even help us to cope with some of the more undesirable people into whose company we are sometimes thrown. Buddhists will be chiefly interested in the first article, by Dr. Layard, on "Boar-sacrifice". Vajravārāhī, the "Adamantine Sow", is an important deity in Tantric Buddhism, and in Tibet the manifestation of Rdo-rje Phag-mo through the abbess of Bsam-lding occupies a high rank in the hierarchy. Dr. Layard now treats the Pig as an archetype, and it is certainly of interest to follow his survey of the range of mental conflicts which are both expressed and soothed when we give full rein to our fancies concerning boars. After he has regaled us with the dream of a schizophrenic, some Mediterranean myths, and the "boar-symbolism in the myth, ritual and social organisation of Malekula", he asks: "What is all this about?" "The answer is: The Mother, and men's efforts to free themselves from her, and from subserviance to women in general". That may very well be so, and perhaps some day someone will go over the ample Tibetan evidence to find out whether, or not, it confirms Dr. Layard's diagnosis.

Generally speaking, those Buddhists who want to go more deeply into the mental mechanisms behind the mythological and magical components of their religion, will be able to learn a great deal from the writings of the Jungian school. Neither Prof. Jung himself, nor any of his disciples, seem, on the other hand, ever to have contributed anything of importance to the analysis of the core of the Buddhist doctrine, which is after all not concerned with gods and demons, with legends or rituals, but with spiritual emancipation by the triple means of morality, trance and wisdom. It appears to me probable that the methods of "Analytical Psychology", derived as they are from clinical observations on bewildered psychopaths, can do no justice to the higher ranges of the spiritual life, to the more transcendental aspects of religious doctrines, or the more world-renouncing aspects of religious practice. It seems to me significant that, for instance Joseph Campbell, in his classic on "The Hero with a Thousand Faces", while admirably dealing with the legend of the Buddha's life, nevertheless bungles his treatment of the "Heart Sutra" on p. 151. I find my suspicions further confirmed when I look at the only full-length study of Buddhism which a Jungian has undertaken so far. It is a German book by H. Guenther, called *The Problem of the Soul in Older Buddhism*, and it was published in 1949. The "explanation" of Buddhist doctrines offered in this book is indistinguishable from their elimination. All Buddhists, so we are told, have always misunderstood the master's doctrine, which was in fact identical with the Upanishadic teaching of the Self. For, so Guenther says, Nirvana and the Self are the same. Such cavalier treatment shows a lack of reverence for the spiritual traditions of the past, and at least suggests that the actually existing Buddhism is inaccessible to the methods of the

Jungian school. The psychology of the people who take up this kind of psychological analysis may well be the clue to their helplessness in the face of the higher spiritual life. Count Keyserling once summed up his estimate of Dr. Jung as a person when he said: "Nobody would feel the need to concern himself with the souls of others as intensely and minutely as analytical technique demands, unless he were unsuccessful in solving his own mental conflicts within himself, but had the gift to become aware of them through their projection on others. And it seems to me significant that in my experience even those analysts who are most clairvoyant with regard to others, have no insight whatsoever into themselves." My own experience, I am afraid, points the same way.

5

PROFESSOR MURTI'S CENTRAL PHILOSOPHY OF BUDDHISM

Under the title *The Central Philosophy of Buddhism*, Professor Murti, of Benares University, has just now published a book[1] which promises to remain the standard work on the philosophy of Nagarjuna and the Madhyamikas for quite a time to come. The typescript of the book was completed already in 1949, when the author deputised for Prof. Radhakrishnan in Oxford. It has taken six years to get the book into print, and its forthcoming publication has from year to year been announced in the catalogues. Those acquainted with the Hindu sense of time were not really surprised at being kept waiting—for what would be the sense of being too much in a hurry about things which concern the timeless wisdom of mankind? It is quite right and proper that publications dealing with the ephemerous concerns of the present day should be rushed through the press at record speed. Quite different is the situation with books such as this one, which is exclusively devoted to the abiding problems of mankind, to its search for wisdom and absolute truth, and to the questions which concern the meaning of life and the final liberation from the bonds of existence.

One of the classical formulations of this wisdom tradition took place in India at the beginnings of the Christian era. It was first worked out in a rather unsystematic form in the Sutras dealing with Perfect Wisdom (*prajñāpāramitā*), and then more systematically by the school of the Madhyamikas who between A.D. 150 and A.D. 1050 produced a considerable number of outstanding thinkers. In my *Selected Sayings from the Perfection of Wisdom* I have pointed out that the Prajñāpāramitā Sutras

[1] Allen & Unwin.

all have only one subject matter: "It is just the Unconditioned, nothing but the Absolute, over and over again" (p. 18). Similarly it was one, and only one, theme which occupied the Madhyamikas over all those centuries, and that was to find the rules which govern the transcendental knowledge or intuition of the Absolute.

Even those, relatively few, Europeans who were interested in this problem, could so far not really benefit from the thoughts of the Madhyamikas because these were expressed in Sanskrit, and a rather difficult Sanskrit at that. It is one of the more remote and unforseen results of the joint activities of two English Lords, of Lord Clive and Lord Macaulay, that we are now given in English a superb re-statement of the views of the Madhyamikas. By its lucidity and comprehensiveness Prof. Murti's book is a real masterpiece of exposition. The letter of the Madhyamika writings holds no terrors for him. He has been trained in the grammar of Patañjali and possesses a proficiency in Sanskrit which only few Europeans can rival. When I knew him in Oxford he was constantly astounded at what I regarded as grammatical and linguistic difficulties.

There is, on the other hand, no greater menace than a mere grammarian let loose on a sacred text, for he will not rest until he has pounded the bloom of its fragrant blossoms into a sad heap of dry and insipid powder. Only those can fruitfully interpret metaphysical texts who are in love with metaphysics, who take it seriously, see its worth, and understand its modes of approach. Only those can make these texts live to whom they are parts of life. And for Murti "the Madhyamika is not an academic system". "It has permeated every walk of life—literature, fine art, social sciences, religion and philosophy". On it "a stable and exalted civilization was built". "The great measure of unity and stability of social structure which still persists (in Asia) is the reflection of the Śūnyatā (Absolutist) conception in the practical affairs of men" (p. 337). When thus viewed in their concrete social context, and when expounded by a man who is equally well versed in Indian and European philosophy, the tenets of the Madhyamikas stand out in their full magnificence. Although he has throughout expressed himself with great economy, Prof. Murti has needed 341 pages to bring out their meaning. It would be idle to attempt to sum up his conclusions in a short article, and all I can do in this respect is to recommend the book wholeheartedly to our readers. May they study it carefully, word by word, sentence by sentence, as it deserves to be studied.

But whereas Prof. Murti's material resists condensation, his opinions invite discussion, and there are at least two points on which the book will lead to controversy. The first concerns the orthodoxy of the Madhyamika system, the second its relation to the doctrines of the Upanishads. By way of tenderly putting the cat among the pigeons I will now say a few words on each of these in turn.

The very title of Prof. Murti's book suggests that he regards the Madhyamika doctrine of Emptiness as the "central philosophy of Buddhism", "the central or the pivotal system" (p. 5). In addition he claims that "the early Buddhist view was like that of the Madhyamikas" (p. 53), that "the evolution of the Mahayana may be said to have begun from the time of Buddha's parinirvāṇa" (p. 77) and that "the Prajñāpāramitās are not innovations; they can and do claim to expound the deeper, profounder teachings of Buddha" (p. 83). This thesis is unlikely to be received with joy by some of the adherents of the Ceylonese orthodoxy. Having convinced themselves that their tradition alone enshrines what they call "the pure Buddha-Dhamma", they will be none too pleased to hear that "the Southern Ceylonese Sect had little or no direct influence on the development of Buddhist schools in India. For our purpose it may be ignored" (p. 69), and, a few pages (p. 78) later, that "the Sthaviravāda (Theravāda), predominant at first, gradually declined in importance and influence from the time of the third Council (Asoka's reign) till it disappeared altogether from the mainland proper". The Pali Canon is said to have been subjected to "careful and partisan revision and editing by the Theravadins". Nevertheless it contains a certain number of anticipations of the Madhyamika position (p. 50), which are set out impressively in this book, although Murti omits those passages in the *Sutta Nipāta* (796–803) which I had always regarded as particularly noteworthy.

Now I find it difficult to see how anyone can, on historical grounds, contest the truth of Murti's position. In the course of its history, the Buddhist community has divided itself into 21 principal schools, and so as to ensure a proper perspective I will here set them out by way of a diagram:

The Buddha's Dharma
/ \\
The Eighteen Schools — The Mahayana
1 2 3 4 5 6 7 8 9 10 11 12 13 14 15 16 17 18 — 19 20 21

It would lead us too far here to add the names of all the schools. By way of example I will be content with eight. As 1 we have the Theravādins, "those who followed the doctrines of the Elders"; as 2 the Sarvāstivādins (*sarvam*—everything; *asti*—exists: those who teach that also past and future events exist), the dominant school in India; as 3 the Pudgalavādins, or "Personalists", the whipping boys of all the other schools; as 4 the Sautrāntikas, who held that only the Sutras are canonical, and not the Abhidharma; as no. 18 the Mahāsanghikas (*mahā*—great, *samgha*—assembly), from whom the Mahayana developed. The Mahayana itself fell into three schools, no. 19 the Madhyamikas (*madhyama*—middle) the Teachers of the Middle Way (between yes and no); no. 20, the Yogācārins, 'teachers of Yoga", and no. 21 the Vajrayāna, or "adamantine career".

Each of these 21 schools can equally well claim to represent the true teaching of the Buddha. Two accidents of historical transmission have, however, combined to distort the perspective of Europeans at present, and to blind them to the merits of many of these schools, The first accident took place in Asia. The 17 "Hinayana" schools, i.e. nos. 2–18, who flourished in the North of India, had about A.D. 1000 the misfortune to encounter the fanatical fury of the Mohammedan invasion which totally destroyed them. One of the eighteen schools, no. 1, the Theravadins, had by then been pushed out into the comparative backwater of Ceylon. By way of compensation they thus avoided the Mohammedans, and, though for a time badly harassed by the Portuguese, they were able to preserve their scriptures and tradition under the rule of less persistently bloodthirsty invaders. The second accident of transmission took place in Europe. One of the eighteen schools, again the Theravadins, were in England favoured by the fact that they caught the eye of British administrators, such as T. W. Rhys Davids and Lord Chalmers, and that their writings have been almost completely translated into English. The Sarvastivadin texts, and so on, which exist in Sanskrit, Chinese and Tibetan, have on the other hand engaged the interest of Continental scholars, and much information about them exists in French, German, Russian and Japanese, but nearly none at all in English. In the perspective of those who only read English the Theravadins have therefore come to occupy a quite disproportionate importance. This second historical accident is bound to be gradually nullified in the course of the next decades. It usually takes 20 to 30 years for new ideas to travel from the Continent to England, and it will then be seen that the Buddha Dharma is a much richer and livelier thing than one has suspected so far. Even on the grounds of antiquity the Theravadins cannot claim to hold a privileged place. All the scriptures we know go back at most 1,900 or 2,000 years, and everything before that is mere surmise. And what zoologist, incidentally, would claim that the Pterodactylus is the one and only true bird, and that swallows, eagles and peacocks must be considered as a "degeneration" of the Archaeopterix? My book on *Buddhism* was written on the assumption that the Dharma had reached its maturity in the Prajñāpāramitā doctrine. In Prof. Murti's book this thesis has now received an important and quite independent confirmation.

The second point on which Murti's book throws a great deal of light is the relation of early Buddhism to the Upanishads. There has been a tendency to attribute to primitive Buddhism the Upanishadic teaching of the Self. This misinterpretation has been due to quite a variety of motives. Among Europeans it can usually be traced back to the difficulties of understanding the orthodox anattā doctrine without practising the meditations which were designed to disclose it. Also a secret hankering after the Christian conception of a soul may have been at work. The European assimilations of the Buddha to the Upanishads are manifestly the work of people "who are removed from him by centuries of time as well as distance of culture and outlook" (p. 25). The minds of their authors have only too obviously drawn their sustenance not from the free air of Himalayan hermitages, but from the anxious cares of the London suburbs.

Hindus, like Radhakrishnan, have, on the other hand, been prompted by their nationalistic ideas to formulate similar theories. In Prof. Radhakrishnan we have the example of a philosopher who can with ease not only attain high political office, but also maintain himself successfully in it, for the simple reason that from the very start he had regarded philosophy as a branch of politics. Just as during the nineteenth century professors in Germany, Eastern Europe, and elsewhere found that the revival of interest in the national literature of the past could act as a powerful stimulus to national consciousness, so in India the glories of indigenous philosophy were mobilised as an eloquent weapon in the struggle for self-government. Professor Radhakrishnan is interested in Indian philosophy because it is Indian, because it is created by Hindus. Since to him it appears essentially to be the work of one nation, he likes to see it as a development of one single tradition, deriving from the Vedas and Upanishads. He then ejects dissentient views, like the Buddhist anattā doctrine, from the history books with the same gentle firmness with which his Brahminic forebears removed the dissenters themselves from Indian history.

Prof. Murti, as a person, yields to no one in nationalist pride and in strict adherence to the taboos of the Brahmin caste. In his book he nevertheless shows conclusively and with a wealth of argument, that there are *two* main traditions in Indian philosophy, and that Buddhism differed from the Upanishads in that it rejected the belief in a self. "If the ātman had been a cardinal doctrine with Buddhism, why was it so securely hidden under a bushel that even the immediate followers of the Master had no inkling of it? The Upanishads, on the other hand, blaze forth the reality of the ātman in every page, in every line almost" (p. 17). Prof. Murti seems to me to have once and for all disposed 'of a soul-affirming primitive Buddhism followed by a soul-denying scholastic Buddhism." For "in attempting to bridge the difference between the Upanishads and Buddha, we would have immeasurably increased the distance between Buddha and Buddhism" (p. 25). Many people are discouraged from probing the depth of the anattā doctrine by the belief that it is not essential to Buddhism. They thereby miss its very core.

One must, however, remember that it is only through

meditation that this doctrine can be understood. And this is equally true of its logical development, the doctrine of Emptiness, which is "the real heart of Buddha's teaching" (p. 51). Prof. Murti has collected with great completeness all the points of view about emptiness which are prompted by philosophical arguments. His book contains nothing, however, about the meditation on Emptiness. It appears that someone drew his attention to this omission and induced him to add at the end as an Appendix a short "Note on the twenty Modes of Shunyata" (pp. 351–56). It is not sufficient to be intellectually convinced of the Emptiness of everything. This knowledge must also be realized in direct spiritual experience. The final note of the book gives some hints in this direction, although one might have wished that Prof. Murti had been more explicit on this point. I cannot, as a matter of fact, think of any occupation which is both as innocuous and as profitable as the prolonged meditation on the almost unlimited subject of Emptiness.

6

PROBLEMS OF BUDDHIST HISTORY[1]

As one of the sublimest religions of mankind, as well as one of the finest creations of the Indian genius, Buddhism has given rise to an enormous amount of literature in the various European languages. The bulk of it is deficient in either scholarship or sympathetic understanding, and it is, generally speaking, a somewhat heart-breaking business to have to review the latest additions to the crop. With some alacrity I therefore responded to the invitation to say a few words about Bhikshu Sangharakshita's new *Survey of Buddhism*. Written from the inside, with an experience of Buddhist meditation, his book is illumined by the sympathetic insight which comes to believers alone, and is guarded against the grotesque misunderstandings which abound in the works of agnostic outsiders, however "scientific" they may deem themselves to be. At the same time he has a scrupulous respect for the letter of the tradition, has spared no pains to ascertain it, and his scholarship is as faultless as it can humanly be. If one wants to mediate between East and West, it naturally helps to be part of both. So it was with Coomaraswamy, and so it is with Sangharakshita. He is a relatively young Englishman, once a Major in the Indian Army, who took the yellow robe after the last war, and ever since has worked indefatigably in India for the Maha Bodhi Society. By acting as his publishers, the Indian Institute of World Culture has lived well up to its name. For whatever the exact shape of the coming world culture may turn out to be, Buddhism is bound to be one of the ingredients which will go into the making of it.

The value of *A Survey of Buddhism* lies in its detail, and there can be no question of giving a brief summary of the 500 pages

[1] *A Survey of Buddhism*. By Bhikshu Sangharakshita. The Indian Institute of World Culture, Bangalore, viii + 500 pp. 1957.

of this valuable and comprehensive work. It must be read and studied from cover to cover, and, as the years pass, the student will be constantly tempted to refer back to its pages here and there. What I propose to do by way of introducing it to the readers of *The Aryan Path* is to say a few words about the fundamental problems of *evaluation* which confront all those who write a history of Buddhist thought. For this, to be successful, is not a mere matter of collecting more and more facts. However objective he may be, an historian must come to a decision on at least two controversial points: First of all he must make up his mind whom to count as a "Buddhist," and which, if any, of the self-styled Buddhists to exclude. And, secondly, not all those who are included are likely to have an equally good grasp of the Buddha's doctrine, and the historian will have to treat some of the doctrines as more orthodox and profound than others. These two weighty questions cannot possibly be shunned, although to tackle them in earnest is like putting one's hands into a hornet's nest.

The use of the word "Buddhism" is in itself not a very propitious beginning. The recent spread of universal education has its good points, and in any case it is inevitable. Nevertheless it has clearly some disadvantages. One of them is the addiction to abstract nouns of uncertain meaning, such as "democracy", "civilization", "Buddhism", "Christianity", and so on. In themselves these terms are incapable of precise definition, and any attempt to give them a definite meaning leads to nothing but ill will and fruitless disputation. "Nobody can be a Christian and support war"; "Christianity forbids divorce and birth-control"; "A belief in the Trinity is essential to all Christians"; and so on, and so on. The only result of such statements is the exclusion of many, if not most, professed Christians from the speaker's definition of "Christianity". Likewise, where "Buddhism" is discussed, we hear that "no Buddhist can eat meat", "married monks are not really Buddhist monks", and "the Pali Canon alone contains the pure Buddha-dhamma". The futility of such remarks is easy to see, for they cannot possibly be based on scriptural authority. In the New Testament the word "Christian" occurs three times in all, in each case as a term used by non-Christians. It would therefore be quite impossible to build up a definition of the word "Christian" from what the New Testament says about it. Likewise, in the Buddhist Scriptures the words, "Buddhist" and "Buddhism" occur nowhere at all. Just as Karl Marx protested against being called a "Marxist", so it is quite possible that the Buddha was not a "Buddhist". In any case, if he was one he did not say so. It is true that the term *Buddha-sasana*, "the Buddha's teaching", is used sometimes, but always in a vague sense, tending more to edification than to precise definition.

Until Europeans wrote about them, the "Buddhists" were happily unaware that they were "Buddhists". What they were preaching, practising and meditating about was not "Buddhism", but the "holy Dharma". This Dharma, or spiritual truth, exists in a number of separate traditions, or schools. Any one who wants to understand it more deeply must entrust himself to *one* of those lines of transmission, which will convey to him a knowledge of the practices by which alone an experience of the Dharma can be gained. It is this spiritual experience which has been the life-blood of "Buddhism", and it is only in particular schools that this life-blood circulates, just as it does in *particular* horses, and not in a general and abstract "horse" as such. "Buddhism" is an abstraction, coined by unbelievers for their own convenience. "Buddhism" in general has never done anything, nor can it ever do anything—except perhaps provide an excuse for a few more international conferences. The true life of the Dharma lies in the quiet of the meditation rooms, and it is directed not by microphones, but by the voice of the *Guru* gently handing down the wisdom of the past. In the very first pages of his book, Sangharakshita explains that "the scientific study of Buddhism" can have "a merely subordinate and instrumental value". No more can be expected of it than a preliminary survey of the field of possible interpretations of the Dharma, which may help to guide some readers to a more thorough exploration of one of them.

Both in Christianity and in Buddhism we can distinguish between a *central* and a *sectarian* tradition. Christanity originated in the Eastern Mediterranean, and it is there that the central tradition developed. In the outlying districts of Europe, e.g., in Wales, Scotland and Sweden, at the confines of the sea, or in Wittenberg and Bohemia, at the very borders of Mediterranean culture, the Christian faith then appeared in quite new and unexpected guises. As the living tradition had not sufficient strength to penetrate quite to this distance, it was replaced by fanciful ideas which claimed to go back directly to the "original gospel", and which represented the battered remains of a mighty tradition as the "only pure" doctrine.

A similar state of affairs can be discerned in "Buddhism", which originated in the North of India. It is thereabouts that its central tradition took shape, and it is near there, in Tibet, that it has been best preserved. This is the *madhyadesha*, the "middle region", where, if we believe the *Astasahasrika* (xvii. 336), a Bodhisattva likes to be reborn, because it is in the centre of things. But when in the course of its expansion Buddhism spread to the *pratyantajanapada*, to the border regions, there, at the confines of the sea, in Ceylon and Japan, its mentality became not unakin to that of the Protestants in the outlying districts of Europe. In fact, Ceylonese Theravada and Japanese Zen both reject the living tradition of Buddhism, the latter in the name of a "direct transmission outside the Scriptures", the former in the name of a Pali Canon which alone is alleged to preserve the original "Buddha-word".

As vehicles of spiritual attainment, the central and the peripheral tradition of Buddhism are both equally effective. Holiness, gentle calm and serenity, wisdom and piety, are not the monopoly of one school, and in this all-important sphere of religious virtue neither side has a perceptible advantage over the other. It is only when we consider the relatively trifling accomplishment of writing a "history of Buddhism" that the central, universalist, interpretation of the Dharma possesses an unquestionable superiority. For it is as good as impossible to write the history of a religion on sectarian lines. Among Christians, such a "history" will consist of three phases: First the original gospel, soon neglected; then a long period of darkness; then a rediscovery of the original gospel by some unlikely individual in some outlying place at the very edge of the civilized world. For the Theravadins it will run like this: The original gospel, spoken in Pali (!) by the Buddha, taken to Ceylon about 250 B.C., then forgotten everywhere else, and preserved alone by virtuous Ceylonese and those others who received it from them. How this reminds us of Calvinism, with its few children of the light, and its vast "mass of perdition"!

The exclusive sectarian method must reduce the history of Buddhism to that of one little sect. The remaining sects fall by the wayside, or are mentioned only for the enormity of their deviations. By contrast the inclusive method would count as "Buddhists" all those who claim to be followers of the Dharma. This inclusive method was practised in Tibet, for instance by Buston in the thirteenth century, and, with a wider geographical horizon, the author has worked on the same lines. It appears to be the only way in which a balanced Buddhist history can be written.

Now as to our second question: Confronted with dozens and dozens of conflicting schools, the historian cannot avoid regarding some of these as more, others as less significant. Sangharakshita believes that the Buddhist doctrine reached its greatest maturity in the Mahayana. He is not alone in this conviction, which is shared by Murti, Conze and Lamotte, to mention only the most recent authors.

But is this emphasis on the Mahayana not a departure from the impartiality which the historian ought to observe? Is it not merely a way of taking sides in the interminable sectarian squabbles which, in fulfilment of ancient prophecies, threaten to tear apart the Buddhist community, 2,500 years after the Lord Buddha's Nirvana? To have avoided these pitfalls is perhaps the most noteworthy of the Bhikshu's achievements. Like the sages of old he manages to hold to his views without excluding or rejecting those of others. His attitude to the manifold formulations of the Dharma is throughout guided by "the simile of the tree", and I can do no better than quote his own words:

> It may be said that the Buddha's transcendental realization is the root, His original Doctrine. . . the trunk, the distinctive Mahayana doctrines the branches, and the schools and the sub-schools of the Mahayana the flowers. Now the function of flowers, however beautiful, is to produce fruit. . . .The Bodhisattva Ideal is the perfectly ripened fruit of the whole vast tree of Buddhism (p. 432).

Nothing could be less contentious. Without hesitation,

without any reservation whatever, I recommend Sangharakshita's book as the best survey of Buddhism we possess at present. The light of the Dharma continues to shine even in the spiritual darkness which has overtaken the present age. An effort to ascertain its true meaning is not wasted if we want to lead serene and meaningful lives. As a first guide to it we cannot do better than study Sangharakshita's sober and reverent survey of a tradition which, in its surprisingly diverse manifestations, has given peace to many millions, and which has not yet lost all power to stir the hearts of men.

IV. REVIEWS

I

Marie-Thérèse de Mallmann. *Introduction à l'étude d'Avalokiteśvara. Civilisations du Sud*. A.S.E.P. Paris, 1948. 348 pp. 32 plates.

The quality of French Orientalist work continues to take our breath away. During this century a living tradition has been built up by men of the calibre of Sylvain Lévi, Paul Pelliot, A. Foucher, J. Przyluski, L. de la Vallée-Poussin, to mention only a few. In order to study Buddhism, it has become almost as necessary to know French as to know Sanskrit. Many of the learned bhikshus of old seem nowadays to seek rebirth in France. In recent years, external conditions have become rather unfavourable. The high cost of printing, Government indifference, the shortage of accommodation, and the slow disappearance of persons with independent means have caused difficulties, but they have not been able to extinguish the flame. De Mallmann's book on Avalokiteśvara, a Thesis submitted at the École des Hautes Études, is a striking witness to the abiding vitality of French Orientalism. It is only the first volume of a larger book. The second volume will be devoted to the career of Avalokiteśvara outside India. In a sense this is a collective work, and that, in part, explains its high quality, which is not easily equalled elsewhere. Throughout the pages of the book we remain in contact with de M's teachers—with P. Pelliot, P. Mus, P. Démiéville, L. Renou, J. Przyluski, J. Hackin, etc., all of whom helped to make this achievement possible.

The book falls into two parts, the first literary, the second archaeological. It begins with extracts from seven representative texts dealing with Avalokiteśvara (pp. 2–56). Then it proceeds to discuss the much-disputed meaning of the name "Avalokiteśvara", surveying nine previous theories and adding a tenth (pp. 59–82). The third literary section considers the figure of Av. in relation to non-Buddhistic trends in India and Iran, and describes the development of the cult of Av. in India (pp. 85–115). This concludes the literary part. The archaeological part falls again into two halves. In the first (pp. 119–205) de M. gives a painstaking chronological study of the Indian images of Avalokiteśvara, and in the second (pp. 209–310) a stylistic study of these images, i.e. a careful description of the gestures, attributes, etc. which are found in all the various figures of Avalokiteśvara. The whole volume is terminated by a short Conclusion (pp. 311–12), a Bibliography, and 32 plates.

The archaeological part of the book deserves nothing but praise. The documentation is extremely full, and, as far as I can see, practically complete. With regard to the Buddha in the head dress, or crown, of Av., de Mallmann is inclined to believe that before the ninth or tenth century that Buddha need not necessarily be an Amitabha, but may be just any Buddha (pp. 124, 308–10). There exist, however, images which undoubtedly represent Av., but which have no Buddha in the crown. On the other hand, de M. assumes that all figures of Bodhisattvas, before the seventh or eighth century, who carry a Buddha in their turban or crown, are necessarily representations of Av. (p. 123). This is plausible enough, but the evidence is not sufficient to prove it. I was glad to see (in footnote 3 to p. 125) that Mlle. de M. proposes to return to the question elsewhere. We would be actually on firmer ground if we could determine the idea which this attribute is meant to symbolize. As it is, we are still in the dark on that point.

In the literary part of the book Mlle. de M. feels obviously much less at home. The literary documentation is, of course, bound to be incomplete, considering the enormous extent of the relevant literature. The actual selection of the passages chosen seems, however, quite haphazard. It is not guided by any scientific principle, but by the accessibility of the texts. Of the *Mañjuśrīmūlakalpa* de M. takes into account only the few passages (26 pp. out of 722) which have been translated into French by Mlle Lalou and J. Przyluski. As to the *Mahāvairocanasūtra*, de M. only knows the French translation of the first chapter. Some of her doubts (e.g. on p. 113) could have been allayed by B. L. Suzuki's competent exposition of the work in the *Eastern Buddhist* for 1935 and 1936. As de M. herself expresses it, she "meets (in her iconographical survey) with a great number of images of Av., clearly marked by attributes and assistants, which correspond to no text. This shows the extent to which we still need an attentive study of the sanskrit manuscripts and of the Chinese recensions" (p. 311). An adequate survey of the literature concerning Av. still awaits the patience of someone with an easy command of sanskrit, and a thorough knowledge of Chinese and Tibetan—if such a one can be found.

We now come to the thorny question of the meaning of the name "Avalokiteśvara". It is very convenient to find in this book a conscientious survey of the widely scattered discussions which have dealt with the problem, and it seems somewhat ungracious to criticize Mlle. de M's efforts. I cannot, however, conceal my opinion that this is very much the weakest part of the book. In this connection I would like to make three points: 1, that there is no problem at all; 2, that, if there were one, philologists approach it in a wrong spirit; and 3, that de M's solution of the problem is not only quite inconclusive, but actually vitiates her understanding of the place of Av. in Buddhist thought and art.

ad 1, in the compound Avalokiteśvara, *īśvara* means "Lord", and *ava-lok-ita* "the compassionate look". Avalokiteśvara is "the Lord who looks down with compassion". In Buddhist scriptures, ava-lok has the unmistakable meaning of "survey with compassion", for instance in *Ashtasāhasrikā* xxii, 403. The meaning "look down" is found in the same text, at xvii, 323, *na ca pareshām krita-akritāni vyavalokayati*, where *vy-ava-lok-ayati* stands for *avekkhati* in *Dhammapada* 50, *na paresam katākatam . . . avekkheyya . . .* (See *R* 80 and 373). This is the meaning of the name as explained explicitly in the *Kārandavyūha*, and as understood by Tibetan, by Mongol, and by most Chinese translators. From the point of view of Buddhist doctrine, and even from that of grammar, it is a perfectly valid meaning, as de M. herself admits (p. 69 "La proposition: Avalokiteśvara . . . seigneur qui regarde (d'en haut) avec compassion . . . *reste valable*"). But if that is so, why look for other, far-fetched, solutions?

ad 2, even if there were a problem, I am not sure that the alternative solutions offered by philologists, including de M., are methodologically sound. When one speaks of the "meaning" of a term—whom does it have that meaning for? Obviously a concrete body of people. The meaning of *colloquial* words can often be deduced by linguistic methods, but to get at the meaning of a *theological technical* term one must ask the theologians themselves. To them Avalokita was the personification of the compassionate look. If modern philologists try to improve on that by lengthy discussions on "roots", etc., they ignore the actual psychology of the monks who actually coined those terms. Anybody who has marvelled at the etymologies of Buddhaghosa and of the Prajñāpāramitā knows that they exhibit a sovereign disregard not only for the niceties, but for the very possibilities of linguistics and grammar. In texts of the early Mahayana a love for puns and for mystification is more pronounced than a concern for grammatical exactitude. One must also remember that most of the actual creative thinking was done in Prakrits, and not in Sanskrit at all. In consequence, once we leave the simple and obvious explanation of a technical term, the possibilities of speculation become literally unlimited, all sure foundations vanish away, and there is no criterion by which to distinguish the true from the false. In the train, between Oxford and Didcot, I managed to think up three more explanations of the name Avalokiteśvara. For reasons of space I am content to offer just one of them, by way of parody, as the eleventh solution of the mystery, as plausible as that of de M.—and as redundant: *Ava-lokita*, "survey", takes in Pali, and other Prakrits, the form *apa-lokita*. The same word, *a-palokita* also means "not liable to decay", or "Nirvana". Now it is the essential attribute of Avalokiteśvara that, from compassion, he never disappears into Nirvana. Therefore, on the principle of *lucus a non lucendo*, he is given the name "Nirvana." Such a mystification would be quite in keeping with the mentality of Mahayanists, who derived *an-uttara* (utmost) from *aṇu* (least), connected *parama* with *aparimāna*, *pāramitā* with *āramita*, and whose sense of humour revelled in constant plays on words.

ad 3, de M. herself derives *ava-lokita* from ava-ruc, "shine", and Avalokiteśvara is said to mean the "luminous, or shining, Lord". M. Fowler in *Artibus Asiae* (12, 1949, 155–158) has shown that this proposal is "possible, but most unlikely". It would, indeed, be but an innocent exhibition of ingenuity, quite suitable and in its place in a Thesis, if it had not led de M. into conclusions about the nature of Av. which seem scarcely tenable. Luminosity is, it is true, one of the attributes of Av. It is also an attribute of many other deities besides. It is continually said in the Scriptures of any and every Bodhisattva that—from the eighth *bhūmi* onwards—he sheds light over many world systems. In this way, radiance or luminosity is one of Avalokiteśvara's attributes, but it is by no means the central and distinguishing one. His distinguishing feature is "compassion," just as "wisdom" is that of Mañjuśrī, "friendliness" that of Maitreya, etc.

In a number of particularly valuable and often striking pages (pp. 86–95, 126) de M. examines the influence of Iran and the Near East on the formation of the conception of Avalokiteśvara and Amitābha. I wish to draw attention to the remarkable parallel between parts of ch. 24 of the *Lotus*, and certain passages in the *Zend Avesta* (p. 93). de M. believes that the kinship between Av. and Mithra strengthens her case that Av. initially was essentially a *Seigneur Lumineux*. If ever Av. was a solar deity of the Iranian type *within* Buddhism, why did the Buddhists not give him a name derived from *avabhāsa*, or *ābhā*, or any of their many synonyms, instead of using the word *avalokita* based, according to de M., on a Vedic root (*ava-ruc*), the original meaning of which was subsequently forgotten (le sens primitif de son nom étant oubliè, p. 80)! At what time *within* Buddhism was this meaning of a Vedic word remembered?

de M. traces out the main stages of the development of Av. At first he is a Bodhisattva who is not easy to distinguish from a Buddha. He then gains a number of cosmic features which assimilate him to the ancient Vedic notion of Purusha-Prajāpati-Brahman. Finally, he becomes a kind of roi-magicien, and progressively a replica of Shiva. "The different aspects of Av. which scholars have so far pointed out and which show Iranian, Brahmanical or Shivaite influences, all correspond to reality. But, instead of being *simultaneous*, they seem rather to be *successive*" (p. 312). This conclusion of the book, when I read it for the first time, seemed to me rather neat, plausible and impressive. On re-examining de M's material, I do not think that her evidence is really conclusive. To begin with, the number of texts which she takes into consideration is far too small to support such a generalization. It would be like deducing the geography of England from 50 pieces of land, each a square mile in extent, chosen at random, without any clear notion of their relation to each other, or to the whole configuration of the country. But even those few texts do not, as they stand, fit into de M's scheme. In consequence she must resort to all kinds of uncertain opinions about the dates of different parts of one and the same text, about interpolations, etc. A particularly glaring example (on p. 101) concerns an inconvenient passage in the twenty-fourth chapter of the *Lotus*, where she hazards the guess (hypothèse, évidemment hasardeuse) that "ce passage appartînt primitivement à un autre texte, aujourd'hui perdu, et qu'il eût été rattaché arbitrairement au Lotus". The transparent honesty with which de M. introduces such guesses is bound to disarm any critic. We must, however, realize the fact that the conclusions which result from an accumulation of "hazardous hypotheses" of this kind are perhaps probable, but cannot be said to be cogently proved.

The time is now ripe for a series of monographs on the various Buddhist deities. With considerable courage and ability Mlle. de Mallmann has tackled the most difficult figure of all. Our knowledge of Avalokiteśvara, one of the noblest creations of the religious imagination, has been immeasurably advanced by her patient and devoted research. We all owe her a profound debt of gratitude for the splendid work she has done, and we must hope that the second volume will not be long delayed.

2

S. Radhakrishnan. *The Principal Upanishads*. G. Allen and Unwin Ltd., 1953. Sri Aurobindo. *Eight Upanishads*. Sri Aurobindo Ashram, 1953, Sri Aurobindo. *Katha Upanishad*. Sri Aurobindo Ashram, 1952.

Among the great and lasting documents of human thought few are more valuable than the Upanishads. While he was ambassador in Moscow for the Republic of India, Prof. Radhakrishnan found the time to write a new translation of the Upanishads which has now been published. It is a truly monumental work, and supersedes all the translations we have had up to now. This is a big book, of nearly 1,000 pp. First of all it gives a most instructive Introduction of 145 pp. The bulk of the book then consists of the text and translation of 18 Upanishads, with many notes from the most authoritative commentaries, and with parallels from other religious and philosophical sources. This goes on up to p. 938, and is followed by 19 pp. of Appendices and Indices.

The Sanskrit text is given in Roman letters which we Europeans read so much more easily than the Devanagari script. Misprints are almost totally absent. The translation is literal and accurate, except for the few occasions when the author's sense of propriety impels him to bowdlerize his rendering (e.g. on p. 165 *yoni* becomes "source", or, on p. 632, *maithuna* "love"). The contents of the Upanishads are of rather unequal interest to us today. About one-third of the volume deals with Brahmanic ritual. "As here hungry children sit (expectantly) around their mother, even so do all beings sit around the fire sacrifice" (p. 445). For non-Brahmins of the twentieth century this archaic lore has no more than an historical interest today. But the remainder of the book is concerned with the great problem of the *ātman*, and there the Upanishads can still teach us a great deal. So different, however, are the linguistic habits of Sanskrit and English, that the one cannot always be made to correspond exactly to the other, and the pitfalls are many. To take the word *ātman* itself: usually it appears as "self", but sometimes as "soul" (p. 714), or as "body" (p. 183), or as "mind" (p. 235). And sometimes there is no *ātman* in the Sanskrit where the English gives a "self", as on p. 630, where "self-caused" corresponds to *svayambhu*. Other technical terms are subject to similar fluctuations. *Anna*, usually "food", becomes "matter" on p. 554, and "earth" on p. 452. Irregularites of this kind are quite unavoidable, and the easy accessibility of the original should here remove the danger of misunderstandings.

The death of Sri Aurobindo has released a flood of posthumous publications from his Ashram. Among these, the two dealing with some of the Upanishads give the text in Devanagari, together with a translation of which I have compared a few pages with Radhakrishnan's rendering. Wherever the two differ I found Radhakrishnan to be more accurate, more readable, and altogether more sound. Perhaps we Buddhists will one day have the enterprise to bring out our own Scriptures in the admirable form in which Prof. Radhakrishnan has presented those of the Vedanta.

It has now become more easy to study the Upanishads than ever before, and we will be impelled to consider anew the relation of their sublime and profound teachings to the doctrine of Buddhism. Prof. Radhakrishnan is one of those who believe that the two are quite closely connected, and that the Upanishads contain the metaphysics which "justifies Buddha's ethical discipline" (p. 949). On the other hand, one could argue that he is not quite as familiar with Buddhism as he is with his own philosophy. On p. 123 he invents a non-existent edition of the *Lankavatara Sutra*, and when he says that the Buddhists "accept the teaching of the Upanishads, though they interpret it in their own way" (p. 25), I cannot think of any fact which he could adduce in support of this statement. The Upanishads, it is true, use a terminology similar to our own and likewise deal with the laws of a spiritual life, and everywhere search for the transcendent, for the Absolute, for immortality. But it should never be overlooked that the Upanishads were a secret doctrine taught to groups of pupils who "sat near" their teacher (p. 19; see also p. 629), and there is no real reason to believe that the early Buddhists were in contact with just these groups of persons who were instructed in the Vedanta. And then, while *ātman* is the key-word of these writings, *anātman* is the key-word of ours. It is, of course, possible that the Buddha always meant "Self" when he said "not-self", but this hypothesis would attribute to him a delight in mystification which ill accords with his compassion for those he wished to instruct.

3

René de Nebesky-Wojkowitz. *Oracles and Demons of Tibet.* Oxford University Press, London: Cumberlege, 1956. xiv + 666 pp. 10 plates.

Tibetan Lamaism blends a sublime transcendental spirituality more or less harmoniously with magical beliefs and practices which do not differ from those current elsewhere. Its magical side is bound up with the "Protective Deities", comparatively inferior godlets "of the eighth, ninth and tenth rank", and lower down, about whom comparatively little was so far known. A young Viennese Tibetologue with anthropological leanings has now collected for us a great deal of information about them. He obtained his knowledge in the neighbourhood of Kalimpong from Tibetan Lamas and officials, and in addition he has consulted about 200 rare block-prints and manuscripts. With great competence he distinguishes throughout the three distinct strands of the tradition—Yellow Hats (Gelugpa), Red Hats (Nying-ma-pa), and Bon. The seemingly endless lists of deities and their "retinues" on pp. 3 to 340 are followed by a description of their cult, with special emphasis on the State Oracle, and on the methods employed for divination and weather making. The 20 plates show his informants, a few local paintings of "protective deities," and a medium going through the stages of trance. In addition there are 25 drawings, copious indices, and in the footnotes an almost complete inventory of the European literature on the questions discussed.

As a scholarly monograph this thorough and erudite contribution to Tibetan studies is an outstanding achievement, packed with reliable facts, most of them new to the West. Non-specialists will, however, find it rather indigestible. Tibetan words, to mention the most obvious difficulty, are translated rarely and sporadically. A large proportion of the book's contents must remain incomprehensible to all but a few highly proficient Tibetan linguists. It would have been a merciful concession to the more average reader if the English equivalents had been added to the extensive Tibetan lists in the indices (pp. 605–52). Even then the reader could not help feeling that after all he has learned very little about either Lamaist magic or Tibetan Buddhism. He is offered a truly staggering quantity of material, but in a raw and unfinished condition. Before it is capable of assimilation into the existing body of knowledge, it must await further historical and philosophical analysis.

Historically speaking, the Tibetan religion of the present day is the result of a fusion of the Indian Buddhist Tantra with manifold indigenous traditions. In the course of his book Dr. Nebesky makes numerous useful suggestions about the influence of the Bon religion, of Shamanism, and of various tribal beliefs. The vast Indian Tantric literature, on the other hand, lies outside his ken. Since thus the starting point remains in the dark, the further stages of the development which took place during the last millennium cannot be either described or analysed. This is a relatively minor omission, and in due course it will be rectified.

Far more fundamental is the fact that Dr. Nebesky's philosophical outlook precludes any insight into the phenomena he studies. He is not alone in this disability, which he shares with most scientific anthropologists of the present generation, who are really at home only with the debris of cultures in a process of rapid decay. With Prof. H. Webster, in his great work on "Magic" (1948), they dismiss all magic as a "barren pseudo-science" (p. 497), and Dr. Nebesky seems, in spite of some hesitations, to concur with their verdict. On one occasion (p. 440) he makes a rather hair-raising attempt at a "scientific" explanation of the phenomena observed, but for the rest he treats them as altogether nugatory. Now it may very well be that the beliefs and practices of the Lamas are quite devoid of any basis in objective reality, mere phantasies conjured up from the void. We still remain curious to know what made this system "tick", what rules governed the conjurings, and what gave them an appearance of coherence and plausibility, however spurious. A scholar who shirks these questions is bound to write an unsatisfactory book, for the beliefs he describes turn into a chaotic, unintelligible, and completely meaningless medley of bizarre absurdities. Six hundred pages are here filled with statements about "cosmic tortoises" and "sky dogs", or about gods dressed in "fur coats" or "tiger skins", living in "iron palaces" or "copper fortresses", and "holding a black trident with four heads stuck on it and a blood-dripping heart, at which two black vipers are sucking". These propositions obviously do not refer to objects of the commonsense world, but if they are fictitious, are they therefore hopelessly nonsensical, or do they have a logic of their own? In order to be fruitful, the study of living beliefs, particularly those different from our own, demands a great deal of both empathy and philosophical profundity. Just the more competent and accurate specialists seem, alas, often to be conspicuously unendowed with those qualities. How much more interesting, intelligible and stimulating their books would be if they could add to their respect for facts a respect for the intellectual integrity of the great thinkers of alien cultures! But it is no use crying for the moon, and we must be grateful to Dr. Nebesky for what he has chosen to give us.

4

K. W. Morgan (Ed.) *The Path of the Buddha.* Buddhism Interpreted by Buddhists. The Ronald Press Company, New York, 1956. x + 432 pp.

At first sight it would seem to be an excellent and most fruitful idea to induce a number of leading Buddhists of Asia to write essays about their own religion, and to publish them all together in book form. Backed by the ample funds of American Foundations, K. W. Morgan, a University Chaplain, accordingly travelled about in Asia, and the result of his labours now lies before us. He has here gathered together eleven contributions—seven Japanese, and one each from India, Burma, Ceylon and Tibet. His position as an American did not, of course, prove an asset in every way. No Chinese authors have been included, for the reason that "Americans are not permitted to travel freely in China".

What then about the Tibetan? He is a Lobsang, a former official of the Tibetan government, now in Kalimpong, and certainly not a trustworthy authority on religious questions. Details of ecclesiastical history are seen through a haze. On p. 241 the author speaks of "a religious debate between the Chinese monk Kamalashila and a disciple of Santarakshita". In fact, Kamalashila *was* the disciple of Santarakshita, and the Chinese monk in question is known as the Hwa Shang. This is a fair sample of the Lobsang's scholarship. If we leave out his many inaccuracies, he is content to just recount the more elementary facts well known to every one by now, and related much better by Bell, and others. His description of the contents of the Prajñāpāramitā Sutra on pp. 270–1 is so extraordinary that he can never have seen more of it than the outside. His 35 pp. on the doctrine of Lamaism are a complete muddle. All I learned from it was that a Tibetan politician need not always be particularly well informed about his holy religion, no more than an English one, for that matter. Somewhat disarmingly he tells us that "the common people of Tibet know little of philosophy", and it would certainly have been better if Mr. Morgan could have induced a proper Lama to write this contribution. Unable to tell us anything new or precise about Lamaism, the Lobsang is all the more ready to take sides, both in the past disputes between Gelugpas and Karmapas (p. 253), and the current ones between Panchen and Dalai Lama. His vigorous condemnation of the Panchen (pp. 255–6) would fit in well with his editor's predilections, but the reader must be disappointed to see it backed up by a mere travesty of the actual position.

Not all contributions are as shoddy as this one, but one alone seemed to me worth reading. It is the Ven. U. Thittila's account of "the fundamental principles of Theravada Buddhism".

As I ploughed my way through these 400 pp. of undistinguished writing, my spirits became increasingly deflated by the uniform mediocrity I encountered on all sides. What, I asked myself, had gone wrong with the Chaplain's excellent idea? The answer, when it came to me, proved surprisingly simple. All these men, with the exception of the Ven. U. Thittila, were unacquainted with the mentality of Westerners, and all of them were made to use a language not their own, i.e. English. No wonder that the result is as distant from Cicero's euphoneous lucidity as it is from Hemingway's racy idiom! No wonder that we are treated to a kind of foreigners' English—constantly saying "which" when "who" would be appropriate, or "not in any way" when "not in every way" is meant, and so on, and so on. And then, habituated to Buddhist benevolence, I placed myself into their position, and I wondered what would survive of my own sublime thoughts if I were forced to put them into Sanskrit, Tibetan, or even Italian. Just the kind of mauled remnants which we have here! No one can expect Oriental thinkers to give their best if they are first of all deprived of their linguistic resources and forced to express themselves in the language of their conquerors. This book modestly calls itself "the first clear, vivid and authentic account of Buddhism for the Western reader". The truth is that it is none of these.

Thirty years ago, J. B. Pratt, an American professor of philosophy, made a pilgrimage through the Buddhist lands of Asia, and in 1928 he published his beautiful classic on "The Pilgrimage of Buddhism". But, then, Pratt used his eyes, his intelligence, his sensibility and his sympathy, and in his book Buddhism lives and throbs, and speaks to our head and heart alike. A reprint of Pratt's work would teach very much more to the present generation than Mr. Morgan's unimaginative piece of book-making can do.

5

G. Tucci. *Minor Buddhist Texts, Part I.* Rome, 1956. Ismeo, Serie Orientale Roma IX. xi + 312 pp.

From his numerous expeditions to Tibet and Nepal Prof. Tucci has brought back a considerable number of Sanskrit manuscripts which are of outstanding importance for the history of Buddhist thought. These finds are now gradually being made accessible to scholars, and in the book before us a beginning has been made by the publication of six documents, all of them pertaining to the later Mahāyāna.

The most important of these is Asaṅga's *Triśatikāyāḥ Prajñāpāramitāyāḥ Kārikāsaptatiḥ*, "The seventy(-seven) stanzas summing up the contents of the *Vajracchedikā Prajñāpāramitā*". Section I, which occupies the bulk of the book (pp. 5–192) is devoted to its elucidation. Not content with publishing the Sanskrit text of his Nepalese palmleaf manuscript (from the Nor monastery), together with the two Chinese translations of Bodhiruci and I Ching, the Tibetan translation from the Tanjur, and an English translation of his own, Prof. Tucci has added a wealth of subsidiary material. So far we had known from the Catalogues that at least eight Sanskrit commentaries to the *Vajracchedikā* had been preserved in the great Chinese and Tibetan collections, but their relation to each other had never been investigated. In a lengthy introduction Prof. Tucci has now done so, and the result can be seen at a glance on p. 22. These commentaries all stem from the same tradition which also produced the *Abhisamayālaṅkāra*, and which attempted, with Maitreya's miraculous aid, to "give some logical order to the ideas expounded in or suggested by the text" of the *Prajñāpāramitā*, building up a "coherent architecture of subtle notions" of which it is rather doubtful whether it really represented the intentions of the original authors of the Sūtras themselves. It is not always easy to avoid getting lost in the numerous divisions and subdivisions of these schemes, and we must be grateful to Prof. Tucci for the additional help he has given us by his analysis (pp. 131–71) of Vasubandhu's prose commentary to the *Vajracchedikā* (T 1510), which he has compared with Kamalaśīla's more extensive commentary, preserved only in Tibetan. For good measure we still have in this section an edition, by Prof. Chakravarti, of the 7 leaves of the very old Gilgit MS. of the *Vajracchedikā*, which contains chapters 13c–14e, and 15b–32 of that text. It shows that many passages in M. Mueller's text are the later additions of pious scribes, and its relation to the Pargiter MS. can be studied with ease in the edition of the *Vajracchedikā* which I am bringing out in the S.O.R. this year (see no. *H*).

The complications which the Yogācārins introduced into the interpretation of the *Prajñāpāramitā* almost pass belief, and a considerable mental effort is needed to maintain oneself in this rarefied atmosphere of metaphysical abstractions. The resources of Prof. Tucci's scholarship are, however, adequate for his exacting task, and his attention seems to have faltered on rare occasions only. It appears to me, for instance, that he has misunderstood verse 13ab:

phalato na mitā buddhaiḥ praṇidhijñānalakṣitāh,

which seems to mean that the qualities of these Bodhisattvas are "not inferred by the Buddhas from the fruits" they produce, and that these Bodhisattvas are "marked by the cognition which results from their vow". Prof. Tucci, however, understands (on p. 99) the *praṇidhijñāna* to belong to the Buddhas, and refers us to the *Abhidharmakośa*. But just there it is expressly stated that the *praṇidhijñāna* is common to all the *āryas*, and Prof. Tucci's rendering would, it seems to me, presuppose *-lakṣitaiḥ*. Likewise the sentence about the bodies of the Buddha at the top of page 30 must also be due to inattention. But apart from these two points, my rare disagreements from Prof. Tucci are confined to matters of opinion, which in any case concern problems too recondite for a review. Ever since Schmidt published the Tibetan *Vajracchedikā*

120 years ago, the contents of this Sūtra have baffled European readers. The new material now at our disposal at last enables us to see some of the meaning behind it.

In the second half of this book we find the Sanskrit text of the *Mahāyānaviṃśikā*, often attributed to Nāgārjuna; Kambalācārya's *Navaślokī*, a not particularly inspiring summary of the *Prajñāpāramitā*, in Sanskrit, Tibetan, Chinese and English, with a few extracts from the Sanskrit commentary; a late commentary, in Sanskrit, on three of the four hymns of the *Catuḥstava*; and finally two late logical texts, of "rather scant importance", but not quite without interest for the specialists in Buddhist logic.

Prof. Tucci's English translations are nearly everywhere accurate, though not always felicitous. For instance, the usage of "Verb" for "Word" on p. 148 is rather harsh in English. One may also wonder whether it is desirable to translate *tathatā* (Suchness) as "the absolute", *abhijñā* (superknowledges) as "mystic intuitions", *gatiṃ yānti* (go to a place of rebirth) as "meet a form of existence", and so on—but then these translations are meant to be read in conjunction with the original, and so no harm is done. There is the usual crop of misprints, all of them trivial, *e.g.* p. 21, l. 6 from below, add *kyi*; p. 24, l. 9 omit "is"; p. 63, l. 3 from below, a syllable is missing; p. 101, l. 13 add "as", p. 153 last line add "if", p. 133 l. 4 from below, read *'dhigama*, p. 147 l. 1 *spraṣṭavya*, 148, l. 11 *deśanādharmakāya*, p. 155 last line *lokadhātur*, p. 205, l. 3 "Homage".

A second volume, containing the Sanskrit original of Kamalaśīla's first *Bhāvanākrama*, as well as Sajjanapada's *Mahāyānottaratantraśāstropadeśa*, is announced for the near future. All Buddhist scholars will look forward with keen interest to this sequel to the superb volume before us which appeared last year (see pp. 176–8 below).

6

F. A. Bischoff. *Ārya Mahābala-nāma-Mahāyānasūtra*. Tibétain (MSS. de Touen-Houang) et Chinois, Préface de M. Lalou. Buddhica, première série: mémoires, tome X. Paris; Paul Geuthner, 1956.

The *Mahābala Sūtra* is a Tantric text which was very popular in early times in Tibet and Central Asia. The Sanskrit original is lost. Mr. Bischoff has now edited the Tibetan translation (pp. 22–49) from fifteen Tun-huang manuscripts, filling in a few gaps from the Kanjur. He also gives us a French translation of the Tibetan version (pp. 50–66), as well as of Dharmapāla's Chinese translation (pp. 67–80). Six long *mantras* form an important constituent of the text, and on pp. 81–102 we find a welcome transliteration and translation of these *mantras* in their Sanskrit form after Dharmapāla, who gives them in the Chinese transliteration current in Sung times. Finally there are a few notes and indexes, and four plates with photographs from the manuscripts.

There is such a dearth of critical editions of Tantric documents that we must be grateful for any new addition to the list. The teaching of the *Mahābala Sūtra* combines a great deal of magic with the metaphysical and soteriological commonplaces of the Mahayana, and to some extent it deserves the epithet "tedious" (*rebutant*) which M. Lalou in her Preface bestows on the Tantras in general.

It is indeed hard to enter sympathetically into their spirit, and while the edition of the documents has been undertaken with meticulous care, the accuracy of their interpretation leaves much to be desired. Closer examination reveals many mistakes, particularly in the restitution of the Sanskrit terms. *Brgya-byin* is of course *Śakra*, and not *Śatakratu*, as we are told on pp. 52 and 87. The *Śatakratudevānāmindra* on pp. 51 and 113 is just *Śakra, devānām indra*. *Yid-la byed* is *manasikaroti*, and not *namas KṚ* (p. 52); *mchod-pa byed* simply means *pūjayati*, and not *abhi-PŪJ* (pp. 54, 55); *byas-pa bzo-ba, kṛtajña*, means "grateful", and not "a fait ce qui est à faire (*ābhoga*)" (p. 59); *luṅ, vyākaraṇa*, "prediction", and not *āgama* (préceptes, p. 59); *phun-sum-tshogs* is *sampat*, "achievement", and not "sublime" (p. 61); *sprul-pa* renders *nirmāṇa* or *nirmita*, and not *vikurvaṇa* (pp. 61, 64, 111); *srid-pa* is *bhava*, "becoming", and not "malsaine" or "mauvaises" (p. 65); and *yoṅs-su sṅo-ba byed do* is the Sanskrit *pariṇāmayati* ("dedicate to"), and to translate "verdoieront entièrement" (p. 65) gives a quite wrong idea of it.

These are all quite elementary points, and a reliable Sanskrit-Tibetan dictionary, if it existed, could help even beginners to avoid such blemishes. Greater familiarity with Buddhist usage would have allowed Mr. Bischoff to see that *mi gYo-ba* stands for *acala* rather than *akṣobhya* (pp. 58, 107), which is usually *mi 'khrugs-pa; chos-kyi sgo* in these texts is more likely to mean *dharmamukha*, instead of *dharmadvāra* (p. 58); and *chos-kyi tshul* is *dharmanaya* or *dharmanetrī*, but certainly not *dharmaśīla* (pp. 60, 111); on p. 58 we are puzzled by the statement that someone enters *samādhi* "indolemment", the Tibetan being *ma thag-tu* "as soon as".

This uncertainty about the meaning of technical terms distorts the translation in many places. There is no point in multiplying the instances, and I will conclude by turning to a few passages of genuine difficulty. On p. 84 *māravikaraṇa* is translated "la transformation magique de Māra"; I would have thought that, in spite of p. 51, it means the "destroyer" of Mara and on p. 93 Mr. Bischoff himself renders *vikara* as "Ruine!" The sentence on pp. 64, ll. 8–10 is unintelligible as it stands. I would suggest "after the Tathagata's

Parinirvana this Sutra will do his work", though "after" is rather harsh for *tshe*. On page 63 we have an enumeration of the marks of all conditioned things, which merely repeats well-known ideas, except where the *saṃskāra* are compared to *k(h)yim*, "maison" as Bischoff translates. This gives no sense, and I would suggest that "sign of the Zodiac" is meant; for the *saṃskāras* have as much inner unity as the signs of the Zodiac which are a mere conventional grouping of disparate elements. This comparison occurs in other Buddhist texts, and may well have been intended here. And finally I would like to draw attention to a passage which neither Mr. Bischoff (p. 61, l. 35 to p. 62, l. 2) nor I have understood, and which offers a challenge to other scholars more skilled in such puzzles. Its meaning seems to depend on some word play on *spyi, mūrdhan* (which occurs at p. 32, ll. 26 and 35, p. 33, l. 2), and which also the Chinese (p. 75) seems to have been unable to reproduce.

After having so far been completely ignored by European scholars, the *Mahābala Sūtra* is suddenly quite in the news. Just now *Oriental Art* (N.S. III 2, pp. 68–70) has published an article describing a Mongol illustrated manuscript of a Mahābala text which is kept in the Bodleian and awaits further study. And there are also still some Central Asian Tibetan documents in the India Office Library (no. 389–391), which will one day have to be compared.

7

Āryasuvikrāntavikrāmiparipṛcchāprajñāpāramitānirdeśasārdhadvisāhasrikā-Bhagavatyāryaprajñāpāramitā. Bearbeitet von Dr. Tokumyo Matsumoto. Verlag Heibonsha, Tokyo, 1956. i–v, 102 pp.[1]

Dr. Matsumoto, who in 1932 and 1935 brought out the first two chapters of this Prajñāpāramitā text, has now edited it in its entirety. His text reproduces with meticulous accuracy the one and only manuscript which has survived, i.e. Cambridge Add. 1543. On a number of doubtful points I have compared Matsumoto's edition with the photographs of that Ms, and neither his eyesight nor his attention have ever been found wanting. Yüan-tsang's translation has been compared throughout, and a number of useful variants from it are given in Sanskrit translation in the footnotes. The Tibetan translation, which is of much greater value for text-critical purposes, has on the other hand not been consulted at all, and it clearly lies outside the field of Matsumoto's interests, as is

[1] This review has been modified and corrected on the basis of a correspondence with Prof. Shoren Ihara in 1959. The points raised here can now be checked against Hikata's edition (see below pp. 168–71) and my full English translation in *T*, 1973, 1–78.

also shown by his falsely attributing it (on p. iii) to the 11th rather than the ninth century.

On quite a number of occasions the Sanskrit text can be corrected from the Tibetan. At 8b, *na-āvedhyate* should be added after *nātra kiṃcid vedhyate*; at 12a, *jñānakarmaṇām* is omitted in the Tibetan, and may be a copyist's gloss; at 12b, (*na ca punar*) *dharmādharma-svabhāvena* (*saṃvidyate*) confirmed by the Chinese reads *chos ni chos-kyi ṅo-bo-ñid-kyis med do* in Tibetan. At 13a a whole sentence is spoiled: *na bodhih satvatayā prajñaptāniḥ sattvānubodho hi bodhir ity ucyate. bodhir satveti, yena jñātā, sa ucyate bodhisatva iti*. Here one must obviously read *niḥsatvā-*, and after *bodhir* and in front of *satveti* a *na* or *a-* must be inserted. For the Tibetan has: *byaṅ-chub ni sems-can-gyis btags-pa ma yin-gyis sems-can med-par khoṅ-du chud-pa ni byaṅ-chub ces bya'o/byaṅ-chub sems-can ma yin-par gaṅ-gis śes-pa de byaṅ-chub sems-dpa' shes bya' o*. At 13a the conjecture *pratividdhā-* seems confirmed by *rab-tu rtogs-pa*. At 24b *ā-jānanā, śes-par 'gyur-ba* is preferable to the *ajānanā* of the Ms; at 27a *jahāti* should, I think, twice by *jānāti* (*śés*); and where Matsumoto gives *yā cāsvabhāva-parijñā* nach dem Chinesischen verbessert as *yā ca*, etc., the Tibetan *ṅo-bo ñid med-par yoṅs-su śes-pa* confirms the Manuscript reading; at 31a *vā'gamanaṃ* should, of course, be *vā-āgamanaṃ* (*oṅ-ba*); at 37a the correction of Ms *vidyāyai* into the meaningless *avidyāyai* (cf. 35b, 62b, 97b) is not confirmed by the Tibetan *ri-g-pa'i*; at 39b *Suvikrāntavikrāmin, nākāśam* should be *Suvikrāntavikrāminn ākāśam*; at 63b the Ms reading *anidarśanena* is confirmed by *bstan-pa ma yin-par*; and *vā nidarśanena* three lines later should be *vā-anidarśanena*; at 66a a word has fallen out after *darśanaṃ vā*, i.e. *ṅes-par bstan-pa*, = *nirdarśanaṃ vā*; the curious negation in *nāpy* is not confirmed by Tibetan or Chinese; at 67a *kaścid aviparyāsaḥ* is required by the sense, and confirmed by the Tibetan (*phyin-ci log gaṅ yaṅ med-pa*). At 70b *sarvārambaṇaparicaryā* should be corrected to *sarvārambaṇa-parijñācaryā*(*dmigs-pa thams-cad yoṅs-su śes-pa'i spyod-pa*), and Matsumoto's correction of the Ms at n. 2 does not improve the sense and is not confirmed by the Tibetan. At 74a the manuscript reads *sarvajñānasamudghātān*, Matsumoto corrects to *-ghātā*, but the Tibetan *śes-pa thams-cad yaṅ-dag-par gshom-pa'i phyir* confirms the Ms. At 76b the Ms has, as a result of the erroneous transposition which I have explained in *JRAS*, 1948, pp. 39–40, *āvaraṇa* instead of *ārambaṇa* (*dmigs-pa*). At 82a, *harati*, following on *maitryā*, should be corrected to *spharati* (*khyab-par byed do*). 84a to 84b are somewhat distorted: *api carati* should be *api na carati* (*yaṅ mi spyod do*) in the first three as in the last three clauses, *vânityena vâdhruvena vâśāśvatena* should be read as *vā nityena*, etc., and *anātmanā* must be corrected to *ātmanā* (*bdag gam*). And at 97a we should read *aviparyāsa*, as at 69a.

These all appear to me to be certain corrections. The Tibetan confirms the Chinese against the Ms at 62b n. 9, 65a n. 4, 67b n. 5,

76a n. 1, 78a n. 3, 81a n. 3, 85 b n. 15, and at 67a n. 2 the Tibetan has, similar to the Chinese, *aviparyāsa-sthita ity ucyate*.

There are other instances where the deviations of the Tibetan from our manuscript seem to point to a different text. This is the case at 13b where the Tibetan omits *asatvasaṃjñāvibhāvanatayā*; at 35b–36a it is difficult to choose between *nāpy ebhir dharmair vinirmuktā prajñāpāramitā*, as confirmed by the Derge Kanjur, and the *chos de-dag-las rnam-par grol-ba yaṅ śes-rab-kyi pha-rol-tu phyin-pa'i phyir ro* of the Narthang. There is also no clear preference at 36b–37a where the Tibetan omits *kāraṇatvena vā akāraṇatvena vā*, and renders *anabhinirvṛttaye* by *mṅon-par 'grub-pa'i*, *upapattisamucchedāya* by *skye-ba kun-'byuṅ-ba'i*, and *nirvṛttaye vā anabhinirvṛttaye vā* by *grub-pa'i* and *mi grub-pa'i*. At 39b the Tibetan omits *vā parinispattyā*, at 40a it reads *mahatā-avabhāsa-*; at 40b it omits *aparinispannā prajñāpāramitā*, at 60b *anabhihāraḥ*; whether at 67a *yaś ca viparyasto* or *gaṅ phyin-ci log med-pa* gives the better sense, I have not been able to decide, and similarly at 77b where *cittānutpādaparijñā* and *sems skye-ba yoṅs-su śes-pa* seem to fit equally well.

A few passages are so corrupt that it is not easy to correct them with any degree of certainty. At 25b *yā āpāramitā sarvadharmāṇāṃ na śakyā nirdeṣṭuṃ* is somewhat unsatisfactory. Matsumoto corrects to *yā*, *ap-*, the Tibetan has *gaṅ chos thams-cad-kyi tshu-rol rtogs-pa ste/de ni bstan-par mi mus* (See now *T* 22). At 62a *nidarśanam upaiti votpaśyati vā* is not so easy to follow, and the Tibetan has: *ṅes-par bstan-par yaṅ ñe-bar 'gro-ba 'am ñe-bar 'gro-bar 'gyur-ba ma yin no*. At 67a the Ms has: *sarvā hi Suvikrāntavikrāmin caryā sa acaryāṃ utthāna-caryā-vikalpad viparyāso*. Matsumoto omits *acaryām*. The Tibetan suggests the correct reading: *spyod-pa thams-cad ni spyad-pa las byuṅ-ba daṅ/spyod-pa-la rnam-par rtog-pas phyin-ci log go* (cf. Hikata). At 74a *tenâlayā* should be: *te' anālayā* (they, without a settling place) /*de-dag gnas med*(!) *ciṅ*. At 76a I cannot see much meaning in *cittajam iti cetasaḥ pratiṣedhah eṣaḥ*, and *sems śes bya-ba de ni sems rab-tu rtog-pa'o* (*pratibodha*) seems easier to understand. Finally, there must be something wrong at 81a, where *bhāvyam* is first translated as *dṅos-po* and then afterwards as *bsgom-par bya-ba*.

The typography is generally excellent. There are, of course, a few dozen misprints, unavoidable in any work of this kind. The only ones likely to cause difficulties are *punaḥ* at 78a, *snigdhā* at 106b, and *yad* for *ṣaḍ* at 108b. At 78a the reading is not easy to decipher with complete certainty. *Ty* and *bhy* are notoriously difficult to distinguish in these manuscripts, and Matsumoto first reads *atyudbhūta* (*mṅon-par 'phags-pa*), and then *abhyudaya* (*mṅon-par'phags-pa*) (see Edgerton s.v.). I note in this context that at 112a the unusual form *ajāneya* for *ājāneya* is clearly attested by the Ms (although I would wish to emend on p. 98 line 16 the *ajāneyānām* into *anajāneyānām*). If Matsumoto has regularly *syand-* for *spand-* in 33a, 86a, 98b *spandanā* (*gYo-ba*), 74a *spandita*)*gYos-pa*), 99b *spanditāni* and 103b *vispānditānām,* he here reproduces an error which is frequent in Sanskrit Mss, but obscures the derivation and meaning of the term. The last two instances pose a delicate problem which faces any editor of Buddhist Sanskrit documents. Should he preserve the idiosyncrasies of his manuscripts, how ever ungrammatical they may be? Or should he at least add the grammatically correct form, so as to aid those who read these books for their contents?

Although they never seem to have found a commentator, the "Questions of Suvikrāntavikrāmin" are a valuable source of Prajñāpāramitā thought. They belong, together with the *Saptaśatikā* and *Vajracchedikā,* to that phase, between the fourth and sixth century, when attempts were made to cut loose from the framework and arrangement of the larger Sūtras and to re-state their message in fairly short works built up on principles of their own. The description of the merit to be derived from Prajñāpāramitā, which takes up excessive space in the *Śatasāhasrikā* and even in the *Vajracchedikā,* is here reduced to reasonable proportions. In the first two chapters we have a fine description of the mentality of those ready to receive this teaching (Partly translated in *E*, 1955, 27–31 and fully in *T*, 1973, 2–4, 18–22, 36–42). But the bulk of the work is devoted to the exposition of the basic metaphysical teachings, generally in the form of "litanies" which apply some given formula to a definite and often repeated number of categories. Fewer categories are listed than in the *Śatasāhasrikā*, and the standard lists show some remarkable peculiarities in this Sūtra. Of special interest is the frequent treatment of advanced Abhidharma problems. It is often allusive, and many of the terms are not fully intelligible to us at present. When we just read the text, almost everything seems fairly smooth and straightforward. The difficulties become apparent when we try to translate it, and soon we find that for quite a number of words no adequate or intelligible English equivalent can readily be found. Some time will therefore have to elapse before we can claim to fully understand the contents of this work. Without Prof. Matsumoto's self-denying labours, which have gone on over so many years, we could however not even begin with its study, and all scholars in this field owe him a profound debt of gratitude.

8

H. V. Günther. *Philosophy and Psychology in the Abhidharma.* Lucknow: Buddha Vihara, 1957. xii + 405 pp.

This study of the philosophical and psychological teachings of the Abhidharma goes beyond most previous works on the subject in that it is based on the documents of more than one school. For each problem the author adduces the opinions of representatives of the three most accessible lines of tradition—the Theravadins, the Sarvastivadins (as represented by Vasubandhu), and the Yogacarins. This method brings out the basic unity of all Buddhist thinking on Abhidharma, and the juxtaposition of the different views of the great Buddhist scholastics is at times most instructive and illuminating.

There are four chapters. The first suveys "Mind and its States"; the second deals with some aspects of "Meditation"; the third is entitled "The Interpretation of the world we live in", and discusses *rūpa*, perceptions and atoms; and the fourth, finally, explains the "Path". In this way all the basic topics of the Abhidharma are covered, and only one problem of general interest seems to have been omitted. Except for a brief remark on p. 6, there is nowhere a proper explanation of what a *dharma* is, and how it differs from a "thing". The epoch-making analysis of Stcherbatsky and his school has remained unnoticed.

The Sanskrit and Pali equivalents of technical terms are always accurately given, and their English translation is usually correct, and sometimes felicitous. A few of Dr. Günther's proposals are, however, unlikely to be generally accepted, as when he wants to render *rūpa* (form) by "Gestalt" (p. 151), *pratipad* (progress) as "attainment" (p. 403), and *prajñā* (wisdom) as "knowledge", or "analytical appreciative understanding" (p. 104), or, what is worse, as "discrimination" (p. 329). Great attention is paid throughout to the accurate definition of all the terms, to the religious significance of the Abhidharma exercises, and to the connections which can be established with contemporary Western philosophers, among whom C. D. Broad of Cambridge and Susanne K. Langer of New York are Dr. Günther's current favourites.

In other words, this new work of Dr. Günther's has all the makings of an excellent book. And yet it is not one, being disfigured by serious faults. We are here given the impression that either the author has had no predecessors at all, or that, if he had any, they were just a lot of fools. The Pali Text Society (e.g. pp. 179, 222), Prof. Murti (p. 322), and the great Prof. Stcherbatsky (p. 159) are each dismissed in short footnotes as beneath contempt. A Buddhist book is also not improved by the repeated use of phrases such as—"has been completely misunderstood", "have completely failed to grasp", etc.—or by the assertion that other scholars are "silly" (as on p. 7 where Günther himself is clearly in the wrong). Convinced that he is a thinker of outstanding genius, Günther constantly strives to distinguish himself from everyone else. He is thus driven to blandly state, without any proof, such absurdities as the following: "The reality of Samsāra has never been doubted and Buddhists never made the fatal mistake of judging it as an illusion (*māyā*)" (p. 291). The emphatic "never", twice repeated, in this extremely dubious sentence, is a good clue to Günther's mentality. It is not given to him to know how much he does *not* know, and so for 400 pp. he always speaks at the top of his voice, whether he is on objectively sure or on uncertain ground. This book is thus really more brilliant than weighty, and, though most intelligent and stimulating, is not fully reliable or authoritative—not only because of the author's lamentable polemical habits, but also because of the many bees (Tantric and others) which buzz about in his head. His remarks on *anattā* (p. 125) and the Buddha's compassion (pp. 307–8) are positively shoddy, his paean in praise of "Love" on pp. 157–9 is a gratuitous piece of special pleading, and when on p. 256 he comes to his well-known hobby-horse of "Sex" there is no holding him back at all.

Who then can benefit from reading this rather uneven book? For beginners it is unsuitable, as presupposing too much knowledge, and as being unsound on too many issues. But for the more advanced student it is a positive feast, to which he should treat himself as soon as he can. He will quickly understand what Buddhaghosa had in mind when he said that "those who study the Abhidhamma literature experience unending joy and serenity of mind".

9

Suvikrāntavikrāmi-paripṛcchā Prajñāpāramitā-Sūtra. Edited with an Introductory Essay by Ryusho Hikata. Kyushu University, Fukuoka, Japan, 1958. i–lxxxiii, 142 pp., 5 Tables.

When we consider the difficulty of getting Prajñāpāramitā texts into print, it is truly remarkable that two years after Matsumoto's publication of the *Suvikrāntavikrāmi-paripṛcchā* another edition of the same text should have been brought out in Japan. It is no reflection on Dr. Matsumoto's scholarship to say that Prof. Hikata's edition is the better of the two, and that scholars will use it in preference to his. The print is larger and easier to read, misprints (except for a few Tibetan words) are quite absent, and, what is most important, the text has been corrected with the help of the Tibetan. The punctuation also is much more rational than that of Matsumoto, which often positively impedes the understanding of the text. The comparison of four blockprints of the Tibetan translation (here also wrongly assigned to the 11th, instead of the 9th, century) has, incidentally, brought to light the interesting fact that "where there exists a disagreement between the Sk. text and the Ch. tr. it frequently occurs that some editions of the above four agree with Sk. and not with Ch., and the others with Ch. and not with Sk." (p. LXXX). This is not at all easy to explain.

Many of the corrections I proposed in my review (above pp. 163–6) have been adopted. Some minor improvements would, I think, still be possible. For instance, at 44, 1 we should read *-minn ākāśam*;

at 64, 9 *dhārayeyur('chaṅ -ba)* and *svādhyāyeran*; at 65, last line, *deva* is an error for *evaṃ* (*de-bshin-du*), and at 82, 1 the Ms reading *-ghātān* should be retained. Not all divergencies of the Tibetan from the Sanskrit have been marked, as for instance *avacanīya* at 9,6. Some occasional untidiness is observable—the exact Ms reading is sometimes not indicated, and many minor deviations from the Ms and from Matsumoto are not specially noted. This is generally harmless, except at 14,15 where the word *pratibuddha* is a conjecture given without a note indicating the pros and contras. Hikata's text has successfully removed many puzzling features of Matsumoto's edition. I am not altogether happy, however, about Prof. Hikata's obsession with classical Sanskrit. The longer I study the earlier Buddhist Sanskrit Mss, the more I come to the conclusion that the scribes' treatment of the Sandhi is not the result of sheer ignorance, but that they followed a definite method which may differ from that of the Brahmins, but is as legitimate and valid as theirs. I can see no useful purpose in the industry which Prof. Hikata has bestowed on "normalizing" the Sandhi throughout, and in the numerous footnotes devoted to this labour. What could be the point of a note like no. 13 on p. 115, "*sañcaya* = *Sk. saṃcaya*"? What else could it possibly be?

In addition to the text, the book contains a Bibliography of the Prajñāpāramitā Sūtras, Tables comparing the different versions of the Sūtra, and a long essay on the Prajñāpāramitā literature. The *Bibliography* is good and adequate for the Chinese material, but for the Sanskrit and Tibetan documents rather incomplete, and not without some errors. The *Tables* are very much superior to the previous ones which we owed to Watanabe (1908, 1933), Kajiyoshi (1944) and Yamada (1958). They will be a great help to all scholars who rapidly want to find their way through the vast material. The only complaint I have to make concerns the treatment of the divisions of the *Abhisamayālaṅkāra* (Table III), which is fairly unintelligible, and which would have been clearer if Prof. Hikata had adopted the numbering of the Tibetan tradition, which also Obermiller and myself have followed.

Now to the *Essay* itself. It first tries to define what *prajñāpāramitā* means, then classifies the Prajñāpāramitā-sūtras, attempts to determine the "Urtext of the Prajñāpāramitā-sūtra", to outline the later development of this literature, to arrive at a decision about the author of the *Ta-chich-tu-lun*, and to give the main facts about the *Suvikrānta* sūtra. As the first treatise in English on the development of the Prajñāpāramitā literature this essay deserves some consideration.

It is, first of all, self-evident to all students of the Prajñāpāramitā that (1) the Smaller Sūtras are the latest of all, and (2) that the Large *Prajñāpāramitā* (in 18,000, 25,000 and 100,000 *ślokas*) is later than the *Aṣṭasāhasrikā*. Hikata has in fact given us a very fine survey of the additions which the Large *Prajñāpāramitā* has made to the

Aṣṭasāhasrikā. Since Japanese scholars are chiefly interested in the Chinese sources, they are apt to unduly neglect the verse version of the *Aṣṭasāhasrikā*, i.e. the *Ratnaguṇasaṃcayagāthā*, which was translated only in A.D. 1001, but which by the archaic character of its language would seem to be one of the most ancient documents, although, of course, in its present form it has been re-arranged by Haribhadra. Japanese and European scholars have so far worked on these problems independent of one another, and it is quite stimulating to compare their results. There are two different suggestions:

1. Kajiyoshi (1943) believed that the original *Prajñāpāramitā* was roughly identical with the first chapter of the *Aṣṭasāhasrikā*, as it exists in Lokakṣema's translation of A.D. 179. This would to some extent agree with Conze's suggestion (1958), that the oldest *Prajñāpāramitā* is to be found in the first chapter, or perhaps in the first two chapters, of the *Ratnaguṇasaṃcayagāthā*.

2. M. Suzuki suggested that the version in 4,000 *ślokas*, or the 5th division of Yüan-tsang, represents the earliest text of the *Prajñāpāramitā*.

Hikata rejects Kajiyoshi's theory on grounds which seem to me unconvincing (p. xxxx), and believes that "the first and most original Prajñāpāramitā contained from chapter 1 to ch. 25 (Parīndanā)" of the translation of Lokakṣema (p. xxxxiv). He adds that "it did not contain as yet those parts concerning Akṣobhya-buddha". In my article on "The composition of the Aṣṭasāhasrikā" (in *BSOAS*, XIV, 2, 1952, = *S*172–5) I came to a very similar conclusion. The only objection I have to regarding a lengthy text like this as the original one stems from the conviction that all Mahāyāna Sūtras were originally very short, as we can see with the *Rāṣṭrapālaparipṛcchā* (when, as Prof. de Jong has done, the Sanskrit text is compared with T 170), with the *Suvarṇaprabhāsa*, etc. No certainty is, however, possible in view of the scanty evidence we possess, and the extremely involved "Pedigree of Mahā-Prajñāpāramitā-Sūtras", which Prof. Hikata gives as Table V, is surely not warranted by the few stray facts at our disposal.

The chronology of the smaller Sūtras, with the exception of the *Vajracchedikā*, is less controversial. Hikata places the *Hṛdaya* at 350, the *Saptaśatikā* at 450, the *Suvikrānta* at 500, and these dates are unlikely to be disputed. As for the *Vajracchedikā*, he claims that "it must have existed before the middle of the 3rd Cent., for, as Prof. Ui recently suggested, the two verses from this Sūtra are quoted in the Ch. tr. (by Dharmarakṣa in A.D. 289) of Vimaladattāsūtra" (lxxxiii). Since there are actually *three* verses in the *Vajracchedikā* (i.e. 26a, b, 32a), I looked up the passage referred to (T 338, vol. xii, p. 92c). All I could find was the verse of ch. 26a, with some hints of the contents of 26b. In the "Diamond Sūtra" this verse has no connection with anything that precedes or follows it, and may well have been annexed from some other Sūtra, particularly as a similar verse has found its way into *Theragāthā* 469. I myself would prefer a later date, (1) because of the term *saṃdhāya* in ch. 6, which otherwise occurs only in the *Saptaśatikā* and *Suvikrānta*; (2) because of the preoccupation with "the last 500 years", quite absent in the earlier Sutras, and more fitting for a period when the original duration of the Dharma for 1,000 years was believed to be nearing its end.

As for the *Ta-chih-tu-lun*, Prof. Hikata, like Prof. Demiéville before him (in *JAs*, 1950, pp. 375–95), proves that parts of the commentary are clearly due to Kumārajīva himself (liii–lxiii). He maintains that Nāgārjuna is indubitably the author of the remainder (lxiii–lxxii), although we may prefer to await Prof. Lamotte's considered judgment before wholeheartedly agreeing to this thesis.

In a work of this kind a few minor slips are unavoidable. On p. xxxxiii *Gaṅgā-upāsikā* is ch. 60, and not ch. 16. On p. xxxiv *Subhūtiparivarta* is at *Aṣṭa* II 44 *Subhūteḥ parivarta*, which *AAA* explains as *nirdeśa*. On p. xxxxii we note that at *Aṣṭa* XXVI 435 the second of the four stages of a Bodhisattva is *caryāpratipanna*, as evident from *AAA* and the Tibetan. Ch. 10 of the *Aṣṭa* is *Dhāraṇāguṇa* (L), and the differences between the original and the revised *Pañcaviṃśatisāhasrikā* are much greater than the author suggests on p. L. The English is remarkably good, and always intelligible. We are indeed greatly indebted not only to Prof. Hikata, but also to those of his colleagues, pupils and friends who have raised the funds which made the publication of this really excellent work possible.

10

A. J. Bahm. *Philosophy of the Buddha.* Rider & Company, London, 1958. 175 pp.

M. Eliade. *Yoga. Immortality and Freedom.* Routledge & Kegan Paul, London, 1958. XXII + 529 pp.

"That Gotama was misunderstood should be clear to everyone" (p. 26)—so Prof. Bahm begins his argument. This lapidary sentence is by no means as self-evident as he seems to assume. The Lord Buddha himself,—somewhat democratically addressed by his first name throughout the book,—was not at all aware of being 'misunderstood'. For 40 years he taught, and gathered many disciples, and on the whole he seems, unlike Hegel two millennia later, to have been fairly contented with them.

But even granting that everyone so far has misunderstood "Gotama",—what then enables just Mr. Bahm now at last, 2,500 years later, to penetrate to the original teachings? On the face of it his qualifications seem to be tenuous in the extreme. A teacher of philosophy at the University of New Mexico, he spent nine months in Rangoon, read English translations of Pali Texts, and acquired some smattering of Oriental languages ("The Pali term, *sangha*, like its Sanskrit ancestor, *sam-gha* . . ." (!) (p. 131). On this basis he comes to the conclusion that the Buddha, an exponent of "our commonsense" (p. 150), taught some of the verities current in the U.S.A. at present. All that his doctrine amounts to is the "very simple" principle that "happiness is to be found in accepting things as they are" (p. 19). Brought up on the current "misunderstandings" of his doctrine, we will be relieved to hear that "to choose to be choiceless is almost on a par with suicide. Gotama did not advocate complete choicelessness, but only relaxed choosing" (p. 154). Nevertheless, the Buddha had not yet reached the full truth as it has meanwhile revealed itself ["Gotama did not wholly understand reality" (p. 27)], and a final chapter (pp. 150–162) criticizes his position as not being sufficiently "realistic", "voluntaristic", "idealistic" and "instrumentalistic". Oh, how far is New Mexico from the Deer Park of Benares!

Prof. Brahm's thesis has no factual basis, and there is no need to discuss it. "The Buddha's original doctrine" is a will-o'-the-wisp which is caught easily by those whom scholarship does not weigh down. It will be chased after by many more to come, and nobody is really any the worse for it, except for a few unsuspecting readers and long-suffering reviewers.

As distinct from Prof. Bahm, Prof. Eliade has superb scholarship, a proper respect for tradition, and a mind flexible enough to learn from other cultures. His book is likely to remain the standard authority on Yoga for our generation. Eliade has a thorough knowledge of the Sanskrit language, he has soaked himself at Calcutta in the traditions of India under Prof. Surendranath Dasgupta whom he describes as his "guru", and he has a sympathetic understanding of Yoga as a system of thought which altogether transcends the limitations of our own civilization. His book falls into roughly three parts: First of all we have two chapters (pp. 3–100) describing "the doctrines and techniques of Yoga, as they are systematized and formulated in Patanjali's *Yoga-sutras* and the commentaries on them." The second part (pp. 101–358) then describes the form which this Yoga takes in the long tradition of Indian thought—beginning with the *Vedas*, then proceeding to the *Mahabharata*, to Buddhism, Tantrism, Alchemy and the aboriginal cults of India. The third part (pp. 367–432) is headed "Additional Notes", and contains a staggering wealth of literary information on the topics discussed in the first two parts. It is followed by a "List of Books Cited" (pp. 435–80) and by a copious Index (pp. 483–529). With increasing fascination I have read every word of the whole book, and it seems to be about as accurate as a book can possibly be. This is, I think, worth stating explicitly, when speaking of a subject like Yoga, in which bogus productions outweigh the genuine statements of the truth by about a thousand to one.

Mircea Eliade, a Rumanian by birth, a Frenchman by culture,

and now an inhabitant of Chicago by economic necessity, is one of the great men of our time,—one of the few who take to spiritual things like the proverbial duck to the water. Convinced of the shallow superficiality of the views and ideals which have led to the noisy turmoil of the present day, he has turned back to the archaic techniques with which the men of the Palaeolithic age mastered the problems of life and death, and of which Shamanism and Yoga are the two most intelligible survivals. He must have incorporated these techniques somehow in his own being, for he never puts a foot wrong, however slippery the path that leads to the central cave. The aim is "to emancipate man from his human condition, to conquer absolute freedom, to realize the unconditioned" (p. 95). That such an aim should have been envisaged, nay, that it should actually have been realized,—that is momentous news, indeed, and Eliade's masterpiece makes us almost believe that it is true.

Readers who see me dismissing Mr. Bahm as nearly illiterate, and praising M. Eliade as nearly faultless, may well believe that my mind is apt to run to extremes. If they will take the trouble to examine the two books for themselves, they may well agree that I have merely spoken the sober truth.

II

Benoytōsh Bhattacharya. *The Indian Buddhist Iconography*. Second Rev. and Enl. Ed. xxxiii + 478 pp., 357 illus. K. L. Mukhodpahyay, Calcutta, 1958.

The first edition of Professor Bhattacharya's book in 1924 was a major event in Buddhist scholarship. Now, thirty-four years later, a second has come out, enriched by much additional material. It must be welcomed as the work of a most distinguished scholar who has devoted his entire life to the elucidation of the Buddhist Tantras. The book is based in the main on two sources, i.e. the *Sādhanamālā* and the *Niṣpannayogāvāli*, two 12th century Tantric manuals which Professor Bhattacharya has edited between 1925 and 1949. To the extent that his book adheres to these sources, it has considerable value. The reader will find many useful extracts from the Sanskrit texts, with translations which, without being over-precise, are generally adequate. Professor Bhattacharya's unconcern with literal accuracy shows itself in his treatment of the term *svābhā*, which is correctly explained on p. 438, but translated in the most variant ways on pp. 44, 52, 84, 226, etc. And, if my own rendering of the *Tārā-sādhana* (in *Buddhist Meditation*, pp. 133–9) is anything to go by, Bhattacharya's translation of the same text on pp. 20–23 contains between 25 to 40 distinct inaccuracies. In addition to his translations, the author has looked far and wide for images which depict these *sādhanas*—statues, manuscripts, etc., in India and as far away as Java and Lamaist Peking, but with a curious neglect of Tibet, China, and Japan. Of China, Professor Bhattacharya only considers the "Two Lamaist Pantheons" described by Clark, and on the basis of these he decides whether an image is "popular in China" or not. In consequence we are told that Kṣitigarbha "is rarely represented" (p. 85), when in fact Ji-zō is about as common as any Bodhisattva can be. Japan completely falls outside the author's ken, although the Shingon pantheon would have been most relevant to his purpose. The choice of illustrations is apparently guided by the rather strange "old Tibetan tradition" which "declares that in the matter of art Bengal comes first, Nepal second, while the Tibetans and Chinese are the worst" (p. 6). It would, I suppose, be uncharitable to assume Professor Bhattacharya to be a Bengali?

On p. 384 the author states the purpose of his work, which is meant to be "a practical handbook for the guidance of Museologists who have to handle large numbers of images of gods and goddesses with strange faces, weapons and poses." This purpose is certainly well fulfilled, and Professor Bhattacharya is quite correct in saying of his book that "within the limited scope, it has enough information of the highest practical value to the students of iconography, and this value is enhanced by the inclusion of photographs of excellent sculptures, bronzes and original Nepalese drawings procured with difficulty and at high cost" (p. 384).

But Professor Bhattacharya has not confined himself to an accumulation of useful and interesting facts. He has also added an interpretation, and that has little to recommend it. In fact, a positive woolliness envelopes all and everthing, and the explanations show little historical sense or philosophical penetration. The assertion that the *Guhyasamāja* dates back to A.D. 300 does not gain in probability from being repeated throughout the book dozens of times, in and out of season, like a wearisome incantation. On p. 143 we are told that "the conception of Avalokiteśvara is as old as the third century B.C. He was first ushered into existence by the Mahāsānghikas, about the time of Aśoka, in their work, entitled, Mahāvastu Avadāna," etc. It is difficult to say anything intelligent in the face of so much self-confidence.

The terminology of the explanations is quite antiquated, and in conflict with that of the texts which Professor Bhattacharya himself has edited. Where they speak of "Jinas", and "Prajñās" or "Bhagavatīs," he always speaks of "Dhyāni-Buddhas" and "Śaktis." Having committed himself to the absurd idea of "Dhyāni-Buddhas," he has to distinguish them from the so-called "Manushi-Buddhas" or "Mortal Buddhas," and feels bound to reproduce uncritically all the misconceptions of Hodgson (1833) and Oldfield (1879), which on p. 79 have hardened into an absolutely impenetrable confusion. The fundamental difference between *Bhaktic* and *Tantric* deities (see my *Buddhism*, p. 189) has not been appreciated, and they are all treated as the same. But if a "Dhyāni-Buddha" was "not required to pass through the stages of a Bodhisattva" (p. 47), then the bhaktic Amitābha and Akṣobhya of the 2nd and 3rd century are quite different persons from the Tantric deities of the same name, because the names which they had as Bodhisattvas are explicitly stated in the relevant texts. Far too much reliance is placed on sources which are out-of-date and unscholarly. Hodgson (1833) alone is the authority for the author's views on the Ādi-Buddha, "the primordial monotheistic god" (p. 42), and Getty is quoted (on p. 43) in support of the thesis that Vajradhara's "Śakti" has the name of Prajñāpāramitā, when the *sādhana* (p. 44) clearly speaks only of *prajñā*, as with all the other deities. Apart from one of Bhattacharya's own works, the Bibliography includes only books published before 1939. In 1949 Mlle. Mallmann gave a rational account of the various manifestations of Avalokiteśvara, (see above pp. 150–4) and on a much smaller scale I have tried to do the same for the Prajñāpāramitā in 1949 and 1951 (ORIENTAL ART II 2 and III 3 = *S*243–68). None of all this has ever reached Professor Bhattacharya. Lately I have been struck by the curiously old-fashioned air which pervades nearly all Buddhist studies produced in India during the last 10 years. Over and over again they reiterate the same old fallacies, and they seem to be quite out of touch with the vigorous research carried on in Europe, North America, and Japan. I very much fear that this is largely due to the restrictions which the Indian government has placed on the import of foreign books. Mr. Nehru ought to realize that the very small saving in foreign currency is paid for by a considerable decrease in India's standing in the world, and so may prove fairly expensive in the end.

In the absence of a rational scheme, the arrangement of the deities in this book is very bewildering, and gives the impression of an unrelieved chaos. The problem is a difficult one, but Gruenwedel (1900) and Pott (1951) have certainly done better. Here, however, the same deity occurs over and over again, and the logical coherence of the Tantric system is completely obscured, although a full Index minimizes the damage to some extent.

Far too many sentences in this book are, I am sorry to say, meaningless, misleading or positively absurd. It is, for instance, hard to know what to make of the statement on p. 440 that "the Buddhas are innumerable and have a hierarchy among them, the different orders being Pratyeka, Śrāvaka (!), Samyak Sambuddha, Jina, Arhat (!), Tathāgata, and the like." Minor inaccuracies are very frequent. For instance, on p. 40 the Dharma and the Samgha are interposed; on p. 392 the *Daśabhūmikaśāstra* should, of course, be a *-sūtra*; and so on, and so on. The illustrations are numerous and interesting, but whereas the drawings have come out well, the photographs often are faint and too indistinct to be of much use. Misprints occur on nearly every page, but rarely distort the sense. On p. 48 I found the astonishing statement that Vajrasattva "is generally regarded as the priest of the five Dhyāni Buddhas," and I assumed "priest" to be a misprint for "first," until I saw the same statement repeated on p. 74.

Generally speaking I rather enjoy writing unfavourable reviews, since they allow me to vent my spleen on the ignorance of mankind. On this occasion I am sad and sick at heart for what I have had to say. For Professor Bhattacharya is a great scholar whose powers have now failed, and who has unfortunately allowed himself to be persuaded by an ambitious publisher to write a book which is unworthy of all that he has stood for in the past.

12

G. Tucci. *Minor Buddhist Texts,* Part II (Serie Orientale Roma, Vol. IX, 2), Rome, 1958.

A. Ferrari. *Mk'yen Brtse's Guide to the Holy Places of Central Tibet.* Compl. and ed. by L. Petech, with the coll. of H. Richardson (Serie Orientale Roma, Vol. XVI), Rome, 1958.

The eighth century Tibetan debate between Indians and Chinese is rapidly becoming one of the best-documented events in Buddhist history. Since Professor Demiéville's work of 1952 it has come to be known as the "Council of Lhasa", but now Professor Tucci (pp. 32 sq.) claims that one should rather speak of the "Debate of Bsam-yas", although it appears from pp. 285–7 that Professor Demiéville only imperfectly concurs with this proposal. Wherever it may have taken place, the debate is of great historical and doctrinal interest. Historically it marked, if it did not decide, the preponderance of Pāla Buddhism in Tibet for more than eleven centuries, and the suppression of the Chinese, especially Ch'an teachings, which had been quite strong until then. Doctrinally, it shows the astonishing variety of religious opinion even within the Mahāyāna branch of Buddhism. A Roman Catholic and a primitive Methodist are more likely to agree on the interpretation of the Bible, than Indians and Chinese on the meaning of the early Mahāyāna Scriptures. In India the teachings of the *Prajñāpāramita*, and so on, had logically developed through Nāgārjuna, "Maitreyanātha" and Candrakīrti into the Pāla synthesis of Haribhadra and Śāntirakṣita. In China the same ideas were transformed out of all recognition by the contact with Neo-Taoism, the vast scholastic apparatus of the Hindus was rejected as so much ballast, and between 400 and 700, through the work of men like Seng-chao, Tao-sheng and Hui-nêng, there emerged an indigenous Chinese quietism, distinguished by the somewhat mysterious and challenging watchword of "sudden enlightenment", which in this form gives no sense from the point of view of the Indian tradition. In 792–4 the two lines of development confronted each other in Tibet, and they could no longer comprehend one another. So great indeed is the divergence of the two viewpoints that even at present no scholar has yet been able to do equal justice to both. To each, one of the two must appear more obvious and plausible. The debate was officially decided in favour of "the Mādhyamikas", and I do not understand why Professor Tucci seems to think that "this did not say very much, because neither school could deny resting on that system for a starting point" (p. 52). It was clearly a verdict in favour of the Indian, as against the Chinese tradition, and the future course of Tibetan Buddhism bears this out.

Kamalaśīla, the spokesman of the "Mādhyamikas", wrote his three *Bhāvanā-kramas* after the debate was over (p. 41). The first explains the doctine of the Mahāyāna, the second how it can be meditated upon, and the third what is the result of that meditation. [The third will be edited by Professor Tucci in *Minor Buddhist Texts*, Part III, S.O.R. XLIII, 1971, 31 pp.] The second seems to survive only in Tibetan. The Sanskrit text of the first has now been edited by Professor Tucci (pp. 187–229), together with the Tibetan translation (pp. 229–82), and an English summary of its contents (pp. 157–82). From the rather indifferent Chinese translation, "Le Concile de Lhasa" (pp. 335–5) had only given an "analyse sommaire", chiefly indicating the quotations it contains. The first *Bhāvanākrama* is now revealed as a straightforward *exposé* of the career of a Bodhisattva according to the tenets of Pāla Buddhism, and its interest lies chiefly in the numerous precise definitions of technical terms. There is little, if any, direct reference to the doctrine of "instantaneous enlightenment", which is not refuted explicitly, but rather disposed of indirectly by the careful enumeration of the steps of the development which gradually proceeds from the "first thought of enlightenment" to the final *buddhabhūmi*, which ensues on the tenth stage of *dharma-meghā* if and when there arises *sarvasmin jñeye sarvākāram asaktam apratihataṃ jñānam.* A further reference to the debate can be seen in the care with which the orthodox meaning of "no-thought" is explained on pp. 211–214.

In addition, Professor Tucci's new book throws considerable light on the history of Ch'an Buddhism in Tibet. On pp. 68–101 he prints the Tibetan text and English translation of an important rÑiṅ-ma-pa document, i.e., the chapters of the *bKa' thaṅ sde lṅa* which record the Ch'an doctrines and their teachers. "This also implies that after the split, which occurred at the death of Hui-nêng in A.D. 713, the Hva śaṅ Mahāyāna considered himself and was considered by his followers as the authentic perpetuator of the teaching of Bodhidharma" (p. 64). Professor Tucci also shows that by no means all the Indians sided with Kamalaśīla, and that some of them, like Vairocana and Vimalamitra, who have had a great influence on Tibetan thought, favoured many of the tenets of Ch'an. Thirdly he maintains that the Ch'an ideas survived, more or less underground, in the rDzogs-chen branch of the rÑiṅ-ma-pa, on which a further study is announced for the future (p. 122). Preparatory to it we find here (pp. 122–53) summarized those works in the Tanjur which are ascribed to persons connected with the Debate. One of the most important sources for the rDzogs-chen doctrines is an extremely rare collection of heretical Tantras, the *rÑiṅ-ma-pa rGyud 'bum.* Professor Tucci possesses a copy, in 25 volumes, of the sDe dge print, and a manuscript of the same collection, probably from Sikkim, seems also to exist in the India Office Library. Professor Tucci gives us here only two pages of extracts (pp. 62, 3), but more is promised for the future. After we have become better acquainted with the contents of this collection, we will be able to decide whether the undoubted similarities between rDzogs-chen and Ch'an are due to borrowing, or to a parallel unfolding of trends latent in Buddhism for a long time.

This brief summary may to some extent indicate the wealth of new material offered in this book. In addition there is much useful and stimulating comment on questions of detail, like the date of the lDan dKar-ma Catalogue (pp. 46–8).

The second publication of the S.O.R. derives from the posthumous papers of the gifted Alfonsa Ferrari, who died in 1954 at the early age of 35. Mkhyen-brtse (1820–92), a rÑiṅ-ma-pa Lama, spent most of his life on pilgrimage in Central Tibet, and from his personal experience and the current *dkar chag* literature he composed his own Guide, which is here edited (pp. 1–33), and translated. Professor Petech has collected an incredible amount of information about places, persons, buildings, and images from the relevant literature, and Mr. Hugh Richardson, for nine years British agent in Lhasa, has added many of his own observations, and also provided 53 photographs. At the end there is a clear map, and three indices (pp. 173–99) facilitate access to the many facts presented here. This sumptuous publication is a model of its kind, and confirms the impression that Rome is now becoming one of the most lively centres of Buddhist learning in Europe, rivalling even the Ecole de Paris in its output.

13

A. F. Wright. *Buddhism in Chinese History*. Stanford University Press (London: O.U.P.), 1959. xiv + 144, pp. 8 illus.

It is a remarkable achievement on the part of Professor Wright that in six lectures which cover no more than 127 small pages, he has given us an account of two millennia of Chinese Buddhism which is readable and accurate, in close contact with recent research and alive to the social forces which dominated the scene at any given time. Although, as he candidly tells us, "modern historical studies of China 'still' amount to little more than a tentative reconnaissance over a largely uncharted field" (p. 5), an interim report on what has become known during the "last four decades" is certainly most welcome.

Professor Wright distinguishes four great periods, which are "given names that suggest successive modes of interaction between

Buddhism and the culture it was invading" (p. 7). First, the "period of preparation" (A.D. 63–317), during which the breakdown of the Han Empire made the Chinese receptive to alien ideas, while at the same time the Buddhists took the first steps towards adapting their religion to Chinese culture. Then there is the "period of domestication" (317–598) when, both in the South and in the North, under widely differing circumstances, Buddhism established itself as a creed widespread among all classes of society, and in the course of which the Buddhists gained a much clearer understanding of what their own religion, as distinct from Taoism, really taught. Next we reach the height of the curve in the "period of independent growth" (*ca.* 589–900) when "Buddhism was fully and triumphantly established throughout China" (p. 82). The great persecution of 842–45 and the revival on Confucianism then "undermined its vitality" (p. 84) and led to the fourth period, that of "appropriation" (*ca.* 900–1900). Buddhist ideas and practices now become more and more "sinified", less and less differentiated from Taoist beliefs, though they continue to persist in an attenuated form and are never quite absorbed, swallowed up, assimilated without trace. In a particularly stimulating chapter (pp. 108–27) Professor Wright finally discusses "the role and significance of Chinese Buddhism in the twentieth century" and also makes some "general observations" "about the characteristics of Chinese civilization" which are to some extent inspired by a concern about the future of Communism, another 'alien religion', in that country.

Professor Wright is a good scholar who makes few mistakes. On p. 4 the quotation from Ranke cannot be right, and on p. 35 n. 10 "visions" must surely be a misprint for "versions". If anything is missing in this book it is perhaps an awareness of the wealth of truly spiritual ideas which Chinese Buddhism generated when it was at the summit of its glory. It may, however, well be held that it is not the historian's function to deal with phenomena as intangible as "spiritual intuitions" usually turn out to be. Also it may seem rather invidious to call the Mahayana "a politically incompetent religion" and unwise to connect its decline with its inability to build a "church" "which could achieve the socio-political dominance that Christianity once had in the Western world" (p. 106). For could it not be argued that at one time the politically "incompetent" just as well as the "competent" religion managed to dominate society, whereas at present both equally are reduced to a position where their pronouncements, outside the areas deficient in industrial power, fall on deaf ears unless they happen to suit the convenience of the actual rulers? Whatever historians may say, I still persist in believing that a religion's unworldliness is its greatest asset. Could there be anything more unworldly than the gospel of Christ as expounded in the *Epistle to the Galatians*? And yet, what power radiated from it, what influence, what modification in the pattern of life!

14

D. L. Snellgrove. *The Hevajra tantra: a critical study*. (London Oriental Series, Vol. 6.) 2 Vols.: xv, 149 pp., front., plate; xi, 188 pp. London, etc.: Oxford University Press, 1959.

For the first time a major Buddhist Tantra has now been edited in such a way as to invite study instead of repelling all but the most hardy. Those who have at one time or other struggled with the corruptions of the *Mañjuśrīmūlakalpa*, the tiny print of the 1919 edition of the *Śrīcakrasambhāra*, or even B. Bhattacharyya's *Guhyasamāja* which is 'critical' without, however, taking the Tibetan into account, will appreciate what Dr. Snellgrove and the O.U.P. have done for us. Vol. II contains a clearly printed Sanskrit text, with the Tibetan translation readily accessible on the opposite page, and followed by the *Yogaratnamālā*, a Sanskrit commentary by Kāṇha, which is easy to use because the words commented upon stand out in italics. The editor must be congratulated on having so successfully coped with the unenviable task of producing a reasonably accurate and plausible text from a few late Nepalese manuscripts.

The introduction (I, pp. 1–46) gives much useful information about the historical background of this text, and also dispels some current misunderstandings such as the belief that the 'feminine partners' are known in the Buddhist Tantras as *śaktis* (I, p. 44). Dr. Snellgrove stresses the presence in this text of 'notions that are not Buddhist, in the sense that they are not properly assimilated, and so seem to exist in contradiction with the wider context' (p. 7, cf. II, 18). This is quite obvious for many of the rites and practices but as far as ideas are concerned I have found only one instance of definite unorthodoxy, and that is rather a doubtful one. I, v, 16 seems to ascribe the creation of the world to Wisdom—an idea possible in Gnosticism, but quite out of place in Buddhism. If, however, the reading of MS. A be adopted, we get the meaning '*Prajñā* is called Genetrix because she generates the Jina of the world', and that is no more than one of the hoary commonplaces of the *Prajñāpāramitā* (e.g. *Śatas.*, ch. 33). The other manuscripts, the metre, the Tibetan translation, and the commentaries, on the other hand, bear out Dr. Snellgrove's interpretation, which no Buddhist could fail to deplore.

Dr. Snellgrove shows convincingly that the Tantra is a legitimate development of Buddhism, and that the charges of 'degeneration' are without foundation. But some doubts remain even after we have given due weight to his arguments. Association with *yoginīs* may well be a useful aid to enlightenment, but the power-seeking magic which is mentioned again and again is bound to disconcert even the most tolerant observer. From the very heights of spirituality we are switched abruptly to childish advice on how to stop armies, and such things. The nature of this transition is not adequately explained here, or anywhere else.

It is only Dr. Snellgrove's translation which may perhaps invite a few critical comments. To begin with, I find it hard to agree with his assertion that 'the work benefits considerably from its transference into English' (I, p. 10). On the contrary, not only has the melody and swing of the Sanskrit verses been lost, but also much of their precision has been blurred. The translation aims at being literal, except for the sexual passages (I, pp. 8, 10) which are either glossed over or wilfully obscured (as at I, x, 5–7). Psychologists and anthropologists must be warned that without recourse to the Sanskrit original they can form no adequate idea of what actually happened. Some of the practices of the Hevajra Yogins seem to have been similar to those depicted in Mulk Rāj Anand's recently published *Kamakala*. In their origin they are clearly non-Buddhistic, and while within Buddhism they may at times have been actually carried out by "fools" (I, pp. 43, 46), they were soon interpreted as mere symbols for spiritual developments within the psyche of the Yogin (I, p. 5, n. 2, pp. 8–9).

Without the aids which Dr. Snellgrove has so copiously provided, few readers would succeed in getting very much meaning out of the Sanskrit text. There are a few occasions, however, when he himself seems not to have caught its sense very well. At I, x, 37 *mahā-bhautikaskandkaḥ* does not mean 'the group of skandhas', but, as also shown by vv. 38–40, "the mass of the great physical elements". The phrase *A-kāro mukhaṃ sarvadharmāṇām ādyanutpannatvāt* is the first sentence of the famous Arapacana alphabet in the *Prajñāpāramitā* (e.g. *Śatas*, p. 1450), and the two alternative renderings at pp. 50 and 109 are both wide off the mark. Important words are sometimes omitted, as at I, viii, 54; II, iii, 2; II, iv, 47 and 93; on occasions the translation is unduly and misleadingly free, as at I, viii, 36 or II, iv, 32–4; and at I, i, 8 and II, ii, 22 and 51 the author seems to employ an obscure "twilight language" of his own. At II, ii, 1 "goad" is a misprint for "gourd", and "waving" on p. 91 should probably be "wavering". To call the Tanjur a "Tenjur" seems to fulfil no useful purpose.

In view of the strange terminology of this text, the elaborate glossary (I, pp. 131–41), is quite invaluable. It is both informative and reliable. The statement that *vidyā* "is used in the *Hevajra tantra* exclusively in the sense of 'feminine partner'"seems, however, not to be borne out by II, ii, 10.

This is an unusually fine pioneer study of a rather obscure phase of Buddhism which has lasted for many centuries. It appears to have left few, if any, works of outstanding literary merit, but its psychological and historical interest is nevertheless surprisingly great. Confronted with the scornful disapproval of their social superiors, the "outcasts and voluntary outcasts" (I, p. 11) who initiated this trend of thought covered up their tracks as best they could. At last historical research is catching up with them. Dr. Snellgrove is, in fact, the first person who has made their mental processes comprehensible, although even he has not succeeded in making them appear either attractive or worthy of imitation.

15

E. Zuercher. *The Buddhist Conquest of China.* 2 vols. vi + 468 pp. E. J. Brill, Leiden, 1959.

It stands to reason that an ancient and mature civilization like that of China must to some extent transform any ideas imported into it from the outside. At the moment there is much speculation on how Marxism will fare in the People's Republic, and how far contact with the pre-existing Confucian and Taoist beliefs will alter its structure. Likewise Buddhism, an Indian doctrine, was after its introduction into China clearly modified by the new environment in which it found itself. It is, however, not at all easy to determine how deep this influence went, and the problem is indeed singularly intractable. Some scholars, convinced that national characteristics are bound to override religious traditions, maintain that the Chinese never actually understood Indian Buddhism, and contend that all that was really alive in the Buddhism of China, especially Amidism and Ch'an, had only slight connections with India and was in fact a creation of the Chinese mind from its own antecedents. This extreme view has recently gained much ground among Sinologues who are only imperfectly acquainted with Sanskrit Buddhist documents.

At the other extreme we have the view that Buddhism is the same everywhere. While a certain number of its Chinese followers may well have misunderstood it, there were always many who did not, and who understood it just as Indians did. The cultural tinge may have affected merely the veneer and not the core of the teaching, and cultural particularities cannot destroy the unity of Buddhist spirituality, which is essentially the same in India, China, Tibet or Japan. A study of Buddhist art would I think, largely confirm this thesis. Where ideas are concerned, the difficulty lies in that we cannot directly look into the minds of Chinese Buddhists who died 1600 years ago. All we have to go by are the words which they used, and they are often Chinese terms taken from the Taoist Scriptures. To take a simple example: Where Sanskrit books speak of *mārga* (The Path), the Chinese have *Tao*. How many of the far-reaching non-Buddhist connotations of *Tao* would then be in the minds of the Chinese who used the term? To merely raise the question shows what we are up against.

For a whole century European scholars had viewed Chinese as a mere perpetuation of Indian Buddhism. In the 'thirties some Chinese scholars, like Hu Shih, T'ang Yung-t'ung and Fung Yu-lan, animated by a re-nascent nationalism, adduced much evidence for the existence of a specifically Chinese Buddhist thinking. Later on, Walther Liebenthal devoted most of his energies to substantiating their suggestions. In 1948 he published in Peking a book of fundamental importance, *The Book of Chao*, about Seng-chao, one of the disciples of Kumarajiva. He followed this up with quite a profusion of further studies, which all tend to stress the uniqueness of Chinese Buddhism. He leaves us in no doubt that to him Chinese Buddhism, if we except a few scholastic and purely monkish developments, seems far more Chinese than Buddhism, and he has stated his opinions quite unmistakably in two articles in 1952 (*Asiatische Studien*, VI, 116–129 and *The Visvabharati Quarterly* XVIII, 3). Dr. Liebenthal's publications have drawn the attention of scholars to the formative years of Chinese Buddhism, and especially the fourth century. Dr. Zuercher's learned monograph is an important contribution to our knowledge of this decisive period.

In an introductory chapter (pp. 18–80) he gives a survey of the little that is known about the history of Chinese Buddhism during its period of "incubation", from the beginning to about A.D. 300. The main subject of the book is the Buddhism of the upper classes in Southern China between roughly A.D. 300 and 400. The possession of a more or less standardized classical literary education was at that period the distinguishing feature of the Chinese governing class, which is usually described as "the gentry". Little useful could in any case be said about early "Popular Buddhism", since the doings of ordinary people, unless they managed to stage a revolt, were deemed unworthy of the attention of Chinese historians. The author's strong sociological interests guarantee that his narrative never strays too far away from social realities, and his intimate familiarity with the original documents is evident on every page.

Five trends must apparently be distinguished in Chinese Buddhism up to A.D. 400. 1. There were those who, attracted by "wisdom", were mainly interested in the doctrine of Emptiness, as propounded in the *Prajñāpāramitā*, the formulations of which show a truly remarkable affinity with the Neo-Taoist "Dark Learning" of the period. The bulk of Dr. Zuercher's book is devoted to this trend. It is admirably done and makes fascinating reading. His perspective is, however, slightly out of focus because he dislikes the "unbearable monotony" (p. 399, cf. p. 101) of the *Prajñāpāramitā*. His lack of sympathy for a Scripture which after A.D. 180 fired the Chinese with so much enthusiasm makes it easier for him to minimize the very real influence which it had, and to exaggerate the relative importance of "Dark Learning". 2. The concern of others was primarily with meditation, or Buddhist Yoga (see the Index s.v. *dhyāna*. 3. Devotionalism had many adherents from early on (see Index s.v.). 4. A number of magicians and shamans cultivated and displayed their supernatural powers (e.g. pp. 103–4), and, 5. Some saw in Buddhism nothing but a system of morality (p. 137). The co-existence of these five approaches is the normal state of affairs, and can with slight variations be found in all Buddhist countries.

Dr. Zuercher describes all this with a scholarship which is extensive, sound and above reproach. It greatly exceeds anything I myself may ever hope to attain. Nevertheless his conclusions are sometimes open to doubt, and readers should be warned against accepting them too unquestioningly. I am sorry if in arguing against them I may seem to detract from the merit of his book. Nothing is further from my mind, and I am merely commenting on a trend of theorizing of which he is only the latest representative, and which in my view unduly overestimates the national peculiarities of Chinese Buddhism.

A rather entertaining example of this mentality occurs on pp. 207–8 where he talks about the Buddhists who retired into mountains "far from the bustle and the impurities of the world". He then goes on to say that "it must be noted that the strong associations between Buddhist monasteries and mountains—especially 'sacred' mountains—is a typically Chinese (!) phenomenon", adds that "the background of the custom is no doubt (!) Taoist", and then enumerates some Taoist notions which strike him as relevant. This surely is "specialist's myopia" at its worst. For contemplatives to want to live on mountains is obviously sheer common sense. One might just as well ascribe S. Bernard's choice of Monte Cassino to a lingering pagan tradition about Diana the mountain goddess, the selection of Mt. Koyasan and the Hiei mountains to a Shinto reverence for high mountains, as exemplified by the cult of Fujiyama, and the Lord Buddha's preference for Mt. Vulture Peak to some weird and wonderful Hindu notions about mountain spirits and Shiva as "The Lord of Mountains". When writing about the spiritual life it is good not entirely to lose sight of its basic laws!

What is more serious is that Dr. Zuercher continually tries to make out that, deeply immersed in their Taoist heritage, the Buddhists of the fourth century "misunderstood" the true principles of Buddhism, and that many of their ideas are "hardly Buddhist". He says of them that "the result of this intense and continuous process of selection and hybridization is widely divergent(!) from the contents of the imported foreign scriptures which were so faithfully copied, memorized and recited by Chinese devotees" (p. 2). What strikes me on the contrary is how well these members of the "gentry" actually did understand Buddhism. To take just one example, on pp. 164–76 we have a translation of Hsi Ch'ao's "Essentials of Religion", which is "a kind of Buddhist catechism composed by a prominent layman. . . . It shows to what extent these persons understood or (what is at least as important) misunderstood the message of Buddhism" (p. 135). On reading as a Buddhist through this catechism, I am astonished to find how thoroughly sound it is. Some of it rings a bit strange, but that is the fault of the English translation. If Chinese ideographs are translated on the basis of their derivation, and not their actual meaning, the most bizarre results may ensue. Often in the past when I heard Sinologues complaining that the Chinese did not understand Buddhism, I have wondered how well they themselves had actually grasped the terminology of the more archaic writings. This, however, is not the place for philological controversies, and I must content myself with drawing attention to just one passage on p. 174, where Hsi Ch'ao remarks that "when the causal (process of) retribution has ended, one enters into No-birth, and since (in that state) one is not born, therefore one is able not to die". This is just ordinary Buddhism, and quite unexceptionable in its orthodoxy. But Dr. Zuercher feels constrained to comment, "Mark the Chinese conclusion: the cessation of birth is a means to attain immortality!" (p. 380). If this is a "Chinese conclusion", I greatly fear that the Buddha himself must have been not only a Mongol, as some say, but even a Chinese, for did he not promise immortality (*amṛta*) to those whose thirst for rebirth had been stilled?

These and other errors of judgment seem to suggest some faultiness in the method applied by Dr. Zuercher and his school. It is a basic tenet of our holy religion that the Dharma itself has no history and is fundamentally identical everywhere. Trained in the appraisal of national characteristics, cultural traditions, racial peculiarities and class prejudices, historians and sociologists only too often turn a blind eye on the working of the Spirit. In our case the Spirit operates through the Samgha, which, well-saturated in a supremely rational doctrine and steeped in the habits of meditation, is the source of all significant thinking, and has kept deviations from the dharmic norm within narrow bounds. But this is a deep question, and I must leave it at that for the time being. Though I do not wish to take leave of Dr. Zuercher without thanking him once more for the instructive, stimulating and valuable book he has given us.

16

E. Dale Saunders. *Mudrā: a Study of Symbolic Gestures in Japanese Buddhist Sculpture.* xxiii + 296 pp., 26 plates, 110 text figs. Bollingen Series LVIII. Routledge & Kegan Paul, 1960.

Everyone who has ever been called upon to identify Buddhist images must have wished for a handbook on the *mudrās* which are so important for determining their place within the pantheon. Some knowledge of about half a dozen of the more frequent hand gestures has seeped through to us during the last 50 years, although even among them we are baffled by some of their variations, particularly as regards the *dharmacakra* and *vitarka*. When confronted with the other, more unfamiliar, gestures we had only the Shingon *Si-do-in-dzu* in its French translation of 1899 to turn to, but since that deals with "ritual" gestures which "form an integral part of religious ceremonies", few iconographers can have consulted it without some measure of disappointment. Otherwise we had nothing to guide us except T. de Kleen's *Mudras* of 1924, and P. de Kat Angelino's *Mudras auf Bali*, 1923, both concerned with the hybrid Buddho-Shivaite ritual of Bali. Now Mr. Dale Saunders has singled out of the multitude of more than 300 *mudrās* eight "principal" and six "secondary" symbolic gestures, and described them in detail with all their manifold subdivisions. In this way he rightly claims to have covered "the principal *mudrā* of the greater part of Far Eastern Art" (p. 4). Two-thirds only of his book are, however, actually devoted to the symbolic gestures of the hand, and pp. 121–95 contain a welcome account of first the principal *āsanas*, i.e. "postures and thrones", and then of 18 attributes of Buddhist figures, such as the alms bowl, rosary, vase, etc.

This is a work of a specialist in Japanese studies, and therein lies both its strength and its weakness. The first-hand material is almost all Japanese. Of great value is the information gathered from Japanese publications of the last 30 years, i.e., from the works of Gonda and Ōmūra, the *Daizōkyō Zuzō*, and so on. This, in fact, constitutes the useful core of the book, which is done conscientiously, though a trifle unimaginatively. The author is less successful in integrating his Japanese material with non-Japanese Buddhist art and thought. Like so many other specialists he overvalues the importance of his own subject, and cannot easily see its relations to what lies outside it. If he chose to approach his problem from the Japanese angle, this was done not for the exalted reason he gives on p. 4, but because of the elementary fact that in 1953–1955 it was very much easier for an American to reside in Japan rather than in Tibet. One might have thought that "Tibet, which is particularly faithful in respect to Buddhist iconography as it has been transmitted from India" (p. 30) would form a quite ideal starting point for an investigation of this kind, but in fact Tibetan Buddhism has been very much neglected, and the author seems to have no direct knowledge of it. It is rather awkward that throughout the *mudrās* are given their Japanese names, and this idiosyncrasy does not exactly facilitate the study of the book. We can only hope that no one will imitate this precedent, because for many valid reasons, Sanskrit, and not Japanese, is regarded as the *lingua franca* of Buddhology. Likewise it is disconcerting to find that the Scriptures are almost invariably quoted only in their Japanese form, and where there is a Sanskrit original this makes the verification of doubtful statements (as on p. 81, 226 n. 9) rather difficult (the Buddha did not "kill" but disperse the demons? To kill a demon would not only be unethical, but also futile, because he would immediately be reborn as a demon again).

The book is beautifully and even sumptuously produced. The printing is excellent, the drawings, obviously executed by Japanese, are wonderfully neat and distinct, and the photographs have generally come out fairly well. Mr. Saunders himself has taken great pains over his text, and at first sight he may seem to be well informed. But the longer the book is studied, the more it turns out to be none too good. Literary expression does not come easy to Mr. Saunders. His style is wooden, graceless and often far from lucid. In fact I have come across dozens of sentences which seemed to hold no precise or even ascertainable meaning.

Mr. Saunders draws his information from a wide range of authorities, but has not always been critical enough in their use. His book would have gained if we heard less of the uninspired guesses of E. J. Eitel, a bewildered China missionary of the 1880's, of Miss Getty, a lady from Boston somewhat addicted to the higher nonsense (e.g., pp. 184, 208, 229) and of Charles Williams whose sturdy commonsense delights in clubbing to death the pretensions of Buddhist symbolism (e.g. on p. 174). Likewise, when assigning a tentative date to the *Mañjuśrīmūlakalpa* and *Guhyasamāja*, Mr. Saunders is content (p. 199) to adduce, without discussion or comment, Bhattacharyya's opinion according to which these two texts are from the 2nd and 3rd centuries respectively. These dates are practically impossible, and the 6th and 7th centuries are more likely (see below p. 209).

It is an essential feature of Buddhism that it has come down to us in distinct, though cognate, traditions. For this reason it is most important to distinguish carefully the different trends—in art Gandhara, China (Wei, T'ang, etc.), Japan, Tibet, and in Tibet again the different schools, Nyingmapa, Kagyutpa, Gelugpa, and so on. The author has clearly seen that the conventions of the art of Gandhara differ from those of China and Japan, but where he has erred is in that he has continually mixed up the Shingon of Japan in one inextricable confusion with what he has gathered from secondary sources about the Tantra of Tibet itself with its several quite distinct lineages. In consequence, on pp. 104–5 the Ādi-Buddha, always on occasion for much woolliness, gives rise to some truly hair-raising statements, which are flatly contradicted by note 38 on p. 209 and note 54 on p. 234. And on pages 66–69 the account of the *vitarkamudrā* is so confused that I have read it four times without being any the wiser.

Mr. Saunders, like other art historians before him, is unfamiliar with the finer points of Buddhist theory (just as the connoisseurs of doctrine are generally unacquainted with the finer points of art!). He faithfully translates from his Japanese sources all sorts of remarks about Buddhist doctrine, but without any intellectual grasp of what they actually mean. Howlers abound, the sure touch is missing, and the outlines of perfectly unambiguous Buddhist concepts are hopelessly blurred.

Everybody by now knows that the *Sūtrālaṃkāra* is not by Aśvaghosa (p. 59) but by Kumāralāta. Likewise, few nowadays believe that the *Pali Jātakas* date back to the fifth century B.C. (p. 13). When we hear that Devadatta "caused an elephant to be drunk"

(p. 59; cf. p. 43; on p. 218 we have more probably a "maddened" elephant), that the *vajra* is "the expression of fulminatory identification with the godhead" (p. 160), that "in India, Vajrasattva, the 'sixth' (!) of the five (!) *dhyāni*-Buddhas, is accepted as the 'priest' of the other five" (p. 191), and that the Dalai Lama is an "incarnation" of Avalokiteśvara (p. 212), we can only wonder. Likewise, when we read about "emptiness" what is said on p. 165, or learn on p. 99 that apparently the attainment of enlightenment and the sermon of Benares took place at the same "precise moment." And in the hope that some day someone will take some notice, may I repeat again that in Buddhist Tantrism there are no *saktis* but *prajñās*, and no Dhyāni-Buddhas but Jinas. This is now definitely established, and all the speculations based on the old misleading terms—to which also Dale Saunders regales us in great detail—are unmistakably wrong.

In our contemporary culture intellectuality is clearly at a discount. This is all very well as far as it goes, and must greatly contribute to the contentment of the masses. But if unsophisticated members of this culture, unaware of the intellectual clarity and spiritual magnificence of Buddhist thought, approach the art of Buddhism as though they were using Geiger counters or classifying butterflies, they are surely bound to make a hash of things. The ant has never yet been a symbol of Buddhist endeavour.

17

F. D. K. Bosch. *The Golden Germ. An Introduction to Indian Symbolism.* Mouton & Co., The Hague, 1960. 264 pp., 20 figs. 84 plates. Indo-Iranian Monographs no. 11.

This important work was first published in Dutch in 1948. Its appearance in English will now at last enable art historians outside Holland to study more closely Professor Bosch's interpretation of some of the basic *motifs* of Buddhist art. The English edition does, however, differ from the Dutch original in that it has been augmented by a discussion of some additional symbols, corrected in response to criticisms, and trimmed by the omission of some passages "concerned too exclusively with Hindu-Javanese matters". Professor Bosch's book is a fine piece of imaginative scholarship. In fact, he names Emile Sénart, Paul Mus and Ananda Coomaraswamy as his three immediate predecessors, all men who used their brains as well as their eyes, and who tried to penetrate beyond the facts of Indian art to the meaning behind them. The task he sets himself is "to explore the world of living and creative thought from which Indian art drew its inspiration" (p. 47), and his exposition, though not entirely free from a certain amount of arbitrariness and repetitiveness, considerably advances our understanding of the background of Indian sculpture.

"The Golden Germ" of the title is the *hiraṇyagarbha* which in the Vedas appears as "the beginning and origin of all creation" (p. 51). The author adduces much evidence to show that the Universe which springs from it is often represented as either a lotus plant, or a cosmic tree. He further arrives at the conclusion that the "*hiraṇyagarbha*, the germ and womb of all that lives, assumes the shape of the root of the cosmic lotus, the *padmamūla*" (p. 63), and that also the root of the celestial tree" is shaped like the *padmamūla* and in symbolism is usually treated in a similar manner" (p. 80). The root of the cosmic lotus becomes, as it were, the cornerstone of his entire edifice, and in that he differs from Paul Mus and others who had "made the Mahāmeru the axis of their interpretation of the Indian conception of life and world" (p. 230). Our author, however, believes that "this macrocosmic system in its turn is rooted in an even older and deeper soil; that it is the expression of a system not built up of lifeless matter but inspired from within by Life itself" (p. 231). Accordingly the Mahāmeru is here interpreted as "the macrocosmic equivalent of the *padmamūla*, just as the Meru-top is the equivalent of the lotus-stem" (p. 96).

To put it briefly, Professor Bosch maintains that nearly all Indian works of art can be understood as transformations of parts or aspects of the Lotus or the Tree. He certainly shows that many puzzling details of ornamentation can be explained on this principle, and he chooses his examples from a very wide range, though with particular emphasis on Indonesia. In addition he discusses the bearing of his hypothesis on such long-standing problems as the evolution of the Stūpa (pp. 167–76), or the origin of the Buddha-image (pp. 197–207). Though the strength of the book lies in the application of the basic principle to the structural details shown on the more than 200 clearly reproduced illustrations.

Most of what Prof. Bosch has to say is fruitful and stimulating, much of it is instructive, and some of it seems to be definitely established. In judging his performance, we must never lose sight of the Protean quality of mythological thinking, which is always diffuse and fluid, without the definiteness of conceptual thought. Sometimes the reader may well feel that nearly everything can apparently be equivalent to nearly everything else. Bosch himself mentions it as a particularity of symbolism that at times "identifications, substitutions, associations, hybridizations and such like run wild unrestrictedly, entwining and enveloping each other till finally they strangle and crush each other to death" (p. 104), and he is constantly aware of the danger that he may be "led astray in the labyrinth of Indian symbolism, as so many have been before us" (p. 106).

At times his evidence is extremely tenuous, and quite unable to bear the weight of the conclusions it is meant to support. To take just two examples. In his effort to show that in "the cult-image" of the Buddha "certain characteristics survive reminiscent of its vegetable origin" he refers to the lists of the supernatural marks on a Buddha's body, and finds that they compare the arm to a "lotus stalk", or to an elephant's trunk, which latter he regards as "identification through a concealed third (!)" (pp. 217, 222). This is a most hazardous way of arguing. The same list of the attributes of a superman tells us that the Buddha's "eye-lashes are like those of a magnificent heifer", that "the hair of his head is as dark as a black bee", and that he had "webbed feet like the royal goose". It would patently be unsound to conclude therefrom that the Buddha image is derived from a cow, a bee or a goose. It may well be that "the human body is the microscopic counterpart of the cosmic lotus-plant" (p. 223), but the comparisons contained in the list of the Buddha's *lakṣaṇas* do nothing to confirm this view.

Likewise on p. 205 the evidence for the statement that "the figure of the *yaksha* and that of the Buddha were generally believed to resemble each other" is so extremely feeble that only Professor Bosch's *esprit de système* can account for its inclusion. Sujātā and her maid may have just been ignorant females, and as for Māra appearing "in the likeness of the Buddha", the Scriptures continually show Māra turning up in the guise of nearly everything and nearly everybody. That only illustrates his great power of transformation, and throws no light on his actual appearance.

These are just minor details. Of greater interest is the author's method. The attempt to account for much that is obscure in later Buddhist thought by going back to the archaic layers of Hindu thought, to the Vedas and Brāhmaṇas, has much to commend it, and also in the hands of Coomaraswamy, Mus and Maryla Falk this approach has led to valuable results. A great deal of Professor Bosch's argumentation is based on Betty Heimann's dictum that "to the Indian there is at the beginning of all knowledge a visible phenomenon, never an abstract idea" (p. 58). The application of this principle to the Dharma-notion of the Buddhists (pp. 122–3) demonstrates, however, its limitations as well as its usefulness. Professor Kuiper in his review of the original Dutch edition spoke of Professor Bosch's method as "a-historical" (p. 57). Quite deliberately Bosch seems to treat the Tree as a sort of Jungian archetype hovering timelessly over the Indian Subcontinent and manifesting itself in "an uninterrupted tradition extending from the first settlement of Indians in the Panjāb till the present day" (p. 239). In consequence he sees no harm in that "when wandering through the fields of Indian art and literature, we took our illustrations from periods hundreds, even thousands, of years apart" (p. 239). On the other hand he is somewhat puzzled to find that art supports his thesis so much more clearly than literature, and wonders "how a tradition embodying these representations could be preserved for thousands of years, without, we may add, there being any trace of its having been set down in writing" (p. 241; cf. p. 93). He explains this (pp. 242–3) by assuming a "taboo" which forbade any mention of the "Tree-motif", thereby reminding us a bit of Freudian reactions to criticisms of their assertions about the Unconscious.

The translation is generally adequate, although in many cases the translator has adhered too closely to the Dutch diction, and sentences must be read twice to be understood. This book will exasperate those art historians who are content with "the scrupulous recording and description of antiquities" (p. 11). It will delight those who are interested in "the significance" of ancient Indian art, which "constitutes its real meaning and *raison d'être*".

18
DR. KOESTLER AND THE WISDOM OF THE EAST

As an admirer of Arthur Koestler's *The Sleepwalkers* I asked for a review of *The Lotus and the Robot,*[1] intending to speak well of it. Alas, the intention cannot be carried out. Koestler here writes on Yoga and Zen. As a Jewish journalist with some scientific training he does not find it easy to do justice to them. Yoga and modern science have no mutual contacts, and no two religions could be further apart than Judaism and Buddhism. In consequence it should not really surprise us to learn that Yoga is just one big fraud, and Zen a bad and pointless joke. The book has met with almost unanimous praise in the press and on the radio. To an expert it nevertheless must appear as a mere travesty of the facts, and there is no valid reason why an expert's voice should not also be heard.

We must first consider the methods which have led Koestler to his conclusions. The study of the vast literature on the Wisdom of the East has not been part of his programme. He himself admits that his "knowledge of the Hindu Scriptures is sketchy" (p. 151), and it is hard not to agree with him. M. Eliade's standard treatise on *Yoga* (1954) has escaped his attention, and he prefers to rely on Ernest Wood's slightly sub-standard Penguin (1959). And no use is made of the translations and expositions which four generations of European scholars have devoted to the elucidation of Buddhism.

But what are books? Perhaps the author has succeeded so well in communicating directly with the wise men of the East that he could dispense with such crutches. After residing for twenty years in this country, he has, however, become so thoroughly anglicized (see also on p. 278 the "we" in line 18!)[2] that he expects everyone to speak English. This may not have been so bad in India, but in Japan Buddhists rarely know English, and Koestler often complains about

[1] London: Hutchinson, 1960. Pp. 296.

[2] In India "we ruled by rape, but influenced by seduction". Since Mr. K. was naturalized only in 1946, he had just one year in which to help "us" rule the Indians by rape. If we see the outcome in 1947, it might have been better for "us" if he had desisted.

his "lamentable translators" (p. 273). So the Phoenician priest came all the way from Tyre to interview Aristotle through an interpreter who knew almost no Greek, and sadly concluded that this philosopher's reputation had been greatly exaggerated. In fact, of course, the sublimer the thought, the more it demands a mastery of the language which expresses it. But how could anybody be bothered to learn Japanese just to find out what these self-styled "Zen masters" are thinking? How, on the other hand, can you hope to achieve intimate contact with a man with whom you cannot talk in his own language, particularly if you are intellectually unprepared for it? There is the further point that sages are not easy to find because they shun big cities and the company of the worldly, and must be sought out in inaccessible places. Those whom he managed to meet may well have remained uncommunicative when they saw his total incomprehension.

For blindness to the mentality of Eastern sages is here almost complete. To take just one example, on pp. 268–70 much "evidence" is adduced to show that the Japanese are an irreligious people. For instance, "among students in a Buddhist seminary" "forty-eight per cent (were) without belief in the immortality of the soul". The Buddhists have for 2,500 years consistently denied the existence of a "soul"—how could they possibly believe in its immortality? They also claim that im-mort-ality, or freedom from death, is an impersonal condition which follows on the extinction of individuality, and is therefore incompatible with an individual soul. Mr. Koestler's figures are taken from a Jesuit publication, and this example shows how different religions can misunderstand one another. If a Vedantist Hindu were to circularize European Christians with the question, "Do you want to become God?", nearly all would reply in the negative. He would be most unwise to infer that all Christians are irreligious atheists.

The remaining 52 per cent who gave a positive answer were just being polite. Confronted with a question which, as phrased, gives no sense from a Buddhist point of view, they would try to think hard what the questioner might have had in mind, and would have thought that he referred to re-incarnation, or survival after death.

It is the *ethos* of these Easterners, strikingly different from the ruthless rough and tumble of European disputants, which has so baffled Mr. Koestler. At Benares he occupied himself with a woman by the name of Anandamayee Ma, whom her followers called "the Mother of the Universe", and such things. Rather unconvinced, he asked her, "Does Mother approve of what has been written about her, claiming that she was of divine origin?" She sweetly replied (or rather, "snapped impatiently" (p. 82)), "Everyone sees in me what he likes". This, Dr. Koestler, strange as it must seem to you, is the long and the short of it. It will not do to say that she *is* the Mother of the Universe, and it also will not do to say that she is *not*. Nor is this aversion to clear-cut affirmations confined to Hindus. "Nothing could be more shocking to a Japanese than the injunction 'Let your communication be Yea, yea, Nay, nay'. He would regard it as inconceivably rude" (p. 219). And why shouldn't he? If our author regards Judaeo–Christian habits of thought as the unfailing standard of all truth, if he refuses even to consider the relative validity of Eastern evasiveness, why should he have bothered to go East at all? A different standard prevails there, and to equate it with "logical confusion" (as on p. 225) does indeed seem "inconceivably rude". Deprived of any food for his Talmudic logomachia, Mr. Koestler was most disappointed to meet again and again with the refusal to fight when attacked. And though he had thus plenty of opportunity to study *ahimsā*, it taught him nothing except contempt.

How then is it that our author, noted for his outstanding intelligence, should have had no clue to the mental processes of the representatives of Eastern wisdom? His autobiographical writings provide an answer. In *Arrow in the Blue* he relates (p. 213) how in Berlin he seemed to be more of a machine-gun than a human being. The machine-gun mind is still very much in evidence. The bullets mow down not only the ideas, but also the great men of the East. Positive disrespect is shown to the overtowering figure of D. T. Suzuki who is revered by all who know him. And the sanctity of the Mahatma is assaulted by scandalous reports about Gandhi's private life, which by Hindu standards do not affect the issue at all. This kind of intellectual ruthlessness may be called for in the natural sciences. When directed against wisdom, it can only destroy. A tank stands up to bullets better than a doe. But that does not prove that it is the more "real" of the two.

Elsewhere (e.g. *Arrow in the Blue*, p. 97) Koestler tells us that he is one of those people who suffer from "Chronic Indignation". This leads me to my last point. Mr. K. is angry with Buddhists for their refusal openly to fight social evils. May I therefore say a few words in their defence? To take a concrete example, atomic bombs must surely seem a great evil to all those who regard the survival of mankind as a good thing. They cannot be laid at the door of Yogins or Buddhists, who were too benevolent, or incompetent, to devise such means of mass destruction. In fact they are clearly a product of our Judaeo–Christian civilization. Who then should be held responsible for them?

While we remain within the political sphere, each charge must generate a counter-change. To emphasize the contributions of the Einsteins, Oppenheimers and Tellers will be regarded as evidence of "antisemitism". Those who accuse the scientists will be charged with "obscurantism", and those who blame the politicians will be told that Truman only enacted the "will of the people" who wanted the war to end soon. Likewise to see Hiroshima as the work of "Anglo-American imperialism" would be a sign of "fellow-travelling", and so on.

Things become quite different when we move into the religious sphere. Then these developments seem quite normal, for they either illustrate "original sin", or confirm the fact that life in this world is *duhkha*, always and everywhere. It would be quite wrong to accuse the Buddhists of condoning the horrors of the present age. To make their point they have only to dwell on the complete futility of those who have tried "to do something" about them. For 30 years Mr. Koestler has greatly added to his literary reputation by ceaselessly denouncing the shortcomings of others, but what good, may we ask, has all this done to the countless victims of violence and oppression? "The temptations of the devil are easier to resist than those in which the tempter appears in the guise of a crusader full of righteous indignation" (*Arrow in the Blue*, p. 100). It may well be that self-righteous indignation merely intensifies the evils which it combats. Einstein, rightly indignant about the Nazis, advised Roosevelt to develop the atom bomb. Now, as a direct result, not only the Jews but all living things on earth are threatened with destruction. What then is gained by all this crying and shouting? At least by sticking to inoffensive *koans* our Zen Buddhists do not make matters worse than they already are.

With *The Lotus and the Robot* we are back in the good old days of "East is East and West is West, And never the twain shall meet". But Kipling, as *Kim* plainly shows, had a feeling or flair for the East. Dr. Koestler's own attitude has been well described in *The Invisible Writing* (p. 291). Someone told him about Mahayana Buddhism and gave him "a German translation of the Pali Scriptures to read. As a prim little materialist, I was fascinated and repelled, as if I had been dragged inside a metaphysical brothel furnished with lotus flowers, pot-bellied sages, transparent ascetics and little white elephants". Far be it from me to deny that here our author has accurately defined his outlook on life! In his latest book he has clearly moved outside the range of his sympathies. After reading it, this reviewer at least remains unshaken in his belief that the Wisdom of the East is a great, though subterranean, force which enables many men and women even at the present time to live fairly fruitful lives.

19

Charles Luk (Lu K'uan Yu). *Ch'an and Zen Teaching, Series One.* Rider and Co., 1960. 255 pp.

After hearing so much about Zen Buddhism, we have naturally become quite interested in knowing more about the Chinese Ch'an sect from which it originated. Our interest is partly historical, and partly inspired by the hope of seeing the spiritual message of the Dhyāna-school exhibited without some of the accretions which it gathered to itself in Japan. Swordsmanship and archery, to take just one example, are at present no more than a couple of outmoded preciosities. But even if they were replaced by bayonet-practice and pistol-shooting, such "religious" exercises would remain offensive to the majority of Buddhists all over the world, as showing insufficient respect for the lives of others. The "Japanese national character", or rather the mentality of the Japanese military class, is one thing, the "direct transmission of the Dharma from mind to mind" is another, and many Buddhists naturally take more kindly to the second than to the first. Even the most fervent admirers of the virtues of the Samurai must admit that in this, as in so many other matters, the Chinese were the creators, and the Japanese the borrowers and imitators. Ideas often undergo subtle changes when travelling from one country to another. When we see how much, for instance, the "humanism" of a man like Gilbert Murray had departed from that of his Greek models, we cannot take it for granted that Ch'an and Zen are automatically and in fact one and the same thing.

Having perceived the gap in our knowledge, Rider and Co., on the initiative of Gerald Yorke, have now decided to fill it with a number of volumes on "Ch'an and Zen Teaching". The first volume has just appeared, and if everything goes according to plan there will be about ten in all. Spiritual information is usually misleading unless it emanates from a living tradition, however enfeebled that may have become. The author of the volume under review is a Chinese lay disciple of the Ven. Hsu Yun, a Ch'an master who died in 1959 at the age of 119 years, and whose photograph and obituary appeared in the last issue of *The Middle Way*. His sole ambition is "to present as many Chinese Buddhist texts as possible so that Buddhism can be preserved at least in the West, should it be fated to disappear in the East as it seems to be". A man of sixty-two who sees China from the British Crown Colony of Hong Kong, Charles Luk may be unduly pessimistic about the future of the Dharma in his native land, but we in the West are unlikely to reproach him for an estimate of the situation which confers the benefits of his instruction upon us.

The book falls into four parts. The first gives Master Hsu Yun's discourses about Ch'an training, delivered about 1930 (pp. 19–117); the second (pp. 121–45) six stories which describe "the concurrent causes producing the awakening of six masters whose inner potentialities had been activated to the full, ready for instantaneous union with the absolute". The stories are taken from the "Imperial Selection of Ch'an Sayings" (*ca.* 1730).

Parts 3 and 4 consist of Han-shan's (*ca.* 1616) commentaries to the "Diamond Sutra" and the "Heart Sutra". The commentary to the "Diamond Sutra" in particular is a very fine piece of work which concentrates on the spiritual meaning as seen by a Ch'an master. Han-shan maintains that the Sutra does not aim at revealing the Wisdom which removes the defilements of beings, but only sets out to cut off people's doubts and awaken their faith. The doubts concern (1) the nature of the true Buddha, (2) the Dharma, which had been expounded in apparently self-contradictory terms, and (3) the student who may well wonder whether he is really qualified for this sublime teaching, and whether he can actually observe it. Han-shan regards the commentary of Vasubandhu, the twenty-first Patriarch of the Ch'an sect, as the only one which is really authoritative. If the Sutra is interpreted as a Remover of Doubts, one must first discover the hidden doubts which Subhuti had in his mind. Because these were not expressed in words, Ananda did not record them, but only the Buddha's replies. Han-shan lists 35 such doubts, as against Vasubandhu's 27. Part I of the Sutra (ch. 1–16) is held to deal with 17 coarse errors, part II (ch. 17–32) with 18 subtle ones. It was thus a continuous string of the disciple's wrong conceptions, from the coarsest to the finest, which the Buddha broke up successfully in his teaching of Prajñā. When all the erroneous views were completely eliminated, the original nature of all living beings, including Subhuti and the Tathagata, was fully revealed.

Readers now have at their disposal two commentaries to the Diamond and Heart Sutras—mine written from the Tibetan, and Han-shan's written from the Ch'an point of view. They will be found to be complementary, and a comparison of our respective treatment of certain crucial passages should be quite rewarding.

The sweetness and the authentic glow of the Dharma tangibly pervade the pages of this book. It should not be missed by anyone of those who were first aroused to the spiritual magnificence of the Dhyāna-school by the resounding sound of the gong which Daisetz Teitaro Suzuki struck so mightily in the thirties of this century. I myself am as pessimistic about the prospects of the Dharma in the West as Charles Luk is about those in the East. Nevertheless I rejoice to see that by some unknown concatenation of circumstances we are being made acquainted with one strand of the holy tradition after another—first Theravāda, then Abhidharma, then Zen, then Prajñāpāramitā, then Tantra, and now Ch'an. May we prove worthy of the opportunities so lavishly showered upon us!

20

Ch'an and Zen Teaching. Second Series. Charles Luk. Rider and Co., 1961, 254 pp.

This "second series" of "Ch'an and Zen Teaching" follows on "Series One", which was very favourably reviewed in *The Middle Way* xxxv 1, 1960, pp. 32–3. It is, I am sorry to say, less useful than its predecessor. The book falls into two parts. First there are the "forty transmission gāthās", beginning with the Buddha Vipaśyin and ending with Hui-neng, "the thirty-third patriarch". They are obviously apocryphal, have no historical basis, and are a *jeu d'esprit* of some monk who attempted to formulate different aspects of the Ch'an doctrine, while at the same time furnishing it with a respectable pedigree. They struck me as rather tiresome, but others may think differently, with equal justification.

Secondly we have "the Stories of the founders of the five Ch'an sects". These sects took shape between 750 and 950, and the "stories" about them are often centuries later. Mr. Luk's extracts are derived from three sources: (1) "The Transmission of the Lamp", by Tao-yuan (*ca.* 1004). (2) "The five Lamps meeting at the Source", compiled by Ling-yin Ta-ch'uan", in the Sung dynasty (960–1279), and (3) "The Finger pointing at the Moon" of 1602.

Of the accuracy of Luk's translation I cannot speak, partly because I know little Chinese, and partly because I have understood no more than perhaps five per cent of the contents of this book. But I could not fail to note that the translation reads at times rather strange. It is difficult to know what to make of the word "avatar" in a Buddhist context (pp. 50, 244), and it is more than unlikely that the Vimalakīrti Sutra should have said of the Dharmabody that it "is beyond all mathematics" (pp. 146–147). Surely the original term is *pramāṇa* which does not normally mean "mathematics", but either "measure", or "means of knowledge", i.e. "logic". There is throughout a certain uncertainty about the meaning of Buddhist terms; for instance, on p. 17 the fourth "Unlimited" is given as "renunciation", on p. 221 as "indifference", when in fact "impartiality" or "evenmindedness" would be the correct rendering. These slight, though numerous, blemishes are, however, as nothing compared with the total effect of the translation which manages to envelop the teachings of the Dharma in a thick fog of total incomprehensibility. I except the sermon on pp. 111–26 which a mere scholar like myself could read with enjoyment. But what can we make of the remainder of the book, which consists of disjointed stories, mostly very brief and always completely unintelligible, just strung together, without any system or logical coherence? How these stories used to charm us when we found Dr. Suzuki adding a few at a time as a kind of seasoning to one of his masterly discourses on the spiritual life! But to have to read hundreds and hundreds of them just by themselves is rather like drinking Worcester sauce neat out of a tumbler.

The Sung masters, of course, never intended these collections of quaint sayings and incidents to be used as "books" read by the general public. In fact this is the most esoteric Buddhist work I have yet come across. Esoteric literature has a definite place in Buddhism, but it should never be forgotten that esoteric writings lose all meaning when severed from the living tradition which sustained them. As subjects of meditation under an acknowledged Zen master these stories should be invaluable. When read by outsiders they are quite incomprehensible, just as private jokes current in a closely knit family when told to those who do not belong to it. Mr. Luk's efforts to explain the alleged "meaning" of these private jokes in innumerable footnotes must remain pathetically ineffective. This book should bring great joy to those few who through their karma belong to the Zen lineage. All others can benefit from it only if they are endowed with the miraculous gifts of a "king goose" who, so the Glossary (p. 242) tells us, "is said to be able to absorb the milk from a mixture of milk and water, leaving the water behind".

21

Alex Wayman. *Analysis of the Śrāvakabhūmi Manuscript*. University of California Press, Berkeley and Los Angeles, 1961, 185 pp. (University of California Publications in Classical Philology, Vol. 17). *The Yogācārabhūmi of Ācārya Asaṅga*. Part I, Edited by V. Bhattacharya. University of Calcutta, 1957, 232 pp.

With exasperating slowness the Sanskrit text of Asaṅga's *Yogācārabhūmiśāstra* is gradually being made accessible to the scholarly world. The following survey of the chief subdivisions of this gigantic *Summa* of the Yogācāra school will show at one glance what has so far been done, and what still remains to be done. (To refers to the Tōhoku-number, Tshi and Dzi to the respective volumes of the Derge Tanjur, and H to Taishō vol. 30.)

I. Bhūmivastu.
(1–5. The basic facts of the triple world)
1. *pañcavijñānakāyasamprayuktā bhūmi* — Bh. 4–10; To 4035
2. *manobhūmi* — Bh. 11–72
3. *savitarkā savicārā bhūmi* — Bh. 73–
4. *avitarkā vicāramātrā bhūmi*
5. *avitarkā-avicārā bhūmi* — Bh. 232
1–5. ed. B. Bhattacharya, 1957
(6–9. Two summary treatments of 1–5)
6. samāhitā bhūmi 7. asamāhitā bhūmi
8. *sacittikā bhūmi*, Tshi 160a, H 344 9. *acittikā bhūmi*
8–9. ed. A. Wayman, *Indogaku Bukkyōgaku Kenkyū*, VIII, 1960, 378–6
(10–12. The Path; mārga, pratipad)
10. śrutamayī bhūmi
hetuvidyā, Tshi 187b–199b, H 356a–360c; cf. A. Wayman, The rules of debate according to Asaṅga, *JAOS* 78, 1958, 29–40
11. cintāmayī bhūmi
paramārtha-gāthā, Tshi 205–10, H 363–5, ed. A. Wayman, *Analysis*, etc., 1961, 163–185
12. bhāvanāmayī bhūmi
(13–15. The three vehicles)
13. *śrāvakabhūmi*. To 4036, Dzi 1–195a, H 395–477[1]

[1] On p. 58 Wayman says that in his "Analysis" the pages of the Derge Tanjur are "labeled C". This is not the case. The Derge pages are prefaced by a T, whereas the C figures refer to the Chinese. This slip causes much bewilderment in the reader until he has spotted it.

Summary in: A. Wayman, *Analysis*, etc., 58–134; also 140–150?[1]

14. *pratyekabuddhabhūmi*, Tshi 279a[2], H 477
ed. A. Wayman, as 8–9, pp. 376–5
15. *bodhisattvabhūmi*, To 4037
ed. U. Wogihara, 1930–6, pp. 1–414. – cf. also: C. Bendall and de la Vallée Poussin, Sommaire et Notes (on Wogihara 1–113), *Le Muséon* vi, 1905, pp. 38–52 (ch. 1–2); vii, 1906, pp. 213–30 (ch. 3–4); xii, 1911, pp. 155–191 (ch. 5–8). – P. Demiéville, Le chapitre de la Bodhisattvabhūmi sur la Perfection du Dhyāna. *Rocznik Orientalistyczny* xxi, 1957, 109–28 (Frch. trsl., with copious notes, of Wogihara 207–11).
(16–17. The fruits of the Paths)
16. sopadhikā bhūmi
17. nirupadhikā bhūmi

II. Viniścaya-saṃgrahaṇī, To 4038;[3]
III. Vastu-saṃgrahaṇī To 4039–40;
IV. Paryāya-saṃgrahaṇī, To 4041;
V. Vivaraṇa-samgrahaṇī To 4042.

Having placed the publications of V. Bhattacharya and A. Wayman into their proper perspective, I will now say a few words about each one in turn. V. Bhattacharya prints the next of the first five sections in Devanāgarī characters from the Sankrityana manuscript. In addition he has appended numerous footnotes, which mostly compare the Sanskrit text with the Tibetan translation as given in the Narthang Tanjur, and occasionally discuss difficult words, make comparisons with other sources, chiefly Pali texts and the *Abhidharmakośa*, and draw attention to probable corruptions and doubtful readings. All this is done very conscientiously, as we would expect of a scholar of the stature of V. Bhattacharya. The editor has further added a number of headings in square brackets, which unfortunately do more to obscure the progress of the argument than to elucidate it. This is particularly troublesome in sections 3–5 (which in both the Ms and the Tib. are treated as one single chapter) and the reader will be well advised to insert in the margins of his copy the true subdivisions of the text, which are as follows:

[1] I have not been able to understand where Wayman places the portion dealing with *bhojane mātrajñatā*. On p. 4 he speaks of it as an intrusion into the Śrāvakabhūmi MS, and from *JBRS* 42, 1956, p. 3 one might be tempted to infer that it belongs to 11. But since it is found in Dzi 29–38 and H 408–11, it must surely belong to I 13? Unfortunately I have no access to the Derge Tanjur, and must rely on inference.

[2] The Peking Tanjur also puts 14, 16 and 17 after 12 and before 13, as shown by the *Catalogue* of the Tokyo reprint, III, 1961, p. 702.

[3] II-V are exactly as long as I, II is a commentary on I, dealing with questions and objections, Wayman, p. 43.

I. dhātu: 1. saṃkhyā 73, 2. sthānantara 74, 3. sattvaparimāṇa 76, 4. āyur 77, 5. sambhogaparibhoga 79; 5a. sukhaduḥkhānubhava 79, 5b. āhāraparibhoga 99, 5c. maithunaparibhoga 100.
II. lakṣaṇam 112
III. yoniśo manasikāro 114. 8 subdivisions.
IV. ayoniśo manasikāro 118, = 16 paravādāḥ.[1]
V. saṃkleśa 160. 1. kleśasaṃkleśa, 9 subdivisions, 2. karmasaṃkleśa 170, the same 9 subdivisions, 3. janmasaṃkleśa 195; 3a. prabheda, 3b. vyasanam 196, 3c. aniyamaḥ 197, 3d. pravṛtti 198, = pratītyasamutpāda.

The edition would, indeed, have benefited from a "synopsis of the contents", such as Wogihara had prefaced to his edition of the *Bodhisattvabhūmi* (pp. 1–24). Without the appropriate headings the reader cannot easily appreciate the intricate architectural structure of these chapters, and is apt to get lost in the jungle of its terms and definitions.

A. Wayman's work is a doctoral thesis which falls into six parts. The first is a useful palaeographic study of the twelfth century Nepalese Ms, the script of which is a popular form of Vartula with many unusual features. The second, called "literary history", discusses the date of Vasubandhu and Asaṅga (*ca.* A.D. 375–430), the life and works of Asaṅga, and the *Yogācārabhūmi genre*. The third makes a few remarks about the language of the Ms. The fourth is the "Analysis of the Śrāvakabhūmi", which is followed by the discussion, edition and translation of "intrusive folios", i.e. the section on Food and the *paramārthagāthā*.

Wayman's book is indubitably a fine piece of work and a valuable contribution to our knowledge of Yogācāra Buddhism. It would be a pity, however, if his method of translating the Sanskrit text were to be imitated by others. His English equivalents are, in fact, often neither lucid nor felicitous, and the Sanskrit is often easier to follow than the English, much of which is almost deliberately ugly, like so many buildings in Manchester, Bradford or Chicago. At times Mr. W. is merely perverse, as when he renders *vijñāna* as "perception" (p. 91), after everybody else seems to have agreed on translating it as "consciousness", reserving "perception" for *saṃjñā*. On other occasions he is positively barbaric, as when (p. 97) *prahāṇa* becomes "elimination-exertion", *dharma* "natures", or (p. 163) *śarīrārthagāthā* "Verses of Corpus Meaning". The translation of *samāpatti* as "equipoise" (p. 67, 134) is backed up by a sentence which seems to be both ungrammatical and meaningless. ("If my translation for these words is successful, it should be regarded as faithful rather than literal"(?). To translate *brāhma*, when on p. 134 it follows on *divya*, as "sublime", seems just to evade the

[1] Bh's headings make it appear that there are 18. Also, at p. 118, 11 the 13th, *nāstikavādah*, has been wrongly omitted in the text.

problem, and so does "productive corruption" (productive of what?) for *utpattikleśa* on the same page. Likewise on p. 134 *sarvaśaikṣasamādhinām* is not "among all learned *samādhis*" (the opposite being probably "illiterate *samādhis*"?) but "among all the *samādhis* of the learners". I also defy anyone to find any meaning whatsoever in the obscurities of the definition of *mātṛkā* on p. 45.

Uncouth and unintelligible translations of this kind constitute a sort of obscurantism which is surely worthy of condemnation. The objective difficulties are, of course, formidable. The English language is not suited particularly well for the exposition of philosophical subtleties or for the description of exalted spiritual states. In addition, Englishmen have rarely bothered to translate Mahāyāna texts, and since the days of M. Müller and H. Kern that job has been left to men who learned English as a second language later in life. If such men have no feeling for the genius of the English language, they may attempt, though in vain, to do justice to the true meaning of Buddhist technical terms by inventing horrifying neologisms. Two Austrians, Guenther and Agehananda, are the principal offenders in this respect, and even want to enrich their English translations with German words like *Gestalt* and *Existenz*. This is not the place for a long dissertation on the principles of a desirable translation. Example is always more valuable than precept, and I believe that in *Buddhist Texts* (1954) Miss Horner, Dr. Snellgrove, Arthur Waley and myself have demonstrated that Buddhist texts of all kinds can be rendered into a language which is readable, clear, euphonous, unambiguous, thoroughly intelligible and generally idiomatic. We had, in fact, hoped that our work would provide a kind of standard for other workers in this field. In France also the bad old days of Sylvain Lévi's jargon (with its *in-fonction, auto-subsumption* and *per-connaissance*) are now over, and Prof. Demiéville and Prof. Lamotte have shown that the most difficult texts can with some good will be rendered into fluent and elegant French. No translation can obviously ever quite match the original, as all those know who have attempted to reproduce in English a simple phrase like *sunt lacrimae rerum*. But then, if anyone should really want to know what exactly the original says, he will have to learn Latin, or in our case Sanskrit. He will not be helped by those who try to pack the meaning of the original word into uncouth verbal monstrosities which convey nothing to the average reader, and tell nothing new to the expert either.

The new material enables us to appreciate Asaṅga's position in the history of Buddhist thought better than we could before. The *Bodhisattvabhūmi* "belongs almost wholly to Mahāyāna theory. Except for mere traces of the latter, the rest of the seventeen *bhūmis* are Hīnayāna. In this sense, Asaṅga's is like Sang(h)arakṣa's work, described by Demiéville as "un fond hīnayāniste avec un appendice mahāyāniste" (Wayman 43). For Asaṅga "the attainment of the 'great vehicle' is actually the attainment of the 'small vehicle' plus an extra attainment". "It does not follow that because Asaṅga was 'converted' to the Mahāyāna he thereby forgot or rejected his former views". It is, indeed, Mr. Wayman's "tentative conclusion that various parts of Asaṅga's *Yogācārabhūmi*, and especially the *Śrāvakabhūmi*, are basically the doctrine of the later Mahīśāsakas" (p. 29), and on p. 140 he says of the section dealing with "Food" that "it is feasible to suppose that Asaṅga has reproduced . . . the paragraph as it occurs in the Sanskrit recension *Saṃyukta-āgama* used in his school".

The portions of the *Yogācārabhumi* which have so far been published in Sanskrit consist chiefly of long lists of technical terms followed by brief definitions. They are of immense interest for our understanding of the Yogācāra school, but the student of Buddhism in general must ask himself what authority can be attributed to them. What lineage do they represent, and for whom do they speak? How far can we assume that these definitions give the meaning of the terms as they occur in the scriptures of other schools?[1] After considering a number of instances, I have formed the provisional opinion that these definitions express only the views of the later Mahīśāsakas and of the Yogācārins, and that, generally speaking, they understand controversial terms differently from all other Buddhist schools.

For instance, I was pleased to find in Bhattacharya's edition on p. 166 an intelligible definition of the three kinds of *vipāryāsas* which had eluded me for years. It runs as follows:

saṃjñāviparyāsaḥ katamaḥ? yo'nitye nityam iti duḥkhe sukham iti aśucau śucīti anātmany ātmeti saṃjñā-parikalpaḥ.dṛṣṭiviparyāsaḥ katamaḥ? yas tatraiva tathā saṃjñāparikalpite kṣānti rucir vyavasthāpana-abhiniveśaḥ.cittaviparyāsaḥ katamaḥ? yas tatraiva tathā-abhiniviṣṭe rāgādi-saṃkleśaḥ.

That sounds quite plausible, though on the negative side we must note that this explanation, which regards each stage as an intensification of the previous one,[2] is obtained by changing the traditional order, in which *cittaviparyāsa* always precedes *dṛṣṭiviparyāsa*. More noteworthy still is the fact that this account is almost completely at variance with those of *Abhisamayālaṅkāraloka* p. 333, *Saddhammappakāsinī* 577–8 and *Peṭakopadesa* 120–1. Though, as regards the latter, it is remarkable that the phrase *khantī rucī* also there occurs in the explanation of *diṭṭhivipallāso*. Did Asaṅga here follow the tradition of the Mahīśāsakas (and we must remember that for some time Mahīśāsakas and Theravādins were one and the same sect, A. Bareau, *Les sectes*, etc., 1955, 183), or did he, ignorant of the

[1] de la Vallée-Poussin has discussed some parallels to the beginning of the *Bodhisattvabhūmi* in *Le Muséon* vi, 1905, 48–52.

[2] So does *Saddhammappakāsinī* 577, 17–18, but it leaves the traditional order intact.

actual meaning of these terms, make up something which seemed plausible to him? There is no way of knowing at present.

Again and again we find that Asaṅga's explanations deviate completely from those current in other schools. Our joy at discovering clear and unambiguous definitions of the 12 branches of the Scriptures, Sūtra, Geya, etc. (Wayman 75–8) is soon tempered by the observation that these definitions have no relation at all to those preserved in the Pali commentaries or in the *Vibhāṣā* (E. Lamotte, *Histoire*, etc., 1958, 158–60). For years I had been puzzled by the usage of the term *vibhāvanā* in the *Prajñāpāramitā*. Here (on p. 118) Asaṅga gives a definition which shows that he understands the word to mean "leaving off the intense contemplation"; the meaning in the *Prajñāpāramitā* (see *R* p. 359). Wayman states expressly that "no evidence has so far come to light that the *Prajñāpāramitā sūtras* were influential in the formation of Asaṅga's *Yogācārabhūmi*" (p. 37), and I quite agree with him on that. In this connection Wayman tries to dissociate Asaṅga altogether from the *Abhisamayālaṅkāra*, and he points out that the first known commentary, that of Ārya-Vimuktisena, does not mention Vasubandhu, Asaṅga or any Yogācāra teacher (p. 38), but that the colophon of the Tibetan translation refers to him as "the principal of many great monasteries of the Kaurukullas of the Ārya-Mahāsaṃmata".[1] The colophon of the Kathmandu Ms. of A.D. 1110 speaks of *mahāyānasaṃsthitasya Śākyabhikṣoḥ Ārya-Vimuktisenasya Kaurukullāryasaṃmitīyasyānye(?)kodāravihārasvāmy.*[2] This connection of Vimuktisena with the Saṃmitīyas had been known since 1932 from Bu-ston, but had seemed so incredible to Obermiller that he weakened its impact by translating" he belonged (at first(!)) to the sect of the Kaurukullas" (II 155). The idea of a Saṃmitīya writing an authoritative commentary on the *Abhisamayālaṅkāra* must come as a shock to our preconceived notions, just as in England we were astonished last year to hear some of our Tibetan visitors describing themselves as both Gelugpa and Bon-po.

Putting it statistically, I would say that perhaps two percent of the terms mentioned in the *Yogācārabhūmi* are defined there in a way acceptable to all Buddhists. Most of the others came into use only at a time when the sects had separated, and when an agreed definition could no longer be expected. In consequence, the *Yogācārabhūmi* explanations of those terms are valid only for the later Mahīśāsakas in the Hīnayāna, and for the Yogācārins in the Mahāyāna sections, and cannot usefully be applied to the interpretation of the scriptures of other sects, whether Hīnayāna or Mahāyāna. Scholars must take extreme care never to transfer the con-

[1] This is how *Mhvy.* renders *maṅ-pos bkur-ba*. But see below.

[2] I have to thank Mr. Corrado Pensa of Rome and Dr. Jaini of London for this information. The colophon also confirms *Buddhadāsa* as the name of the nephew.

ceptions of one "lineage" to another "lineage", and never to explain Mādhyamika terms by anything else except Mādhyamika definitions, Yogācāra terms by anything else except Yogācāra definitions, and so for Sarvāstivādins, Theravādins, Mahīśāsakas and all the other sects.

22

Himalayan Pilgrimage. D. L. Snellgrove. B. Cassirer, Oxford. 1961 xvi + 304 pp. 45 plates.

This book is a sequel to Dr. Snellgrove's "Buddhist Himalaya", which was reviewed in *Oriental Art* in 1958 (*zaq*). It "tells of a journey made through the Tibetan regions of Western Nepal in 1956". These almost inaccessible districts had rarely, if ever, been visited by European travellers. The journey lasted seven months; and, travelling everywhere on foot with Pasang, his Sherpa assistant (and for the author "to lose Pasang would be like losing both my hands"), Dr. Snellgrove covered more than a thousand miles of mountainous country and crossed some fifteen major passes of between 17,000 and 20,000 feet. The areas which he explored included Dolpo, "the highest inhabited region in the world".

Snellgrove's narrative is concerned with four different themes. (1) He offers much new information about the Nying-ma-pa and Bon beliefs still prevalent in this part of the world. (2) He gives a delightful account of the incidents which marked his journey, and in this respect his is one of the most pleasant and stirring travel books to have appeared in recent years. (3) He indulges in constant polemics against mistakes in the Survey of India maps. And (4) he makes a few remarks about the history of Nepal, and its social and political life. These latter amount to very little, and are really quite incidental. Likewise the "radical criticisms" of the Survey of India maps, which Dr. Snellgrove puts forward with so much feeling, are of no interest to the general public, although they may excite a few geographers. The value of the book lies in themes (2) and (1).

The description of the difficult and arduous journey is extremely readable. It does great credit to the humanity of the author—a Roman Catholic student of Buddhism—and also reveals the characters of those who either participated in this expedition or who met it at the various stages of its journey.

From a scholarly point of view, however, the real core of the book lies in the information it contains about the more primitive and archaic strata of Tibetan religion, i.e. the Nying-ma-pa and Bon practices which, in a fossilized form, are comparatively well preserved in this area. Originally converted to Buddhism by missionaries from the Sa-kya-pa and Karma-pa sects, the inhabitants of these remote parts of the Himalayas remained totally unaffected by the subsequent reforms of Tsong-kha-pa, and are now inclined to revert to Nying-ma-pa observances which centre around Padmasambhava (p. 78). Dr. Snellgrove's account of the images, scriptures and rituals to be found in the many monasteries he visited is of great value to all students of Tibetan beliefs. As everywhere else, Buddhism is also here in a state of general decay. Most monasteries "tell the sad story of past glory and present ignorance and neglect" (p. 91). It is to Dr. Snellgrove's credit that he brings to life the past glory as well as the present decline.

Exceptionally important are also the indications given about the Bon-po, the indigenous religion of Tibet, which is still largely unknown and which seems to be much alive in Western Nepal. The relentless pressure of Lamaism has for centuries forced the Bon-pos to closely imitate Buddhism in order that they might survive at all. Scholars are therefore inclined to think little of the latter-day Bon-po religion and to regard it, in the words of Prof. Hoffmann, as "a dead branch of Tibetan culture". Nevertheless on the basis of his constantly repeated observations Dr. Snellgrove tells us that "I doubt if any religion could be 'debunked' so easily, yet its practice has every appearance of validity and I certainly learned not to regard these p'ön-pos just as foolish imitators of the Buddhists. It seemed in fact that their religious practice excelled that of all the other monasteries of Dolpo" (p. 126).

The plates show a number of works of art, and also many of the scenes encountered on the journey, as well as the persons who took part in it. On plate XXI Dr. Snellgrove himself can be seen, and his appearance is not unlike that of the people whom he visited. To believers in reincarnation this will furnish the clue to the evident sympathy which he shows for the Tibetan inhabitants of these border districts. To others his sympathetic understanding must remain somewhat of a puzzle, although they will be grateful for its results as presented in this book.

23

G. Tucci. *The Theory and Practice of the Mandala.* Rider & Co., London, 1961. ix + 147 pp. 4 plates.

"Mandalas", nearly unknown in Europe 50 years ago, are gradually coming into their own. The harmonious beauty of Tibetan Mandala paintings easily appeals to our esthetic sense. From 1929 onwards G. G. Jung and his school have written much about Mandalas as affording important indications of unconscious processes. In 1949 B. Bhattacharya made accessible Abhayākaragupta's *Niṣpanna-yogāvalī* (*ca.* A.D. 1100), one of the most important Buddhist treatises on the subject. Nine years later E. Haarh contributed some more material from Tibet (see *Acta Orientalia* xxiii, pp. 57–91, where also references to most of the further non-Japanese literature can be found). What was still needed was a comprehensive survey of the often obscure metaphysical and psychological assumptions which actuated the minds of those Indian and Tibetan thinkers who regarded Mandalas as a means of salvation. Prof. G. Tucci, equally at home in Tibetan and Indian thought, supplied this want in 1949 with his *Teoria e pratica del mandala*, which has now faithfully and skilfully been translated into English with a few additions here and there.

The book falls into five chapters. The first deals with "the doctrinal basis of the Mandala", and describes the opinions currently held in India about the process of salvation, with particular emphasis on the Yogācāra school of Asanga and Vasubandhu. The second, "the Mandala as a means of reintegration", explains how Mandalas can help to bring about a revulsion from all the illusory things of the samsaric world, and effect a reunion with the light of the one absolute consciousness. This method requires that, first of all, cosmic and mental processes should be expressed in *mythological* form. "*Māyā* is an individualizing force, which personifies. Therein lies its strength, but also its weakness. *Māyā* assumes forms and figures by means of which contact may be established between it and consciousness, and it may be, in this way, limited in its power. The cosmic process is expressed in images, pictorially. Its successive phases . . . are imagined under the form of deities, male or female, peaceful or terrible. They are almost always deities borrowed from popular religious experience. Often they are very ancient mythographs which have survived among the lowest and most uncultured classes, and which therefore preserve primitive and barbarous intuitions. Alternatively such images have been purposely invented in order to express, with the efficacy which symbols have, the intricacy of the psychological forces underlying the multifarious movements of the world" (p. 21 cr. to p. 29 of the original). Symbols allow us to "grasp, dominate and dissolve" the forces of the universe. "Through them one can give form to the infinite possibilities which lie in the depth of the unconscious, to inexpressed fears, to primordial impulses, and to age-old passions" (p. 22).

Given this assumption, the Mandala provides a "scheme which represents, in complex and symbolical fashion, the drama of disintegration and reintegration", and it expresses that twofold process "by means of symbols which, if they be wisely read by the initiate, will induce the liberating psychological experience" (p. 22). Tucci then clearly and concisely describes the system of archaic magical concepts which our somewhat over-intellectualized modern mind has begun to lose sight of: the idea of a diagram of the cosmos, considered "as a vital process which develops from one essential Principle and rotates round one central axis, Mount Sumeru, the axis of the world" (p. 23); the reproduction of this diagram in ritual vases, royal palaces, Stūpas, temples or Mandalas, and its employment for the representation of the psyche, wherein the drama of the universe is reproduced in each one of us; the universal magical practice of marking off a sacred, ritually pure, spot by means of a circle; the more specifically Indian symbolism of the lotus, and the evocation of deities by means of syllables which "constitute their occult (*arcano*) principle" (pp. 30–37); and finally the vast complex of magical identifications, correspondences, transformations and transfigurations which is woven round these basic ideas.

Chapter 3, "the symbolism of the Mandala and of its various parts", first deals with the fivefold division of all cosmic forces adopted by both Śivaism and the Vajrayāna. It then proceeds to consider the significance of the fearsome figures who guard the Mandala, of the letters or syllables by which deities may be approached, the status of the deities" who have no reality of their own, but are mere creations of our karmic state" (pp. 65–70), and finally their function which is to "indicate the various stages of return" to the absolute consciousness, as well as the psychological forces which effect it (p. 68). The chapter concludes with some remarks about the decisive and indispensable role of the Guru, and with a fine survey of the division of people into four temperamental types, to which a four-fold division of the esoteric scriptures is made to correspond. The fourth chapter, "the liturgy of the Mandala", is devoted to the ritual observances connected with the construction and designing of Mandalas and with the evocation of the deities. In the last chapter, "the Mandala in the human body", Tucci shows how, in accordance with the equivalence of events in macrocosm and microcosm, the human body can be regarded as a mandala, as the scene of the quest for enlightenment, and how the body can be made into an instrument of salvation. This leads to a brief description of the physiological theories and methods of *Haṭhayoga*, and some attention is also paid to the sexual implications of several Tantric systems.

Nearly all extant examples of Mandalas are Tibetan, and belong to the Buddhism of the "Adamantine Vehicle". In their works of art the Tibetans have, however, faithfully carried out the instructions of their Indian teachers (p. 45). In India itself the Buddhists alone seem to have known elaborate Mandalas which represent well-defined deities in their visual form. In Hinduism their place is taken by Yantras, which consist of geometrical lines and Sanskrit letters, for reasons which Tucci has explained on pp. 46–8 and 60–1. The metaphysical and soteriological ideas behind the Buddhist conception of Mandalas were, however, shared by other mystical schools in India, and Tucci's survey includes the relevant teachings of the Upanishads, Jains, Śivaites, and even Vishnuites.

The beginnings of the Tantra are a mystery much discussed by historians, who are often inclined to believe in a non-Indian origin. In *The Art Quarterly*, 1950, pp. 107–19, Schuyler Camman has published a most interesting and suggestive article which attempts to trace the Buddhist Mandalas back to the Chinese TLV mirrors of the Han dynasty. It is noteworthy that Tucci also seems to have observed the striking similarity in pattern between Buddhist Mandala and TLV mirror, since he publishes a photograph of such a mirror as Plate IV, and describes it on p. 141. I have, however, failed to find in his text any hint as to the significance which he attaches to this similarity. Where he attempts a historical derivation, Tucci goes back much further than the Han, and refers to the Assyro–Babylonian *zikurrats* and to the imperial cities of the Iranian kings (pp. 23, 43). It may well be that he regards the TLV mirrors as just one example of a widely diffused magical pattern, of which the origins are lost in pre-historic times.

Tucci's book is a really authoritative treatise on a mentality which must seem exceedingly strange to this present age. His arguments are substantiated by lengthy quotations from the Indian and Tibetan literature, like the *Sādhanamālā*, the *Tantrasāra*, the *Guhyasamāja* and the *Book of the Dead*. In a book of this size there was, of course, no room for the detailed description of more than one Mandala (that of rDo-rje-can). Others can be found in Tucci's large work on *Tibetan Painted Scrolls*. It is only once, I think, that the author has slightly nodded. The Italian text on p. 112 associated the irreversibility of a Bodhisattva with the 10th stage of his career whereas that is usually said to be achieved on the 7th or 8th stage. Either the author or the translator perceived that something was amiss, and the English translation combines truth with error in the following confusing sentence: "Thus a Bodhisattva, when he attains the seventh(!) land(!), the tenth(!) stage of the spiritual ascent which he must effect (quando è giunto alla decima terra, al decimo stadio dell'ascesa spirituale che deve percorrere) is *avinivarttanīya*, he never turns back again" (p. 112). On page 99 Samayatārā, to judge from the text of the *Guhyasamāja* (p. 2), is an oversight for Māmakī, and on p. 53 Amoghavajra should be Amoghasiddhi. On pp. 7, 102, 135 and plate I the transliteration of Tibetan words is unsatisfactory. On p. 123 one should read "non-initiates" for "initiates", on p. 59 "skull" for "skill". This is not a very fat book, but its importance should not be measured by its bulk. It can be wholeheartedly recommended.

24

Lu K'uan Yü (Ch. Luk). *Ch'an and Zen Teaching. Third Series.* Rider & Co. 1962. 306 pp. 3 illus.

The third volume of Luk's ambitious series on "Ch'an and Zen" contains three translations. On pp. 15–102 we have the famous "Altar Sutra" of Hui-neng, known as "the sixth Patriarch", previously (in 1931) translated by Wong Mou Lam of Shanghai. Students of Zen literature will be pleased now to have an alternative rendering of this famous classic. Secondly, on pp. 116–145 Luk gives us Yung Chia's "Song of Enlightenment" together with his own comments. Suzuki's translation of this Song can be found in the

"Manual of Zen Buddhism" (1935, pp. 106–21), and Luk's explanations are useful when treated as a gloss on Suzuki's so much more distinguished version.

Thirdly, on pp. 159–278 Luk translates "The Sutra of complete enlightenment" (Taisho 842), a Sanskrit work translated into Chinese about A.D. 650, together with the commentary of the Ch'an master Han Shan (*ca.* 1600). This Sutra has never before been done into a European language, and we now have a rough idea of what it says. As a translator of Mahayana Sutras from the Sanskrit I must add, however, that Luk has given us only a first draft. Much of his translation fails to ring true, and Mr. Luk is clearly fairly unacquainted with the Sanskrit language. He may well have considered a knowledge of Chinese alone as sufficient for his task, in view of his staggering assertion that "the ancient Sanskrit in use at the time of the Buddha has disappeared and is now completely unknown in India and in the West" (p. 44). Normally it is generally assumed that the canons of ordinary scholarship demand an intimate knowledge of Sanskrit on the part of those who translate Sanskrit Sutras, even if from the Chinese or Tibetan. Otherwise their work is apt to remain unconvincing.

25

A. Macdonald: *Le Maṇḍala du Mañjuśrīmūlakalpa*. (Collection Jean Przyluski, tome III). i + 190 pp. Paris: Adrien-Maisonnaeuve, 1962.

Students of the *Mañjuśrīmūlakalpa* (= MMK) require great patience and self-denial, because the text is badly transmitted and often tedious. Of the 55 chapters of the Sanskrit original, Mlle Lalou has translated chs. IV–VI (not IV to VII, as stated on p. 1; cf. M. Lalou, *Iconographie*, etc., 1930, p. 6), and ch. XXXIX (or XLI) in 1932. Now Mme. Macdonald, one of her pupils, has translated the bulk of ch. II (from MMK 36, 21 onwards; MMK 25–36 are summarized on pp. 77–81) and the whole of ch. III, and has also printed the Tibetan text of those two chapters as far as translated (pp. 154–74). No student of later Buddhism can withhold from her a feeling of gratitude for what she has attempted to do.

The author has prefaced her translation with an Introduction of 95 pages. First of all she determines (on pp. 2–20) the literary affiliations of this scripture, its date (700–1500) and the discrepancies between the Sanskrit, Chinese and Tibetan versions. The remainder of the Introduction gives us much varied information, of which the most valuable are long quotations from Tibetan masters about the *Kriyā* Tantras. Generally speaking this information tends to bewilder. The author has read greatly in excess of her understanding, and much that was obscure before remains as obscure as it was. The documentation is fairly extensive, though mainly French. Our own Dr. Snellgrove is either ignored (his *Hevajratantra* is never mentioned, even on 70!), or snubbed (pp. 13 and 36, n. 1, where the omission of a decisive comma (between "*vajra*" and: "in") in the quotation from *Buddhist Himālaya* makes him appear more foolish than he actually is).

With Mlle. Lalou and Prof. Edgerton Mme. Macdonald belongs to the school of thought which stricly abides by the objective linguistic data, and refuses to enter into the spirit of the texts. Though not without its strong points, this method leads to frequent misinterpretations of the teaching. I will give just three examples, one minor though typical, and two major.

(1) On p. 21, in a passage preserved only in Tibetan, the *samādhi* called *yul rnam-par 'jig-pa* is translated as *destructeur du pays*. In fact, *yul* has *two* main Sanskrit equivalents, *deśa* and *viṣaya*. Obviously the second is meant here. The *viṣaya* are the range, domain, sphere or province of the senses and their objects, which are shattered (*vidhvaṃsana*, Mhvy. 622) by this *samādhi*.

(2) Page 141 presents us with the absurdity of a Buddha reborn several times as a Buddha, i.e. *pour cette vie même, dans les renaissances successives jusqu'à la dernière incarnation, toujours (l'initié) atteindra l'état de Buddha*. The Sanskrit has (MMK 51): *ihaiva janmai parasparāsu ca yāvat paścimakaṃ niyataṃ buddhatvaṃ prāptavyam iti*, which means, "in this birth already, and in his successive (births) until the last he can be quite certain that he will win Buddhahood". Mme. M. could have caught the idea from the Tibetan which speaks of *eight* births preceding Buddhahood (p. 170). Her translation, i.e. *pour cette vie-ci et ensuite pour les huit renaissances (qui suivront) il obtiendra l'état de Buddha*, is doctrinally impossible. The passage in question refers to the *abhiṣekha* of the Śrāvakas and Pratyekabuddhas which confers the state of an *ārya* (but cf. p. 133, n. 6), equivalent to the "Streamwinner" of the older traditions, who is reborn seven times at the most (*saptakṛdbhavaparama*). The text therefore tells us that the person in question, *before* he becomes a Buddha, will have eight births, counting his present as the first.

(3) Like other Tantric specialists Mme M. might have paid closer attention to the technical terms commonly used by Buddhists. By failing to do so she has caused on the subject of what she calls the *dieux Laukika et Lokottara* a confusion which pervades her entire book, and which I cannot unravel within the compass of a brief review. Her own quotations fail to bear her out. At p. 139 *laukika* means "worldlings", and not (*dieux*) *Laukika*. On p. 33 *sarvāśca laukika-lokottarāḥ sāsravānāsravamantrā* means clearly, "and all the mantras worldly and supramundane, impure and pure", and not *tous les mantras purs et impurs, de tous les dieux Laukika et Lokottara*. Neither the Sanskrit nor the Tibetan has anything about *dieux* (=*devā*?). A similar passage from MMK 51 is translated correctly on p. 141 l.7, but distorted on p. 68 by the arbitrary insertion of (*dieux*). Having once saddled herself with these *dieux*

Laukika et Lokottara, whom she regards as a fourth *kula* in addition to the three generally recognized in the MMK (pp. 35–6), Mme M. desperately tries to find out who they are. She devotes a disproportionate part of her Introduction to a series of unconvincing guesses, and at one point even assures us that *le clan des Lokottara ne se distingue pas des Laukika dans le MMK* (p. 60). Well, well! The reader must be warned that apart from initial mistranslations there is no substance to these lengthy speculations.

Taking it all in all, this is a painstaking study, but a greater breadth of vision would have preserved its author from many errors.

26

J. Ph. Vogel. *The Goose in Indian Literature and Art.* E. J. Brill, Leiden, 1962. vi + 74 pp. 12 plates. Memoirs of the Kern Institute, no. II.

Some of the most satisfying contributions to scholarship are those which take up just one simple and manageable problem and solve it once and for all. A good example is the brilliant article which Prof. Brough published in 1950, and which showed beyond any possible doubt that the initial phrase of Buddhist Sutras should be translated as "Thus have I heard at one time", and that all those are mistaken who translate "Thus have I heard. At one time the Lord dwelt at etc." Likewise in this book Prof. Vogel seems to have proved for all time that the Sanskrit word *haṃsa* always means a "goose", and never a "swan" or "flamingo". "We may", as he puts it, "therefore be quite certain that the Sanskrit word *haṃsa* always designates the goose and nothing else" (p. 74). The difficulty lay chiefly in that in Western Europe we are mainly acquainted with the domestic, and therefore degenerate, goose, and also in that different cultures attribute to birds quite different characters and personalities, as I have shown for the cuckoo and the lark in my study of *The Buddha's Law among the Birds* (1955). So, whereas to us the goose is a pretty ignoble, clumsy and stupid bird, to the Indians it has always appeared as an embodiment of the highest virtues, noted for its graceful gait and charming voice, and as a divine though not sacred animal.

For the rest Prof. Vogel's relatively brief monograph is built up on the same lines as his famous masterpiece on *Indian Serpent Lore* (1926). He collects the relevant facts about the goose first in the Epics, then in Buddhist literature, then in Indian fables and fairy tales, and finally in Indian art. The plates, which are very clearly printed, show that wherever the *haṃsa* is mentioned in writings, it is a goose which is shown on the corresponding sculptures. There can be, in my mind, no doubt that Prof. Vogel has proved his case. From my own special field of study I may perhaps add one further example to his material. The MS. Oxford, Bodl. a7 (R) shows the *Prajñāpāramitā* seated on a throne (this painting has been reproduced in

Oriental Art I, 1948, p. 8 and also on p. 313 of *The Concise Encyclopedia of Living Faiths*, ed. R. C. Zaehner, 1959). In the middle of the throne there are on the right and left two distinctly frisky lions jumping forward and grinning happily, whereas above them there are two quacking geese. We all know that the "lion's roar" is one of the similes commonly used to describe the Buddha's teaching, and now we learn from Prof. Vogel that the goose was a symbol for non-attachment and psychic power (pp. 30–1). All students of India owe a debt of gratitude to the author for the painstaking care with which in his old age he has collected the main facts about one of the most outstanding figures of Indian mythology.

27

R. B. Ekvall. *Religious Observances in Tibet: Patterns and Function.* xiii + 313 pp. University of Chicago Press, Chicago and London. 1964.

The author's knowledge of Tibet stems from two sources: (1) he spent much time in China first as a missionary and then as an intelligence officer with the U.S. Army; and (2) he has had many opportunities to consult Tibetan refugees in Berkeley and Seattle, among them the Dezhung Rinpoche, a man of quite outstanding ability, charm and erudition. The bulk of his book is devoted to the "six religious attitudes and acts" which he regards as characteristic of the Buddhism of Tibet, i.e. faith, expressed verbalized religion ("CHos aDon"), offerings, salutations, circumambulation and divination. Without being particularly original, Ekvall's account, within the limitations of "cultural anthropology", is generally sensible. The linguist will, however, not be altogether happy. The translations of technical terms are often awkward and quaint, to say the least; e.g. a Bodhisattva becomes a "Purged (!) Permeated (!) Hero Mind" (pp. 61, 232). Where the terms are derived from the Sanskrit, which the author has never learned and for which he professes a lofty disdain (on p. 45), they are sometimes positively wrong. To take one single example, "rNam Shes" is rendered as "manner known" (p. 82). In fact, the *rnam* does not stand for *rnam-pa*, "manner," but for *rnam-par*, Sanskrit *vi-*, in *vijñāna*! Mr. Ekvall is an honest man who does his best by Tibetan Buddhism, although the subtleties of a not particularly earthbound philosophy constantly elude him, and his assertions should be believed only where they are corroborated by other and better scholars.

28

A. Foucher. *The Life of the Buddha. According to the Ancient Texts and Monuments of India.* Abridged trsl. by S. B. Boas. xiv + 272 pp. 25 illus. Wesleyan University Press, Middletown, Conn., 1963.

Ever since its publication in 1949 I have regarded A. Foucher's

La vie du Bouddha as a real masterpiece and as the best account we have at present, if not of the life of the Buddha, then at least of the legend of the Buddha in its earlier stages. In consequence I welcomed the appearance of an American translation when I first heard of it. On closer examination I have changed my mind, and come to the conclusion that neither Mrs. Boas nor the Wesleyan University Press have given a fair deal to their readers.

First of all, how much of the book has actually been translated? We are assured that "the translator has shortened or omitted a few passages that seemed cumbersome in English or of no immediate interest to the general reader—excisions amounting to perhaps a dozen pages altogether". To demonstrate the fraudulent nature of this claim, I am content to submit a few figures: An average page of Foucher's *Vie* has 48 closely printed lines; an average page of the translation has 37 loosely printed lines. Foucher's French book has 381 pages, the translation only 267. How can anyone say that only 12 pages have been omitted, when 17,288 lines are rendered by 9,879 shorter lines? Nearly one half of Foucher's text has obviously fallen underneath the table.

Next, what about the fidelity of the translation, and how far does it "preserve the quality of Foucher's style"? Three examples must suffice. Puzzled by "At once there were six earthquakes and a sound like that of the gong particular to the (!) Magadha resounded" (p. 113) we turn to the French and find: "Aussitot celle-ci (= la terre) tremble de six manières (!) et résonne comme résonne sous le maillet (!) un gong du pays (!) de Magadha" (p. 159). At p. 175 we read that "the saints are the saints, and the martyrs are those who live with the saints". The whole point is lost, because the text says that "the saints are the saints, and the martyrs are those who *have to* live with the saints (sont ceux qui *ont à* vivre avec les saints," p. 231). Shocked by a sentence on p. 111 which says that "For the Buddhist ascetic, as for the whole monastic community, the spirit of love can only be the devil," we turn to p. 153 of the original, and there Foucher actually said that "pour le samgha bouddhique, comme pour toute communauté monastique, le Génie de l'Amour ne peut être que le Démon"—followed by three pages of explanations omitted by Mrs. Boas. In other words although Mrs. Boas may well be "a native of France", her command of the English language leaves much to be desired. In fact, her translation throughout is a mere travesty of the admirable original.

Finally the translator, Simone Brangier Boas, described as a "sculptor", is innocent of all scholarly accomplishments. On p. 261, for instance, she gives us the following instructive note: "The Four Noble Truths are: (1) birth is suffering, (2) old age is suffering, (3) disease is suffering, and (4) death is suffering." We did not know that before! Further elementary mistakes occur on pp. 110 (cf. p. 151), 261, 269, 270 (cf. p. 257) and 272, and "The Wheel of Life" on pp. 12 translates *avidyā* as "Unknowable."

To sum up: If the Wesleyan University Press cherishes its reputation it ought at once to withdraw this book from circulation. People who can least afford it, such as my students in Wisconsin University, are made to part with nearly nine dollars for something which is not worth a hamburger.

29

Bhikṣu Thich Minh Chau. *The Chinese Madhyama Āgama and the Pāli Majjhima Nikāya* (A Comparative Study). The Saigon Institute of Higher Buddhist Studies, Publ. Dpt., 1964. 388 pp.

The Sutras, which contain by far the largest part of the Buddha's teachings, have been handed down to us in two distinct recensions,—that of the Theravādins of Ceylon which is preserved in Pali, and that of the Sarvāstivādins of the North-West of India which we possess partly in the original Sanskrit, and partly in Chinese and Tibetan translations. By a series of historical accidents, the English-speaking public has for many years been able to read translations of the Pali scriptures, but all work on the Sarvāstivādins has been published in French or German and has therefore remained largely unknown in this part of the world. That is a great pity because the Northern scriptures are as authentic and as old as the Southern ones, and both "are based upon a common heritage", "upon an original text which is lost now" (p. 1). The situation has, however, changed now that Bhikshu Thrch Ming Chau, a member of the Samgha of Vietnam who has previously published a comparative study of the Chinese and Pali versions of the "Questions of King Milinda", has given us his Ph.D. thesis approved by the Bihar University and produced under the guidance of Prof. S. Mookerjee. In it he compares the *Madhyama Āgama* of the Northern Buddhists with the Pali *Majjhima Nikāya*, and Prof. Mookerjee's introduction is well justified in saying that "his work is that of a scholar, critical, cautious and faithful to the truth" (p. 2).

The Northern version of the "Middle Length Sayings" contains 222 Sutras, as against 152 in the Pali. Of these, 98 Sutras are common to both. Minh Chau's book is concerned only with them and he subjects them to a fourfold comparison: (1) He singles out 22 points of difference of a more general character (pp. 18–37) which are connected with the sectarian preferences of the two schools concerned. (2) He considers their literary form (pp. 45–78) and discusses their arrangement, their titles, the circumstances under which they were preached, the interlocutors to whom they are attributed, and so on. (3) He compares the two versions "as far as the doctrine is concerned", i.e. first the teachings about the path to Nirvana which, following Buddhaghosa, he distributes under the headings of morality, concentration and wisdom (pp. 81–150) and then those which concern the Buddha and the Samgha (pp. 153–82), followed by some remarks about verses and similes, and about the conclusions of the Sutras (pp. 183–207). And fourthly (4) he compares section by section fifteen particularly important Sutras (i.e. Pali M.N. 1, 2, 6, 7, 18, 20, 26, 32, 43–4, 56, 61, 82, 91, 93) and carefully notes all their similarities and divergences (pp. 209–320). The book concludes with 10 "Appendixes", among which Appendix 10 "Pali-Chinese-English Equivalents" is particularly welcome.

This brief survey shows the richness of the contents of this book which is indeed a publication of quite unusual merit and importance, indispensable to all those who are interested in the problems surrounding the standing and authority of the Pali Canon. Its scholarship is beyond reproach, and it fulfills a need which many have felt for a long time. It is, in any case, heartening to know that discrepancies between the two versions, though very numerous, nowhere affect the substance of the teaching. But even in the case of a basic and venerable text like the *Satipatthānasutta* the verbal differences between the Chinese and the Pali are so great (pp. 87–94) that neither can reasonably claim to literally represent the words of the Buddha himself. "Of this application on mindfulness, both versions offer almost the same materials, as the basic approach to the contemplation is identical. But the compilers of both versions seem to have (had) a free hand in collecting materials and this explains the difference in details we witness here. We can safely conclude that both versions were derived from the same source but the selection of details was left to the compilers more or less freely" (pp. 94–5).

Here it will be sufficient to say a few words about the differences of a more general character which form the first part of Minh Chau's study. Some of these concern trifles—e.g. the Chinese adopts a twelvefold division of the Scriptures, as against the ninefold division of the Pali. In other cases the Sutras are made to support specific sectarian tenets, e.g. to the Sarvāstivādins Mahākāśyapa was "the foremost disciple", but to the Theravādins it was Śāriputra; in the Pali the Buddha explicitly designates his doctrine as *theravāda*, but the Chinese omits the passage; the Chinese, on the other hand, contains references to the existence of past and future things, and to the possibility of Arhats falling back, which are lacking in the Pali. So it appears as if in these respects the Sutras had been "doctored" at some time or other in the course of their transmission. Of particular interest are those occasions on which the Sarvāstivādins are nearer to the Mahayana than the "Elders" were. They lay greater stress on compassion and the observance of vegetarianism, they are more liberal in their interpretation of the monastic rules, they describe more frequently the display of miraculous powers on the part of the Buddha and his disciples, and are prone to rather overdo their descriptions of the majesty of the Buddha and the size of his retinue and audience. The author is not quite clear in his own mind how to account for these similarities. In one passage he says that "all the above considerations testify to a later stage of Buddhism, into which some Mahāyānic ideas were already slowly creeping in" (p. 37), and we must, of course, bear in mind that Sanghadeva's actual Chinese translation was made in A.D. 398, though that does not tell us much about the date of his original which was probably written in Prakrit (and not Sanskrit). But when he refers to the stress on compassion, the Ven. Minh Chau seems to think that" this tendency towards compassion which was already latent in the early texts of Sanskrit Buddhism might account for the stress on Maitrī or compassion taken by the Mahāyānists" (p. 31). The author's indecision accurately reflects the present state of our knowledge which does not enable us to be sure where the priority lies.

30

Friedrich Weller. *Zum Kāśyapaparivarta*, Heft 2: *Verdeutschung des sanskrit-tibetischen Textes.* (=*Abhandlungen der sächsischen Akademie der Wissenschaften zu Leipzig, Philologisch-historische Klasse*, Band 57, Heft 3) Berlin, Akademie Verlag, 1965.[1]

Few reliable translations of Mahāyāna Sutra had appeared before 1950. Max Mueller had dealt adequately with some smaller texts like the *Hṛdaya*, *Vajracchedikā* and *Sukhāvatīvyūha* (1894). But Kern's *Saddharmapuṇḍarīka* (1884) and Bendall-Rouse's *Śikṣāmuccaya* (1922) are often very misleading, and also D. T. Suzuki's *Laṅkāvatārasūtra* (1932) will have to be completely re-done. After 1950 we have, on the other hand, J. Ensink's good *The Question of Rāṣṭrapāla* (1952), E. Lamotte's excellent *Vimalakīrtinirdeśa* (1962), a number of tolerably accurate *Prajñāpāramitās* from E. Conze (1957–64), and now there is F. Weller's superb *Kāśyapaparivarta.*[2] So there has been some progress though it is not very fast, and only a tiny section of the Mahāyāna Sūtras is as yet accessible in European languages.

In its bulk the *Kāśyapaparivarta* is one of the earlier Mahāyāna Sūtras, though, like most others, it grew over the years (pp. 8–27). On pp. 6–8 Prof. Weller gives a fine survey of its contents. It is in the main devoted to two themes only—the ideal of a Bodhisattva and a new conception of emptiness. The first was a development of the bhaktic trends in Buddhism—to some extent represented in the literature by the Jātakas—and the other of the Abhidharma. It was the combination of these two mutually unrelated trends which

[1] Heft 1 = *Mongoischer Text* (= *Abh. d. sächsischen Akad. der Wissenschaften zu Leipzig, Philologisch-historische Klasse*, Band 54, Heft 2) (Akademie-Verlag, Berlin, 1962).

[2] J. Nobel's *Suvarṇaprabhāsa* (1958) would have been much more authoritative if (1) he had translated it from his own almost perfect edition of the Sanskrit text, instead of using I-Ching's translation, and if (2) he had taken more interest in Buddhist doctrine.

constituted the Mahāyāna. An early date for the *Kāśyapaparivarta* may be surmised from the uncomplicated simplicity of the doctrinal statements and also from the almost total absence of polemics against opponents, who only now and then are chided for adhering to a *prādeśika-yāna* (p. 65 n. 6, cf. *Aṣṭas.* i 9 about Śreṇika's *prādeśikajñāna*).

What we must ask ourselves is whether its doctrine departs not only from that of the Hīnayāna, but also from genuine and original Buddhism. It is here that I reluctantly differ from Prof. Weller. At the end of his Introduction (pp. 54–8) he has, tentatively and with many reservations, put forth the thesis that the *Kāśyapaparivarta* has modified the teachings of the older Buddhism in response to the ideas of the Vedānta. His reasoning seems to me wrong on three grounds: (1) Weller *ipso facto* equates the older Buddhism with the Hīnayāna. I myself see the dogmatic Hīnayāna as that re-interpretation of the older Buddhism which subordinates everything strictly to the analytical categories of the Abhidharma. It took shape about 500 years after the Buddha's death and represented a narrowing of outlook because it could do no justice to those "pre-canonical" elements of the heritage which fitted none too well with the Abhidharma analysis. The Mahāyānists were those who reacted against this narrowing and stressed just those factors which it neglected, just as the Mahāsaṃghikas, Sautrāntikas and Pudgalavādins had done long before the rise of the Mahāyāna. (2) Weller assumes that the dogmatic conviction that all entities are 'not-self' belongs, not only to the dogmatic Hīnayāna, but also to archaic Buddhism. This, I think, is not the case, and I have given my reasons in *Buddhist Thought in India*, pp. 37–9, 122–34, 208–9. (3) Weller assumes that "mich bedünkt der alte Buddhismus habe eines solchen Positivums auch gar nicht bedurft, das als unverganglich dem Vergänglichen des Saṃsāra gegenübertrat" (p. 56). Nevertheless, even in the Pali scriptures Nibbāna is described as *accutam*, *niccam*, *dhuvam*, etc. He also repeatedly assures us that early Buddhism has an "agnostic" attitude to what is beyond this life. It seems to me that the Mahāyāna has not departed from it, but merely expresses it slightly differently. Whereas early Buddhism showed its agnosticism by just making few (mostly negative) statements about the Absolute, the Mahāyāna did so by making innumerable statements which it all declares to be equally meaningless.

Prof. Weller's translation is done with so much care that it must seem churlish to criticize it at all. On the many occasions when the meaning of Buddhist Sanskrit terms is in doubt, he appends alternative renderings in the footnotes. Nevertheless, since scholarship is a co-operative effort, I do not think that it will be amiss if with due respect I suggest some objections to some items in his translation, although for reasons of space I cannot give many reasons to support my queries.

To begin with, *evaṃ mayā śrutam ekasmin samaye* can no longer be translated as "So habe ich gehört: Einmal" (p. 61). Prof. Brough has in my view convincingly shown fifteen years ago that this preamble to all Sutras must be construed as "Thus have I (=Ānanda) heard at some time," and if subsequent scholars dissent from him they ought to give their reasons in a footnote. The word "Geschlecht(er)" is being rather overworked. At p. 66 n. 2 "die Geschlechter" renders *kulāni*, 'the families of the faithful'; at p. 67 n. 14 the "Geschlecht der Edlen" is the *āryavaṃśa*, 'the lineage of holy men' (also p. 132 n. 9), and at p. 122 n. 10 "Geschlecht" makes do for *gotra* ('clan'). On p. 91 "ausgereift zu", *pariṇāmitam*, should be 'dedicated to', as shown by *Aṣṭas.* ch. vi. The treatment of philosophical terms like *saṃskṛta*, etc. seems to me distinctly awkward. On p. 98 *saṃskṛtāsaṃskṛta* is rendered as "die summierten und die nicht summierten", and a note (n. 5) tries to show why the usual translation as "bedingt und unbedingt" is insufficient. I do not understand it, and against it I set Buddhaghosa's clear definition of *Visuddhimagga* viii 245; *saṅkatā vā asaṅkhata vā ti saṅgamma samāgamma paccayehi katā vā akatā vā*. Readers must be greatly puzzled when they find *saṃskāra* translated as "Summe" (p. 116 n. 16, p. 122 n. 8), or *asaṃskṛta* as "das Unsummierte" (p. 122 n. 9) or as "nichtsummiert" (p. 134 n. 18, p. 136 n. 2). On p. 160 n. 8 *āyuḥsaṃskāra* appears as "die Summen die das Leben ausmachen", whereas in fact in the *Mahāparinirvāṇasūtra* and elsewhere it means the factors which determine the length of someone's life-span. Equally ugly and meaningless is the rendering of *prajñapti* ('concept') as "Nominalismus" (p. 140 n. 20, p. 142 nn. 2–4). On p. 161 n. 12 Prof. Weller translates *prahāṇa* ('forsaking') as "Streben" (Tib. *spoṅ-ba*!), although on p. 134 n. 20 he correctly has "aufzugeben" (Tib. *spaṅbar bya-ba*). At p. 78 n. 6 "Masse der Wesen" for *sattvakāya* is not quite right, because it may seem to be in contrast with the "Elite der Wesen"; I would suggest "Gesamtheit der Wesen", or something like that. *Viṭhapayati* (p. 88 n. 1) normally does not mean "zustande bringt", but "fabricates", or "manufactures", as shown by F. Edgerton's examples and by Haribhadra's comment (*abhūtaparikalpaprabhavatvāt*). At p. 101 n. 16 *niḥsaraṇa* ('way out') should not be "Befreiung", which Weller usually employs for *mokṣa*, but "der Ausweg aus". At p. 122 (n. 1) *samatikrāntam* means "what has transcended", and not "ausserhalb", and at p. 122 n. 4 *nāsty utpāda* "is not produced", or, according to the commentary, "is not reproduced", and not "entwickelt sich nicht" (it is possible not to develop any further after one has reached some kind of existence!). The important distinction between *jīva* and *ājīva* is blurred. At p. 139 1.22 *pariśuddhājīvaḥ* appears as "der ein völlig lauteres Leben führt", at p. 143 n. 4 *mithyājīva* is one "der ein verkehrtes Leben führt", at p. 67 n. 13 *sarvamithyājīvaparivarjitaḥ* "ist frei allem falschen Leben", at p. 68 n. 11 *ājīvaśuddho* "geläutert in seiner Lebensführung" and at p. 143 1.10 *na jīvārthiko* is "legt keinen Wert auf sein Leben". I would say that in every case *ājīva* is, with Monier Williams, not "life" but "livelihood".

So far about the technical terms. As to Buddhist doctrine I noted that on p. 96 n. 6 the five *skandhas* are described as "die Dinge welche zusammen den menschlichen Körper ausmachen". This will do for behaviourists, but for Buddhists only one of the five is corporeal and the other four non-corporeal. "Alleged personality" would be better than "Körper". Likewise, it is not really true to say (at p. 99 n. 3) of *sparśa*, "darunter wird im allgemeinen verstanden, dass es die Berührung von Sinnesobject und Sinneswerkzeug bedeutet, wir sagten vielleicht, dass das Object einen Reiz auf das Sinnesorgan ausübt". In fact, it means the collocation of *three* factors, i.e., sense-organ, sense-object *and sense-consciousness*, as witness *Visuddhimagga* xiv 134 and *Triṃśikā* 20,2. By leaving out 'consciousness' at this point, Weller makes Buddhist epistemology nearly imcomprehensible.

There are also a few small inconsistencies. For the difficult *īryāpathā* the "Gehen, Stehen, Liegen und Sitzen" of pp. 82 n. 20, 85 n. 20, 132 n. 8 is surely preferable to the "vier Arten sich aufzuführen" of p. 133 n. 4. And for *kaukṛtya* the "Gewissensskrupel" of p. 161 n. 10 is better than the "Skrupel" of p. 64 n. 2. Note 9 on page 87 is badly formulated. For "statt *dharmān* sei—das setzt auch der tibetische Text voraus (which has *chos-la* E. C.)—*satvān* zu unterstellen", read: "statt *dharmān*, welche auch der tibetische Text voraussetzt, sei *satvān*, etc.". Throughout his book Prof. Weller equally considers the Sanskrit and the Tibetan text, and he generally holds the balance evenly between the two. Nevertheless I believe that on two occasions the Sanskrit text is definitely to be preferred, i.e., at p. 73 n. 17 and at p. 89 n. 7.

Misprints are very rare. In p. 83 n. 14 the second "um" is puzzling (and why should the four *saṃgrahavastūni* have been given in Pāli; the same applies to 141 n. 4); on p. 84 1.24 the notes should be numbered 22) and 23) respectively; on p. 89 the first note 16) should be 10); on p. 93 the last part of note 15 has got moved on to p. 94; at p. 108 n. 5 I do not understand "der"; at p. 127 n. 6 "Gedenken" should be "Gedanken"; at p. 134 n. 20 one should read *prahāṇāyābhiyukto*, and at p. 143 n. 4 "Leben" instead of "Lebens".

On innumerable occasions Prof. Weller has been able to correct the text of Stael-Holstein's unique Central Asian manuscript, and it is to be hoped that on the basis of his corrections someone will soon re-publish this text in a more accurate and readable form. After living for more than thirty-five years with the *Kāśyapaparivarta* (his "Index to the Tibetan Translation" appeared in Cambridge, Mass., in 1933), Prof. Weller has placed all students of Buddhism in his debt by producing an outstandingly conscientious and accurate study of this important Mahāyāna work.

31

Corrado Pensa, *L'Abhisamayālaṃkāravṛtti di Ārya-Vimuktisena, primo abhisamaya. Testo e note critiche* (=*Serie Orientale Roma* XXXVII). Rome, Istituto italiano per il medio ed estremo Oriente, 1967. xv + 135 pp.

This is a welcome and careful edition of approximately one half of a unique Nepalese manuscript of *ca.* A.D. 1000. The manuscript is rather corrupt, and the editor has regularly compared it with the Tibetan translation of the *vṛtti* and the Sanskrit text of the first *abhisamaya* of the revised version of the *Pañcaviṃśatisāhasrikā* as edited by N. Dutt in 1934. The result of his critical labours is a satisfactory text throughout.

Vimuktisena (the *Ārya* serves to distinguish him from the more shadowy *Bhadanta* V.[1]) comments on both the *Abhisamayālaṅkāra* (=*AA*) and the *Pañcaviṃśatisāhasrikā* (=*P*) side by side. As for the first, it now becomes clear that Vimuktisena was Haribhadra's principal source and that the *Āloka* took from him much more than is indicated by the few occasions when Vimuktisena is actually quoted, and C. Pensa has everywhere noted numerous passages which have been absorbed by Haribhadra. Nevertheless the doctrine is, as one would have expected, here in a more underdeveloped state, and, to give just one example, the elaborations of Haribhadra on the divisions of *pratipattyālambanam* (H 78–9) are here absent (pp. 78–9), as they are also in the *Ta chih tu lun*, and therefore constitute a late scholastic elaboration.

As regards *P*, Vimuktisena has set himself three tasks: (1) He has coordinated the text of *P* not only with the divisions given in the *AA* itself, but with the hundreds of later subdivisions which must have developed at some time in the oral tradition and which agree in all details, except for a few trifling exceptions (e.g. at I, 2, 5), with the headings and sub-headings of the Nepalese manuscript of *P*. (2) He indicates the passage of *P* which corresponds to some item in *AA* by usually quoting its beginning and then summing up the remainder of its contents (3) He picks out a number of individual terms and explains them. The commentary must have been addressed to an audience fairly familiar with brahminical Sanskrit and all the terms commented upon have some Buddhist flavour. In the present state of our knowledge these comments are the most valuable part of the work and teach us most about the thinking of the *Prajñāpāramitā*. Vimuktisena goes here often beyond Haribhadra, because he deals with words which occur in *P*, but not in the shorter *Aṣṭa* which Haribhadra had in view.

Some of the lesser technical terms are treated at quite inordinate length and it is interesting that some of these uncalled-for excursions

[1] See my *The Prajñāpāramitā Literature* (1960), p. 111. What I say there about Vimuktisena's *vṛtti* is only approximately true, based as it was on a few hasty glimpses of the Rome manuscript.

lead to the Yogācāra tradition. At the end of a description of *ṣaṣṭyaṅgopetaḥ svaro*, two pages long (pp. 113–5), Asanga is expressly quoted as the source. Two pages on the five *mithyājīva* (pp. 23–6)[1] are dragged in because, though absent in both *P* and *AA*, the explanation of the eight *mahāpuruṣavitarkā* (of *P* 21) contains the words *alpeccha* (cf. p. 23 l.19) and *saṃtuṣṭa* (cf. p. 25 l.19)[2] and corresponds to the *Bodhisattvabhūmi* and so does the explanation of the four *dharmoddānāni* (p. 21), mentioned not in *P*, but in *AA* I 1, e 20. These observations do, as C. Pensa (p. XIV n. 2) points out, bode ill for A. Wayman's attempt to completely dissociate Asanga from the *AA*. (cf. above p. 203).

There are a few very minor blemishes. Misprints have slipped through at 26,6; 40,21; 52,14; 60,25; 74,9; 77,8; 80,1 and 10; 90,11; 93,2; 106,14; 108,16; 112,7; 126,16 and 18. 126,15–18 should have been printed as verse. It is not quite correct to say at p. 70 n. 2 that "H ha *vijñānam*", when in fact one of two manuscripts, C, has the more probable *vijñāpanam*. And in this age of microfilms, the quotations from later parts of *P* should have been made from one of the many Nepalese manuscripts of that text, and not from the Tibetan translation in the *Tanjur*. The long quotation on pp. 12–13, for instance, is from folio 476a–b of the Cambridge Ms Add 1628 and fits as V 6e, 1–3 into the scheme of the *AA*.

We must hope that Dr. Pensa will soon bring out the second volume of Vimuktisena's work, which is such an important link in the unfolding of the Prajñāpāramitā literature in India.

[1] These are not just *falsità*, as C. Pensa says, but a monk's wrong ways of getting a living.

[2] In the lay-out of Pensa's text this far-fetched connection is not made very clear.

BIBLIOGRAPHY

BOOKS

A. CONTRADICTION AND REALITY, 32 pp., 1939. (Out of print).

B. BUDDHISM. Its Essence and Development. 224 pp. B., Cassirer, Oxford, 1951. Repr.: 1953, 1957, 1963. Paper back edition: 1960, 1963. Harper Torchbooks, 1959. French trsl., 1952, 1971, Payot. German trsl. 1953, Kohlhammer. Repr.: 1956; 1962 (+ Nachwort and Wort- und Sachverzeichnis), 1966. 1971—Italian trsl. 1955, Mondadori. Dutch trsl. 1971.

C. (Ed.) BUDDHIST TEXTS through the Ages. In coll. with I. B. Horner, D. L. Snellgrove, A. Waley, 323 pp., 1954. B. Cassirer, Oxford. Harper Torchbooks, 1964. German trsl.: Im Zeichen Buddhas, Fischer Bücherei n. 144, 1957. (Out of print.)

D. ABHISAMAYĀLAṄKĀRA. Trsl. & Sanskrit-Tibetan Indices. 223 pp. Serie Orientale Roma VI. 1954. (Reprinting).

E. SELECTED SAYINGS FROM THE PERFECTION OF WISDOM. 133 pp. The Buddhist Society, London, 1955. 1968.

F. THE BUDDHA'S LAW AMONG THE BIRDS. Trsl. from Tibetan & Commentary. 65 pp. B. Cassirer, Oxford, 1956. (Otto von Taube, Tibetanisches Vogelbuch, Verlag der Arche, Zürich, 1957.)

G. BUDDHIST MEDITATION. 183 pp. Allen & Unwin, London. 1956. Reprinted: 1959, 1968. Unwin Books 1972. Harper Torchbooks 1969.

H. VAJRACCHEDIKĀ PRAJÑĀPĀRAMITĀ. Ed. and trsl., with Introd. and Glossary. 114 pp. Serie Orientale Roma XIII, 1957. (Reprinting).

I. BUDDHIST WISDOM BOOKS. The Diamond Sutra. The Heart Sutra. 110 pp. Allen & Unwin, London, 1958, 1966. Harper Torchbooks 1972.

K. AṢṬASĀHASRIKĀ PRAJÑĀPĀRAMITĀ. Trsl. (The Perfection of Wisdom in Eight Thousand Slokas), 225 pp. The Asiatic Society, Calcutta, Bibliotheca Indica no. 284. 1958. 1970.

L. BUDDHIST SCRIPTURES. The Penguin Classics, L. 88, 250 pp. 1959. Repr.: 1960, 1966, 1968, 1969, 1971, 1973.

M. THE PRAJÑĀPĀRAMITĀ LITERATURE. 123 pp. Indo-Iranian Monographs no. VI. Mouton & Co., 'S-Gravenhage 1960. (Reprinting).

N. A SHORT HISTORY OF BUDDHISM. xii, 117 pp. Chetana Ltd., Bombay (1960). 1961.
O. THE LARGE SUTRA ON PERFECT WISDOM, with the divisions of the Abhisamayālaṅkāra. Part I. L, 203 pp. Luzac & Co., London. 1961. [Parts II and III. vii, pp. 205–663. Madison, 1964—Seattle, 1966, pp. 584–7, 642–50 re-done].
P. THE GILGIT MANUSCRIPT OF THE AṢṬĀDAŚASĀHASRIKĀ PRAJÑĀPĀRAMITĀ. Chs. 55 to 70, corresp. to the 5th Abhisamaya. Ed. & trsl. xxvi + 390 pp. Serie Orientale Roma XXVI, Ismeo, Rome. 1962.
Q. BUDDHIST THOUGHT IN INDIA. Three phases of Buddhist Philosophy. 302 pp. G. Allen & Unwin, London. 1962. Ann Arbor Paperback, 1967.
R. MATERIALS FOR A DICTIONARY OF THE PRAJÑĀPĀRAMITĀ LITERATURE. vii + 447 pp. Suzuki Research Foundation, Tokyo. 1967, 1973.
S. THIRTY YEARS OF BUDDHIST STUDIES. xii + 274 pp. B. Cassirer, Oxford. 1968. University of South Carolina Press, 1968.
T. THE SHORT PRAJÑĀPĀRAMITĀ TEXTS. viii + 217 pp. Luzac & Co., London, 1973.

ARTICLES[1]

†1. Prajñāpāramitā-hṛdaya. Trsl. The Middle Way, xx 5, 1946, 105 (Reprinted in C, no. 146 and in E.)
2. The Hṛdaya Sūtra; its scriptural background. The Middle Way, xx 6, 124–7; 1946, xxi, 1, 9–11, 17.
3. Social and spiritual values. "Values", 1946, 16–18.
4. Buddhist values and the West. "Values", 1946, pp. 12–15.
5. On omniscience and the goal. The Middle Way, 1947, pp. 62–3.
†6. Text, sources and bibliography of the Prajñāpāramitāhṛdayasūtra. JRAS, 1948, pp. 33–51 (Repr. in S).
*7. Remarks on a Pala Manuscript in the Bodleian Library. Oriental Art, I 1, 1948, pp. 9–12.
8. An exhibition of Tibetan art in Leiden. OA II 1, 1949, 25–7.
†9. The iconography of the Prajñāpāramitā. OA II 2, 1949, pp. 47–52 (Repr. in S).
10. Preliminary Note on a Prajñāpāramitā Manuscript. JRAS 1950, 32–6.
†11. Rahulabhadra, Hymn to Perfect Wisdom. The Middle Way, xxvi 1, 1951, pp. 24–5 (Repr. in C as no. 142; and in L).
†12. The iconography of the Prajñāpāramitā. OA III 3, 1951, 104–9 (Repr. in S).

[1] **Items previously reprinted are marked with a †, those reprinted here with an asterisk.**

†13. Selected Sayings from the Perfection of Wisdom 1–4. "Stepping Stones", II 10, 1952, pp. 271–6 (Repr. in E).
†14. The literature of Perfect Wisdom. The Middle Way, xxvii 1, 1952, pp. 20–3 (Repr. in E).
†15. The composition of the Ashṭasāhasrikā Prajñāpāramitā. BLSOAS, XIV 2, pp. 251–62 (Repr. in S).
†16. The teachings of Prajñāpāramitā. The Middle Way, xxvii 3, 1952, pp. 89–90, 105 (Repr. in E).
†17. The doctrine of emptiness. The Middle Way, xxvii 4, 1953, pp. 124–7 (Repr. in E).
†18.19.21. The way to wisdom. I, II, III. The Middle Way xxviii 1, 1953, 11–14; xxviii 2, 1953, 58–61; xxviii 3, 1953, 95–8 (Partly repr. in G and Q). (see no. 86).
*†20. Compassion and Sympathetic Joy. "Self-knowledge," IV 4, 1953, 106–11 (Partly repr. in Q).
†22. The ontology of the Prajñāpāramitā. Philosophy East and West, III 2, 1953, 117–29 (Partly repr. in Q).
*†23. Love and Compassion in Buddhism. I. Love. MV xxviii 4, 1954, 134–7 (Partly repr. in Q).
†24. Hate, love and perfect wisdom. The Mahabodhi, v. 62, 1954, pp. 3–8 (Repr. in S).
*†25. II. Friendliness and compassion. MW xxix 1, 1954, pp. 8–11, 36 (Partly repr. in Q).
26. The sixth Buddhist Council. Manchester Guardian, 11.5.1954.
†27. The triple world. The Aryan Path, xxv 5, 1954, 200–4 (Partly repr. in Q).
†28. Conditions and the Unconditioned. The Mahabodhi, v. 62, 1954, 159–64 (Largely repr. in Q).
*†29. III. On selfless love. MW xxix 2, 1954, 62–6 (Partly repr. in Q).
†30. A Prajñāpāramitā Rupa. MW xxix 2, 1954, 49–50 (Repr. in E).
†31. The Holy Religion among the Birds. MW xxix 3, 1954, 118–21 (Repr. in F).
†32. Maitreya's Abhisamayālaṅkāra. East and West (Rome), V 3, 1954, 192–7 (Largely repr. in M).
†33. Buddhaghosa's Meditation on Death. I. Translation. MW xxix 4, 1955, 159–63 (Repr. in G, S).
†34. Buddhaghosa's Meditation on Death. II. Commentary. MW xxx 1, 1955, pp. 15–8 (Repr. in S).
†35. The Frontispiece to the "Diamond Sutra". MW xxx 1, 1955, pp. 1–2 (Repr. in I).
†36. Meditations on Emptiness. The Mahabodhi, v. 63, 1955, 203–11. (see no. 69) (Repr. in Q).
†37. Buddhaghosa's Meditation on Death. III. Commentary. MW xxx 2, 1955, pp. 54–7 (Repr. in S).

†38–†41. The Heart Sutra Explained. I. MW xxx, 1955, 104–7, 119; II. MW xxx, 1956, 147–53; III. MW xxxi, 1956, 20–4; IV. MW xxxi, 1956, 76–81 (Repr. in I).

*42. Professor Murti's "Central Philosophy of Buddhism." MW xxx 3, 1955, pp. 114–7, 136.

†43. Tantric Prajñāpāramitā Texts. Sino-Indian Studies, V 2, 1956, pp. 100–22. Visva Bharati, Santiniketan (Partly repr. in M).

44. Buddha's Anniversary. Decline or Revival? The Manchester Guardian, 21.5.1956.

45. Mystic Art of Tibet. Oriental Art, II 2, 1956, pp. 68–9.

45a. A Buddhist Student's Manual, 1956, pp. 243, 251–60.

†46. Philosophers and Techniques. The Hibbert Journal, LV 1, 1956, pp. 14–9 (Largely repr. in Q).

†47–†50. The Diamond Sutra Explained. I. MW xxxi, 1956, 109–14; II. MW xxxi, 1957, 166–70; III. MW xxxii, 1957, 8–12; IV. MW xxxii, 1957, 48–53 (Repr. in I).

†51. On "perverted views". East and West VII 4, 1957, 313–8 (Repr. in MW xxxii, 1957, 91–6).

†52. Marginal Notes to the Abhisamayālaṅkāra. Liebenthal Festschrift, Sino-Indian Studies, V 3–4, 1957, 21–35 (Pp. 6–11 repr. in M).

†53. Shakyamuni's Meeting with Dipankara. MW xxxii, 1957, 54–6 (Repr. in L).

†54. The Oldest Prajñāpāramitā. MW xxxii, 1958, 136–41 (Repr. in 75).

†55–58. The Road to Omniscience. (Astasāhasrikā, ch. 1–2). MW xxxiii, 1958, 8–12.57–9.99–101. xxxiii, 1959, 130–4, 129 (Repr. in K).

59. BUDDHISMO. Le Civiltà dell'Oriente. III, 1958, 745–848 (For the English version see N).

†60. Recent Progress in Buddhist Studies. MW xxxiv, 1959, 6–14 (Repr. in S).

†61. Buddhism: The Mahayana. In: The Concise Encyclopedia of Living Faiths, ed. R. C. Zaehner, 1959, 296–320 (Repr. in S). [Repr. 1964, 1971].

†62. The Buddhist "Personalists", The Mahabodhi 67, 1959, 118–26 (Repr. in Q).

*63. The Buddha's Bodies in the Prajñāpāramitā. Akten des 24ten Internationalen Orientalistischen Kongresses München. 1959, 530–1.

†64. Recent Progress in Mahayana Studies. The Middle Way xxxiv 4, 1960, pp. 144–150 (Repr. in S).

65. (Obermiller's *Ratnaguṇasaṃcayagāthā*), Corrections and Sanskrit-Tibetan-English Index, Mouton & Co., 'S-Gravenhage, 1960, 127–57.

66. The Calcutta Manuscript of the *Ratnaguṇasaṃcayagāthā*. Indo-Iranian Journal IV 1, 1960, pp. 37–58.
†67. The Development of Prajñāpāramitā Thought. In: Buddhism and Culture. Dedicated to D. T. Suzuki in Commem. of his 90th Birthday. ed. by S. Yamagucchi. Kyoto 1960, pp. 24–45 (Repr. in S).
†68. Recent Work on Tantric and Zen Buddhism. The Middle Way xxxv 3, 1960, pp. 93–8, 110 (Repr. in S).
†69. Meditations on Emptiness. The Middle Way xxxv, 1961, pp. 141–6 (Repr. in Q).
†70. The Three Doors to Deliverance. The Middle Way xxxvi, 1961, 10–16 (Repr. in Q).
†71. The Wishless Bliss (of Nirvana). The Middle Way xxxvi, 1961, 105–112 (Repr. in Q).
†72. Dharma and Dharmas. The Middle Way xxxvi, 1962, 142–6 (Repr. in Q).
†73. Dharmas and the Self. The Middle Way xxxvii, 1962, 186–191 (Repr. in Q).
†74. The Mahāyāna Treatment of the *Viparyāsas*. Oriens Extremus, IX 1, 1962, 34–46 (pp. 35–46 repr. with minor alterations, in Q).
†75. The Accumulation of Precious Qualities. Indo-Asian Studies, Part 1, ed. Raghu Vira, 1962, 126–78. (Repr. in K-A).
†76–†79. Saddharmapuṇḍarīka, chapter 5. trsl. The Middle Way. I. xxxvii, 1962, 95–6. II. xxxvii, 1963, 157–160. III. xxxviii, 1963, 15–7. IV. ibd. 49–51. (Repr. in S).
†80. The Perfection of Wisdom in Seven Hundred Lines. Kalpa I 2, 1963, 4–10, Kalpa I 3, 1963, 11–20 (Repr. in S and T).
†81. Buddhist Saviours. In: The Saviour God, ed. by S. G. F. Brandon, 1963 (Manchester University Press), pp. 67–82 (Repr. in S).
†82. Buddhist Philosophy and its European Parallels. Philosophy East and West, xiii 1, 1963, 9–23 (Repr. in S).
†83. Spurious Parallels to Buddhist Philosophy. Philosophy East and West, xiii 2, 1963, 105–115 (Repr. in S).
*84. (The present state and future prospects of) Buddhism. In: Asia, A Handbook to the Continent, ed. G. Wint, 1965, pp. 528–32. Repr. in Asia Handbook, 1969 (Penguin Reference Books), pp. 383–8.
85. Jataka. Encyclopedia Britannica, xii 969.
86. The Way of Wisdom. The Five Faculties. The Wheel Publication No. 65/66. Kandy, 1964. (Repr., with add., of no. 18, 19, 21).
87. The Buddha's lakṣaṇas in the Prajñāpāramitā. Journal of the Oriental Institute (Baroda), XIV, 1965, 225–9.
†88. The Adhyardhaśatikā Prajñāpāramitā, translated. Studies of Esoteric Buddhism and Tantrism, ed. by Koyasan University, 1965, 101–15. (Repr. in T).

*89. Buddhism and Gnosis in: Le origini dello gnosticismo. The Origins of Gnosticism. (Studies in the History of Religions, Supplements to "Numen"), xii, 1967, pp. 651–67.
90. "Maitreya's Questions" in the *Prajñāpāramitā*. Mélanges d'Indianisme à la mémoire de Louis Renou, 1968, pp. 229–42.
*91. Dharma as a Spiritual, Social and Cosmic Force, In: The Concept of Order, ed. P. G. Kuntz, pp. 239–52, University of Washington Press, 1968.
92. Introduction to: D. T. Suzuki, On Indian Mahayana Buddhism, pp. 1–29, Harper & Row, 1968.

REVIEWS

a. W. Ruben, Indisches Mittelalter; Die Philosophen der Upanishaden. OA I 3, 1948, pp. 148–9.
†b. S. Ringgren, Word and Wisdom. OA I 4, 1948, pp. 196–7 (Repr. in S).
c. S. Akhilananda, Hindu Psychology. OA II 1, 1949, pp. 40–1.
d. E. Lamotte, Le traité de la grande vertu de sagesse de Nagarjuna. OA II 4, 1950, pp. 167–8.
*e. M-Th. de Mallmann, Introduction à l'étude d'Avalokiteśvara. OA III 1, 1950, pp. 41–3.
f. H. Zimmer, Philosophies of India. MW xxvii 3, 1952, pp. 108–9.
g. H. de Lubac, Le rencontre du Bouddhisme et de l'Occident. MW xxvii 4, 1952, p. 152.
h. H. Harrer, Seven Years in Tibet. MW xxviii 3, 1953, p. 122.
*i. Radhakrishnan, etc., Upanishads. MW xxviii 4, 1954, p. 166.
k. Ceadel, Literatures of the East. MW xxviii 4, 1954, p. 167.
l. P. L. Landsberg. The Experience of Death. Aryan Path, 1954, pp. 83–4.
m. W. Liebenthal, The Sermon of Shen-hui. MW xxix 1, 1954, p. 45.
n. W. Y. Evans-Wentz, The Tibetan Book of the Great Liberation. MW xxix 1, 1954, p. 46.
o. S. Hummel (Three Books on Tibetan Art). OLZ 1954, 3/4, pp. 167–9.
p. K. Reichelt, The Transformed Abbot. MW xxix 3, 1954, p. 142.
q. L. P. Elwell-Sutton, Persian Proverbs. MW xxix 4, 1955, p. 179
r. R. Robinson, Chinese Buddhist Verse. MW xxix 4, 1955, pp. 180–1.
s. L. Bryson, Symbols and Values. MW xxix 4, 1955, p. 182.
t. S. Hummel, Geschichte der tibetischen Kunst. OLZ 1955, 3/4, pp. 175–7.

u. Runes, Treasury of Philosophy.—Spirit and Nature. MW xxx 1, 1955, p. 38.

v. A. Waley, The Nine Songs. The Aryan Path, 1955, p. 320.

w. D. T. Suzuki, Studies in Zen. The Aryan Path, 1955, pp. 321–2.

x. A. K. Gordon, Tibetan Religious Art. M. Lobsiger-Dellenbach, Nepal. O. Monod-Bruhl, Peintures Tibétaines. Tsung-lien Shen, Tibet and the Tibetans. OA, N.S.I 2, 1955, pp. 91–2.

y. Some recent books. MW xxx 2, 1955, pp. 84–6.

z. J. LeRoy Davidson, The Lotus Sutra in Chinese Art, MW xxx 3, 1955, pp. 125–6.

za. Chou Hsiang-Kuang, Indo-Chinese Relations. MW xxx 3, 1955, p. 126.

zb. W. Heissig, Mongolische Blockdrucke, A(sia) M(ajor). N.S. 5, 1956, p. 115.

zc. T. R. V. Murti, The Central Philosophy of Buddhism, Luzac's Oriental List. LXVI 4, 1955, pp. 61–2.

zd. (3) Books on Indian Art. MW xxx 4, 1956, pp. 176–8.

ze. H. P. Shastri, Scientist and Mahatma. MW xxi, 1956, pp. 58–9.

zf. E. Sarkisyanz, Russland und der Messianismus des Orients. MW xxxi 1, 1956, p. 61.

zg. Philosophy East and West. MW xxxi 1956, p. 62.

zh. Anil de Silva-Vigier, The Life of the Buddha. OA II 1, 1956, pp. 36–7.

zi. R. A. Stein, L'épopée tibétaine de Gesar. OA II 2, 1956, pp. 74–5.

zk. T. R. V. Murti, The Central Philosophy of Buddhism JRAS 1956, pp. 115–6.

zl. A. Bareau, Les sectes bouddhiques, etc. JRAS 1956, pp. 116–7.

*zm. Jungian Psychology and the Dharma. MW xxxi 2, 1956, pp. 95–6.

*zn. R. de Nebesky-Wojkowitz, Oracles and Demons of Tibet. MW xxxi 2, 1956, pp. 102–3.

zo. R. de Nebesky-Wojkowitz, Oracles, etc. Hibbert Journal (= HJ) LV, 1956, pp. 95–6.

zp. Buddhism and Jodo Shinshu. MW xxxi 3, 1956, pp. 135–6.

zq. T. Lobsang Rampa, The Third Eye. MW xxxi, 1957 pp. 182–4.

*zr. G. Tucci, Minor Buddhist Texts. I. MW xxxi, 1957, p. 184.

zs. The Travels of Fa-hsien. MW xxxi, 1957, p. 184.

zt. Morgan, The Path of Buddha; Hilliard, The Buddha, the Prophet and the Christ, HJ LV, 1957, pp. 312–4.

zu. A Buddhist Bible, ed. Goddard, MG 26.4.57.

zv. R. Collin, The Theory of Eternal Life. MW xxxii, 1957, pp. 36–7.

zw. S. Radhakrishnan, The Recovery of Faith. MW xxxii, 1957, p. 38.
zz. N. de Wojkowitz, Oracles and Demons of Tibet. OA N.S. III 2, 1957, pp. 75–6.
*zaa. Morgan, The Path of the Buddha. OA N.S. III 2, 1957, p. 76.
zab. P. Levy, Buddhism: a "Mystery Religion"? HJ LV, 1957, pp. 420–2.
zac. A. Govinda, Grundlagen tibetischer Mystik. MW xxxii, 1957, p. 81.
*zad. Problems of Buddhist History (Sangharakshita, A Survey of Buddhism). Aryan Path, July 1957, pp. 318–21.
*zae. G. Tucci, Minor Buddhist Texts. I. AM NS VI 1, 1957, pp. 122–3.
*zaf. F. R. Bischoff, Ārya Mahābala-nāma-Mahāyāna-sūtra. AM VI 1, 1957, pp. 128–9.
zag. D. Seckel, Buddhistische Kunst Ostasiens. OA III 3, 1957, pp. 113–4.
zah. Bareau, Les premiers conciles bouddhiques. JRAS 1957, pp. 273–4.
zai. D. L. Snellgrove, Buddhist Himalaya, MG 17.1.1958.
zak. J. M. Clark, Meister Eckhart. MW xxxii, 1958, pp. 160, 162.
zal. D. L. Snellgrove, Buddhist Himalaya. MW xxxii, 1958, pp. 162–3.
zam. Buddhism and the West (four books). MG 21.2.1958.
zan. D. T. Suzuki, Mysticism, Christian and Buddhist. The Aryan Path, 1958, p. 180.
zaq. G. Tucci, To Lhasa and Beyond; Snellgrove, Buddhist Himalaya. OA IV 1, 1958, p. 35.
zar. A. David-Neel, The Secret Oral Teachings. Luzac's Or. List LXIX 3, p. 45.
zas. Sis and Vanis, Tibetan Art. OA IV 3, 1958, p. 122.
zat. W. Y. Evans-Wentz, Milarepa. MW xxxiii, 1958, pp. 119–20.
*zau. Suvikrāntavikrāmīparipṛcchā, ed. T. Matsumoto. Indo-Iranian Journal II, 1958, pp. 316–8.
zav. R. Linssen, Living Zen, Luzac's Or. List LXIX, 1958, p. 69.
*zaw. H. V. Guenther, Philosophy and Psychology in the Abhidharma. MW xxxiii, 1959, pp. 163–4.
zay. Meister Eckhart, J. M. Clark and J. V. Skinner. MW xxxiii, 1959, p. 167.
*zaz. B. Bhattacharya, The Indian Buddhist Iconography. OA V 1, 1959, p. 31.
*zba. Bahm, Philosophy of the Buddha; M. Eliade, Yoga. HJ LVII, 1959, pp. 295–6.
zbb. Meisezahl, Die tibetischen Handschriften. OLZ LIV, 1959, Nr. 3/4, pp. 202–4.

zbc. The Cultural Heritage of India. HJ LVII, 1959, pp. 410–1.
zbd. G. Tucci, Minor Buddhist Texts II; J. Blofeld, The Wheel of Life; D. T. Suzuki, Zen and Japanese Culture. Luzac's Or. List LXX, 1959, pp. 53–6.
zbe. E. O. James, The Cult of the Mother Goddess; A. K. Gordon, The Iconography of Tibetan Lamaism. HJ LVIII, 1959, pp. 94–6.
*zbf. Suvikrāntavikrāmīparipṛcchā, ed. R. Hikata. IIJ III, 1959, pp. 232–4.
zbg. Sgam-po-pa, The Jewel Ornament of Liberation. MW xxxiv, 1959, pp. 133–4.
zbh. A. Czoma-Koros; Lamotte, Histoire; Symonds, Blavatsky. MW xxxiv, 1959, pp. 135–6, 138, 139.
zbi. A. K. Gordon, Iconography of Tibetan Lamaism. OA V 3, 1959, pp. 123–4.
zbk. B. Gray and J. B. Vincent, Buddhist Cave Paintings at Tun Huang. OA V 3, 1959, pp. 126–7.
zbl. W. Rahula, What the Buddha Taught. Luzac's Oriental List, LXX 4, 1959, p. 82.
*zbm. G. Tucci, Minor Buddhist Texts II; A. Ferrari, Mkhyen Brtse's Guide. Asia Major VII 1–2, 1959, pp. 230–1.
*zbn. (The Orthodoxy of Chinese Buddhism). Review: E. Zuercher, The Buddhist Conquest of China. MW xxxiv 4, 1960, pp. 173–6.
zbo. E. Zürcher, The Buddhist Conquest of China. Luzac's Oriental List, LXXI, 1960, pp. 4–5.
*zbp. A. F. Wright, Buddhism in Chinese History. HJ LVIII, 1960, pp. 317–8.
*zbq. Ch. Luk, Ch'an and Zen Teaching, Series One. The Middle Way xxxv 1, 1960, pp. 32–3.
zbr. J. Blofeld, The Wheel of Life, JRAS 1960, p. 100.
zbs. Ratnakīrtinibandhavālī, JRAS 1960, pp. 100–1.
zbt. Ch. Luk, Ch'an and Zen Teaching, First Series. Luzac's Oriental List LXXI 2, 1960, p. 26.
zbu. Ch. Luk, Ch'an and Zen Teaching, First Series, HJ LVIII, 1960, pp. 411–2.
*zbv. F. D. K. Bosch, The Golden Germ. Oriental Art VI 3, 1960, pp. 114–5.
*zbw. E. Dale Saunders, Mudrā. OA VI 3, 1960, pp. 115–6.
*zbx. D. L. Snellgrove, The Hevajra Tantra. BSOAS xxiii 3, 1960, pp. 604–6.
zby. Buddhism and the West (5 reviews). The Guardian 4.11.60, p. 7.
*zbz. Dr. Koestler and the Wisdom of the East. The Hibbert Journal LIX, 1961, pp. 178–181.
zca. M. Pallis, The Way and the Mountain. A. Govinda, Foundations of Tibetan Mysticism. HJ LIX, 1961, pp. 202–4.

zcb. D. Seckel, Einführung in die Kunst Ostasiens; F. Sierksma, The Gods As We Shape Them, OA vii, 1961, pp. 41–2.
zcc. N. Smart, A Dialogue of Religions. HJ LIX, 1961, pp. 301–2.
zcd. Govinda, The Psychological Attitude of Early Buddhist Philosophy; S. Dutt, Early Buddhist Monachism. HJ LIX, 1961, pp. 376–7.
zce. Govinda, The Psychological Attitude of Early Buddhist Philosophy. Luzac's Oriental List LXXII, 1961, p. 23.
zcf. R. Thapar, Asoka and the Decline of the Mauryas. The Middle Way xxxvi, 1961, p. 134.
*zcg. Ch. Luk, Ch'an and Zen Teaching. Second Series. The Middle Way xxxvi, 1961, pp. 136–7.
zch. R. Gnoli ed. The Pramāṇavārttikam of Dharmakīrti. JRAS 1961, p. 144.
*zci. G. Tucci, The Theory and Practice of the Mandala, OA vii 5, 1961, pp. 197–8.
*zck. D. Snellgrove, Himalayan Pilgrimage. OA vii 4, 1961, pp. 198–9.
zcl. Anthology of Zen. Ed. W. Briggs, Luzac's Oriental List LXXII, 1961, p. 62.
zcm. G. Tucci, The Theory and Practice of the Mandala. Luzac's Oriental List LXXII, 1961, pp. 62–3.
zcn. P. S. Jaini, Abhidharmadīpa. MW xxxvii, 1962, p. 226.
zco. Wen Fong, The Lohans and a Bridge to Heaven. OA viii 2, 1962, p. 94.
zcp. S. Tachibana, The Ethics of Buddhism; Nyanaponika, The Heart of Buddhist Meditation; A. W. Watts, The Way of Zen; Ch. Luk, Ch'an and Zen Teaching. Third Series; J. Mascaro, trsl. The Bhagavad Gīta. Luzac's Oriental List, LXXIII, 1962, pp. 26–8.
zcq. J. Blofeld, The Zen Teaching of Hui Hai; The Lion's Roar, by D. Maurice. Luzac's Or. List LXXIII, 1962, pp. 46–7.
zcr. Abhidharmadīpa, ed. P. S. Jaini. JRAS 1962, p. 161.
zcs. Jñānaśrīmitranibandhāvali, ed. A. Thakur. JRAS 1962, p. 162.
zct. G. Tucci, The Theory and Practice of the Mandala. JRAS 1962, pp. 162–3.
zcu. A Wayman, Analysis of the Śrāvakabhūmi Ms. JRAS 1962, p. 163.
zcv. A. Dahlquist, Megasthenes and Indian Religion [This review was foolish. See J. Kuiper in IIJ xi 2, 1969, 142–6]; T. O. Ling, Buddhism and the Mythology of Evil; G. Tucci, The Discovery of the Mallas. Luzac's Or. List, LXXIV, 1963, pp. 3–4.
zcw. C. C. Chang, trsl. The Hundred Thousand Songs of Milarepa. The Middle Way xxxviii, 1963, pp. 39–41.

*zcx. J. Ph. Vogel, The Goose in Indian Literature and Art, OA N.S. ix, 1963, p. 107.
zcy. E. Lamotte, L'enseignement de Vimalakīrti. B. Phillips, ed. The Essentials of Zen Buddhism; S. Dutt, Buddhist Monks and Monasteries in India. Luzac's Or. List LXXIV, 1963, pp. 22–3.
*zcz. A. Macdonald, Le Mandala du Mañjuśrīmūlakalpa, BLSOAS xxvi, 1963, pp. 440–1.
zda. Rgyan-drug mchog-gnyis. JRAS 1963, p. 294.
zdb. Buddhism. Studia Missionalia XII. MW xxxviii, 1963, pp. 128–9.
*zdc. A. Wayman, Analysis of the Srāvakabhūmi Manuscript; The Yogācārabhūmi, Part I, ed. V. Bhattacharya. IIJ vii, 1964, pp. 226–231.
zdd. D. Schlingloff, Die Religion des Buddhismus, I. IIJ vii, 1964, pp. 231–2.
zde. H. V. Guenther, The Life and Teaching of Nāropa. JRAS 1964, pp. 123–4.
zdf. P. V. Bapat, Vimuktimārga Dhutaguṇa-nirdeśa. MW xxxix 4, 1965, p. 190.
zdg. T. Vimalananda, Buddhism in Ceylon, Luzac's Or. List, LXXVI, p. 3.
zdh. K. S. Ch'en, Buddhism in China. MW xl 2, 1965, pp. 94–5.
*zdi. A. Foucher, The Life of the Buddha, trsl. S. B. Boas. JAOS 84, 1964, pp. 460–1.
zdk. S. Kramrisch, The Art of Nepal, OA xi, 1965, p. 177.
zdl. F. Fourcade, Peinture Murale de Touen Houang, OA xi, 1965, p. 177.
*zdm. R. B. Ekvall, Religious Observances in Tibet. JRAS 1965, p. 133.
*zdn. Bhikṣu Thich Minh Chau, The Chinese Madhyama Āgama and the Pāli Majjhima Nikāya. MW xl 3, 1965, pp. 140–1.
zdo. D. Schlingloff, Die Religion des Buddhismus, II. IIJ ix 2, 1966, p. 159. cf. no. zdd.
zdp. D. Schlingloff, Dogmatische Begriffsreihen; Tripathi, 25 Sūtras. JAOS 85, 1965, pp. 463–4.
zdq. P. V. Bapat, Vimukti-mārga Dhutaguṇanirdeśa. Luzac's Or. List.
*zdr. F. Weller, Zum Kāśyapaparivarta. IIJ x 4, 1968, pp. 302–5.
zds. Dh.N. Shastri, Critique of Indian Realism, JAOS 87, 1967, p. 337.
zdt. Books on Buddhism. Pacific Affairs XL, 1967, pp. 170–2.
zdu. R. H. Robinson, Early Mādhyamika in India and China, BLSOS xxxii, 1969, 630.
zdv. Y. Karunadasa, Buddhist Analysis of Matter, BLSOS, xxxiii, 1971, 411–2.

zdw. Th. Merton, The Zen Revival, MW XLIV, 1971, p. 92.
*zdx. C. Pensa, L'Abhisamayālaṅkāravṛtti di Ārya-Vimuktisena, IIJ xiv, 1972, 123–4.

MISCELLANEOUS

ma. The New Buddhist Encyclopedia. Manchester Guardian (July 1955?).
mb. Foreword to Berkeley Galleries, Exhibition, Mystic Art of Tibet. April 1956.
md. Foreword to E. Beswick, Jataka Tales, 1956.
me. Buddhist Literature Outside India. Broadcast for All-India Radio. (18.5 and 2.6, 1956).
mf. Saluting the Supernatural. BBC.22.9. 1956.
mg. The Circle of Becoming. MW xxxi, 1957, pp. 145–6.
mh. Foreword to G. H. Sasaki, A Study of Abhidharma Philosophy, Tokyo, 1958, pp. v–vi.
mi. The Yogācārin Treatment of Prajñāpāramitā Texts (25.8.54). Proceedings of the 23rd Congress of Orientalists, Cambridge, 1954, ed. D. Sinor, pp. 230–1.
mk. Buddhist Teachings by Buddhist Stories. Australian Broadcasting Commission. October 1959.
ml. Prefatory Note to F. W. Thomas, The Flower-Spray of the Quodammodo Doctrine, 1960, p. 3.
mm. Buddhism in the Soviet Union. The Middle Way xxxv 3, 1960, pp. 113–4.
mo. Art. Abhisamayālaṅkāra (1), Encyclopedia of Buddhism, 1961, pp. 114–6.
mp. Letter to "Observer," 10.9.61.
mr. Introductory Note to: F. W. Thomas, Tibetan Literary Texts and Documents Concerning Chinese Turkestan, Part IV: Indices, 1963.
ms. (The) Buddha's Recipe for Mental Peace. Faith and Freedom, 17, 1963, no. 49, pp. 41–4.
mt. Preface to: W. L. King, A Thousand Lives Away, 1964, pp. 5–6.
mu. German trsl. of no. 82–83 by M. Deuring. Yāna xviii, 1965, 53–55, 144–153, 183–196. xix, 1966, 24–30, 56–64.
mw. D. T. Suzuki,—a personal tribute. The Eastern Buddhist. NS II 1, 1967, pp. 84–5.
mx. Tibetan Art, in: The Oxford Companion to Art, ed. H. Osborne, 1970, pp. 1135–7.
my. La doctrine de la vacuité d'après la Prajñāpāramitā. Hermes 6, Le Vide, 1969, pp. 204–209, =E pp. 19–24.
mz. The Legend of the Buddha Shakyamuni. Noted by the International Buddhist Association. Shinozaki Shorin, Tokyo (1967?), iii + 71 pp. = I pp. 35–66.

SOME NON-BUDDHIST PUBLICATIONS

01. Der Begriff der Metaphysik bei Franciscus Suarez, S. J. Leipzig 1928. v, 72 pp. F. Meiner. Forschungen z. Gesch. d. Philosophie und d. Paedagogik, Bd. 3, H. 3.
02. Der Satz vom Widerspruch. Hamburg, 1932.
*03. Social Implications of Logical Thinking. "Proceedings of the Aristotelean Society". xxxv, 1934–5, pp. 23–44.
*04. The Objective Validity of the Principle of Contradiction. "Philosophy", 1935, pp. 205–18.
05. The Scientific Method of Thinking, 1935.
06. An Introduction to Dialectical Materialism, 1936.
07. Spain to-day, 1936.
*08. Social origins of Nominalism. "Marxist Quarterly", 1937, pp. 115–24, 431–436.

BOOKS JUST PUBLISHED

K–A. THE PERFECTION OF WISDOM IN EIGHT THOUSAND LINES AND ITS VERSE SUMMARY. xxii + 325 pp. Four Seasons Foundation, Bolinas, Cal., 1973.

O. Add: All the three parts together: University of California Press, Berkeley, 1974.

P. Add: Chs. 70 to 82 corresp. to the 6th to 8th Abhisamayas, xii + 254 pp., Ismeo, Rome, 1974.

INDEX

Abhidharma 26, 140, 166sq., 196, 216–17
Abhisamayālaṅkāra 30, 114, 169, 203, 220
Absolute 2, 3, 20, 25, 32, 37, 47, 65–7, 138, 155, 217
Ādi-Buddha (Primordial Buddha) 75, 187
agnosticism 217
aggressiveness 39
ahiṃsā (non-violence) 6, 7, 197
ālayavijñāna (store consciousness) 27
ambiguity 83sq.
ambivalence 36
anattā (not-self) 141–2, 168, 217
antinomianism 24
anxiety 48
archetype 132, 134, 190
Aristotle 45, 56, 63, 66, 80–1, 84–5, 88, 92–3, 99, 101–2, 106–7, 109, 112, 116, 192
Asaṅga 198sq., 206, 221
asceticism 40, 51
Asoka 3–7, 115, 139, 174
astrology xiii, 11, 12, 27, 162–3
ātman (self) 142, 155
Aurobindo, Sri 155
Avalokiteśvara (the Bodhisattva of compassion) 121, 150sq., 174–5, 188

Bahnsen, J. 69, 70
Bergson, H. 63, 70
bhakti (devotion) 35, 37, 121, 174–5, 216
Bodhisattva 30, 118, 121, 147–8, 153, 160, 177, 212, 216
Bon 204–5
Borobudur 13
Buddha-nature 19, 20
Buddha's triple body 30, 113sq., 160

cakravartin (universal monarch) 6
Calvinism 20, 148
Candrakīrti xii
capitalism 93sq.
Ch'an 26, 176–8, 182, 194–5, 208–9
charity 34, 41, 46–7
chochma (wisdom) 20, 21
compassion 39sq., 52sq., 119, 120, 152–3, 156, 168, 215–16
Confucius 83–86
contradiction(s) 26, 49, 56sq., 77–8, 98, 112, 180, 195
cosmos 11–14, 16, 25, 103, 129, 189, 206
cruelty 52–3, 55

Dalai Lama 10, 125, 158, 188
demiurge 25
Devadatta 29, 187, 188
Dharma 1sq., 21, 40, 113, 117, 122–4, 129, 141, 146–9, 175, 185, 190, 195, 197
dharma-kāya (Dharma-body) 113, 197
dharmas (impersonal events) 49, 167, 200
dhyāna (transic concentration) 48, 183

Dhyāni-Buddha 174–5, 188
dialectics 67–8, 71, 104, 112, 129
Docetism 22–3

ego 70
egoism 39
Erastianism 5
Eleatics 84
emptiness 49, 50, 69, 118–23, 139, 143, 183, 188, 216
esoteric 115, 133, 197, 207
existentialism 32

feng-shui 11–12

gaings 10
E. Gellner x
Gnostics 15sq., 133, 180
Godhead 25
grace 47

H. Günther 135, 166–8, 201
hatred 39
Hegel 67–8, 71, 171
Heracleitism 63–4, 67, 69

icchantika (those finally doomed) 19, 20
identity 78–81
ignorance 17, 27
impartiality 49, 50
impermanence 69

Jung, C. G. viii, ix, xii, 132sq., 190, 205

Kali Yuga 126

Lamaism 156sq., 158, 205
language 75, 76
love 33sq., 213

Mādhyamikas 56, 69, 118, 137sq., 177, 204
magic x–xiii, 6, 9sq., 28, 81sq., 111, 118, 128, 156–7, 162, 180–1, 183, 206sq.
Mahāyāna 40, 64, 116, 118, 129, 139, 140, 148, 152, 162, 170, 176–7, 179, 194, 201, 209, 215–16, 219
Mahīśāsakas 202–4
Maitreya 116, 153
maitrī, mettā (friendliness) 34, 45–6, 51, 216
mandala 13, 205sq., 209sq.
Mañjuśrī (the Bodhisattva of Wisdom) 5, 121, 153
mantra (spell) 27, 118, 122–3, 161
Māra 3, 25, 162, 190
marks, of the superman 114–15
Milarepa 41–2
Mithra 153
Monism 26
mudrā (symbolic gesture) 186sq.
Murti, C. R. V. 137sq., 167
mystery religions 133–4
mystical pantheism 64–7, 70
mythological thinking 189, 206

Nāgārjuna xii, 26, 114, 137, 161, 171, 176
natural law 4
Neoplatonism xi, xiii, 16sq., 28
neurotic 45
Nicholas of Cusa 65–6, 71, 93
Nietzsche, F. 92
nihilism 32
Nirvana 3, 10, 18, 22, 25–6, 31, 35, 69, 135, 148, 152, 214, 217
Nominalism 93sq., 218
no-thought 177
Nying-ma-pa 131, 156, 177–8, 187, 204–5

Occam, W. of 93, 97–101, 103, 105–6, 108–11
occult 12, 14, 50
One, the 17, 26, 28, 64–5

Pāla Buddhism 117sq., 176–7
pāramitā, perfections, six 118
pietas 4
prajñā (wisdom) 21–2, 174–5, 188, 196
prajñāpāramitā (perfection of wisdom) 21–2, 28–9, 113sq., 116sq., 131, 133, 137, 139, 141, 152, 158, 159sq., 163sq., 168sq., 175–6, 180–1, 183, 203, 211–12, 217, 220sq.
Prodikos 84, 87
Protagoras 63, 70, 84, 87–8
Pyrrho 107

Radhakrishnan, S. 142, 154–5
revelation 17
ritual 47, 135, 155, 185, 207
Roscellinus 107–10

sādhana (evocation of a deity) 122, 173sq.
śakti (female power) 22, 174–5, 180, 188
salvation 16–19, 24, 29
sāmbhoga-kāya (Enjoyment Body) 113–15
saṃdhābhāṣya (hidden intent) 25
Sammitīya 203
Sangharakshita 144sq.
Sarvāstivādins 140–1, 167, 204, 214sq.
Schopenhauer, A. ix, 15, 69, 70
self 36, 38, 44, 49, 51, 142, 155
Self 17, 19, 135, 141
self-deception 53
self-evidence 57, 73
self-extinction 37, 46–7, 49, 50
self-hate 45
self-identical 64
self-interest 41–2, 46
selfishness 37–8, 47
selflessness 44sq.
self-love 45
self-preservation 69
self-sacrifice 37
self-seeking 37, 46
sense of guilt 45
Shamanism 157, 173, 183
skandhas 219
skill in means 41
Socrates 87, 89
Sophia 20–2, 132
Stcherbatsky 167
Stūpa 12–13, 189, 206
śūnyatā (emptiness) 138, 143
Suzuki, D. T. 36, 193, 196–7, 208–9, 216
sympathetic joy 53sq.

Tantras 12, 21–3, 26–8, 31, 47, 115, 117–18, 121, 131, 134, 156–7, 161sq., 168, 172, 173sq., 180sq., 187–8, 196, 207–8
Theravādins 127, 139–41, 147, 158, 167, 196, 202, 204, 214sq.
Thomas a Kempis 46
Tucci, G. 13, 19, 27, 31, 159sq., 176sq., 205sq.

Unlimited, the 42–3, 197
Upanishads 64, 135, 139, 141–2, 154–6, 207

vajra (thunderbolt) 131, 188
Vajracchedikā ('Diamond Cutter') 113, 159sq., 166, 170–1, 195–6, 216
Vajravarāhī (The Adamantine Sow) 134–5
Vajrayāna (the adamantine vehicle) 140, 207
Vasubandhu 69, 160, 167, 196, 200, 203, 206

wisdom 20sq., 35, 37–8, 45, 48sq., 51, 54, 69, 90, 118, 123–4, 132, 137, 153, 167, 180, 183, 191, 194, 214

Yoga 172–3, 183, 191
Yogācārins 25, 113, 140, 160, 167, 198sq., 206, 221
Yoga Sūtras 52, 172

Zen 47, 131, 147, 191–2, 194sq., 208–9